IMAGINING THE POSSIBLE

Imagining the Possible

Radical Politics
for Conservative Times

Stephen Eric Bronner

ROUTLEDGE
NEW YORK & LONDON

Published in 2002 by
Routledge
29 West 35th Street
New York, NY 10001

Published in Great Britain by
Routledge
11 New Fetter Lane
London EC4P 4EE

Routledge is an imprint of Taylor & Francis Group.

Printed in the United States of America on acid-free paper
Design and typography: Jack Donner

10   9   8   7   6   5   4   3   2   1

Library of Congress Cataloging-in-Publication Data

Bronner, Stephen Eric, 1949–
    Imagining the possible : radical essays for conservative times / Stephen Eric Bronner.
        p. cm.
    Includes bibliographical references and index.
    ISBN 0–415–93260–2 — ISBN 0–415–93261–0 (pbk.)
        1. Post-communism. 2. Socialism. 3. Democracy. 4. Internationalism. I. Title.
HX44.5 .B76 2002
335—dc21
                                                    2001048114

TO

FRANCES FOX PIVEN

In Memory of Richard Cloward

(1927–2001)

CONTENTS

Part III: In Pursuit of Progress

INTRODUCTION

IMAGINING THE POSSIBLE is not always so simple as it might seem. Especially when one thinks about politics, the imagination is usually associated with utopia while the possible is identified with the acceptance of existing constraints and the "art" of brokering compromises without any sense of long-term gain or loss. There is something valuable in setting high the standard of change and remembering the utopian hopes raised of the past. But, too often, this occurs at the expense of fully appreciating the fight for reforms attendant upon fostering democracy, shortening the workweek, and improving the quality of life. Neither principle nor compromise has an exclusive claim on truth. The imagination and the possible should not be placed in rigid opposition with one another: the one often inspires the other. Under present circumstances, however, the connection between ideals for creating the best life and plans for creating a better one is becoming increasingly tenuous. Progressive forces have been enmeshed within the agenda set by their opponents for decades. Reinvigorating the left calls for reasserting precisely this connection. Thus, *Imagining the Possible* will highlight the shifting *intersection* between radical goals and immediate demands, the exercise of freedom and the constraints of necessity, where we would like to go and where we are now.

Its essays were written under different circumstances and for different audiences. They stretch back over more than twenty years. A few would serve as drafts and the rest revolve around themes and thinkers important for my larger projects. All the essays have been more or less heavily edited in order to correct minor mistakes, mitigate redundancies, and, occasionally, bring them into line with contemporary developments. But the original arguments and claims have essentially been left intact. These essays share a common concern with expanding the opportunities for democratic participation, radicalizing the commitment to economic justice, and furthering international solidarity. Which received primacy when depended upon the subject under consideration and a judgment of the context in which the essay was written. Each exhibits facets of an overarching worldview and each, after its fashion, explores both the existential and practical importance of socialism, democracy, and internationalism.

Such ideals were not exactly *en vogue* during a period in which most progressives were trying to suppress ideological differences and the right was sharpening its intellectual tools and implementing its reactionary agenda. With its assault on the interventionist state and support for military spending, its attack on the experimental values of the 1960s and its championing of individualism, its nationalism and its commitment to a planetary free market, its privileging of elites and its use of populist rhetoric, the new conservatism generated internationally during the last quarter of the twentieth century offered an explicitly ideological—if profoundly contradictory—program.

Rather than enter the fray, however, the left countered with the consensual and "non-ideological" strategy of self-styled "pragmatists." "New Democrats" and the partisans of "New Labor" became intent upon seeking a "new middle" or a "third way" between traditional social democracy and the free market. They turned their back on the tradition of radical reform associated with the New Deal, the Popular Front, and the 1960s. They rejected "socialism," domesticated "democracy," and identified "internationalism" with globalization. Nevertheless, in retrospect, the pragmatists appear not to have been very pragmatic at all.

Indeed, when the left finally took power in the United States, England, and Germany, its representatives found themselves working within the framework of those they had once claimed to oppose. Some have now shifted in response to popular pressure from below. Still, the current agenda has clearly been set not by the purely reactive politics of sophisticated "new progressives" like Bill Clinton or Tony Blair but, by those we often mistakenly caricature for their stupidity or rigidity: Ronald Reagan and Margaret Thatcher. This situation is what led me to collect some essays capable of offering some historical background, some controversial theoretical perspectives, and some practical ideas that might facilitate the emergence of a radical politics for conservative times

Imagining the Possible understands "democracy," "socialism," and "internationalism" in regulative terms; it does not identify them with any particular institutional arrangement. These ideals are seen as retaining their salience insofar as they still underpin any progressive confrontation with the structural imbalances of power in capitalist society. They also frame the "project" of liberation by offering a conceptual backdrop for appropriating the contributions of other movements, including feminism, environmentalism, and the myriad postcolonial undertakings of the non-Western world. In my opinion, without a willingness to privilege these ideals, the exploited and marginalized will become ever more susceptible to the appeals of right-wing ideology and no genuinely progressive movement will even be conceivable.

This volume is divided into three complementary parts in which the essays, more or less, logically follow one another. "Radical Impulses," the first part provides a historical overview for the volume by highlighting certain events and movements that shaped left politics during the twentieth century. "Words and Deeds," the second section, critically engages the thinking of certain individuals who influenced my intellectual development and who, I believe, still have something to offer the future. "In Pursuit of Progress," the third part, is comprised of essays dealing with the institutional constraints and certain crucial tasks for building a progressive politics. Having said this, however, considering the essays themselves might prove useful both for gaining a sense of the structure of the volume and the coherence of its parts.

"Radical Impulses" begins with an early draft of what, in 1990, would become my first larger effort in political theory: *Socialism Unbound* (2nd Edition: Boulder, Colorado: Westview Press, 2000). Influenced by the ultra-left *gauchiste* perspective of the 1960s, with its emphasis on the self-administration of the working class, "The Socialist Project" probably retains a certain antiquarian flavor given the neoliberal shift in social democracy and the new commitment to democracy on the part of many Western ex-communist parties. The problem is indeed now not the prevalence of reformism but its absence, and not the inability to perceive the virtues of democracy, but the willingness to tame its radical potential. Published in 1980 and dedicated to Rudi Dutschke, the great orator who was also a moral compass for the international student movement, "The Socialist Project" is informed by the belief in a "third way" that attempts to move "beyond" social democratic reformism and communist authoritarianism rather than "beyond" left and right. Aside from providing a certain framework for what follows, indeed, it provides both a sense of how the self-understanding of the left has changed and an attempt to retrieve a lost radical tradition.

"Persistent Memories: Jewish Activists and the German Revolution of 1919" examines how this tradition received practical expression. The libertarian revolts of 1919 occurred amid the revulsion produced by World War I and the euphoria generated by the Russian Revolution. Nineteen nineteen was the year in which both the imagination and the possible were pushed to the limit. Attempts were undertaken in many countries to introduce workers' councils, and intellectuals played a decisive role. In Germany, many were Jewish: Rosa Luxemburg, Kurt Eisner, Eugen Levine, and others. Anti-Semites saw them as part of the supposed worldwide conspiracy against "Christian" civilization that I would treat extensively in *A Rumor about the Jews: Reflections on Anti-Semitism and the "Protocols of the Learned Elders of Zion"* (New York: St. Martin's Press, 2000). This essay shows how certain cosmopolitan and secular trends within Jewish culture blend with the best values of the radical labor movement.

Libertarian socialism has always had an uneasy relationship with the communist movement. The Russian Revolution may have initially inspired many of its partisans, but there was nonetheless a certain moral incompatibility between the communist and anticommunist wings of the left. This becomes abundantly evident in the work of Albert Camus.

He was not a man of the ultraleft, but he was more radical than the social democratic mainstream. Camus was concerned with placing limits on action, countering the burgeoning technocratic ethos, and contesting the ambitions of utopian revolutionaries. He is now perhaps best remembered for his existential concerns as well as the "Mediterranean moderation" and the anticommunist attitude exhibited in his famous debate of the early 1950s with Jean-Paul Sartre. Nevertheless, there is more to consider.

"In the Shadow of the Resistance: Albert Camus and the Paris Intellectuals" proved the sketch for what would ultimately become an intellectual biography titled *Camus: Portrait of a Moralist* (Minneapolis: University of Minnesota Press, 1999). It deals with the political maturation of Camus in the brilliant intellectual circle of Paris following World War II, his efforts in the realm of theory, and some of the most important political controversies of his epoch. Camus is presented here as a genuine humanist with progressive convictions whose political judgments were often flawed. "In the Shadow of the Resistance" also explores the way in which real constraints can inhibit progressive political action. It indeed suggests that not every political conflict has room for a positive solution and that history can undermine the ability of even the most insightful to link interest with principle.

"The Sickness unto Death: International Communism before the Deluge," by the same token, insists that the attempt itself has an intrinsic political value. Surrendering principle in the name of interest succumbing to an unreflective realism or pragmatism, corrodes civic virtue and political commitment. The essay, in this vein, examines how communists wasted the moral high ground inherited from the "heroic" period of the Russian Revolution that extended from 1917–23. Arguably more than the bureaucratic incompetence of a tottering state, or even the self-serving economic policies of its elites, it claims that a growing abandonment of radical ideals— always justified by recourse to the demands of "necessity" and the need to understand what is "possible"—produced the existential exhaustion and collapse of the communist imagination that culminated in 1989.

Originally written for an East European audience, informed by the arguments of *Socialism Unbound* and *Moments of Decision: Political History and the Crises of Radicalism* (New York: Routledge, 1992), "The Sickness Unto Death" was an attempt to undercut any lingering nostalgia for the communist movements and regimes of times past. Uncritical nostalgia for even the best of movements, in fact, can only prove self-defeating. Attempting some mechanical transfer of radical strategies from one period into another is always self-defeating. This pertains not merely to the organizational approach of a decrepit communist tradition, and the economism of social democracy, but even to the 1960s.

Such a strategy involves a betrayal of the imagination and, necessarily, a misperception of the possible. Ideals should take on a new content and organizations a new form in new circumstances. How traditional radical ideals and questions of organization were adapted to confront new conditions and new expressions of protest by new constituencies becomes particularly clear when one considers the 1960s. What I termed a "mass association," more than a simple coalition of interests yet less than a party, appeared on the horizon as the civil rights movement allied itself first with the antiwar movement and then with the "poor peoples' movement." It became possible to envisage a linkage between the extension of democratic participation, a new foreign policy, and the demand for economic justice. Traditional notions of democracy, socialism, and internationalism took a new form and received a new content. Indeed, if only to contest the increasingly sanitized image of Rev. Martin Luther King Jr., I included a short speech dealing with his radical legacy titled "Looking Backwards."

Action is inspired by ideas and, in this regard, the purveyors of ideas still have a role to play. "Critical Intellectuals, Politics, and Society" investigates the way they have been interpreted, the constraints upon them, and some of the tasks they face. It suggests that there is not just one form of intellectual work and that intellectuals can intervene in any number of ways. There is room for the humanist intellectual in support of pluralism, the technocrat with a conscience, and the universal thinker who somehow always winds up interfering in what is supposedly not his business. But there is also something common to critical intellectuals no matter what their field or approach: the refusal to compromise their knowledge, their ability to face the new, and their commitment to foster the will to know. Thus, I think, "Critical Intellectuals, Politics, and Society" serves as an excellent transition to the next section.

"Words and Deeds" constitutes an expression of gratitude to a few people and works that influenced the left in general and my own thinking in particular. This second part of *Imagining the Possible* begins with a speech, given the day before the retaliatory bombing of Afghanistan began, which deals with Gandhi and his legacy of nonviolence. It makes reference to the tragic events of 11 September 2001, the day of the attack on the World Trade Center and the Pentagon by Islamic fanatics, in evaluating the salience of his views in developing a secular rule of political conduct for our time. Gandhi saw recourse to violence as an expression of weakness and nonviolence as an expression of strength and a way of developing moral maturity on the part of the individual. His was a philosophy and a movement that would have profound influence on Martin Luther King Jr., Nelson Mandela, and among many in my generation. But the lingering moral and practical question involves whether nonviolence should be seen in absolute terms. It is incumbent to consider whether the use of nonviolence by a mass movement intent upon reforming or seizing a state is appropriate as the strategy for a state faced with an egregious assault on its citizens, an occasion in which crime blends with war, and a situation in which a lack of symmetry exists between the intentions of actors and the consequences of their actions.

The next essay deals with Rosa Luxemburg. She has been with me since I first translated a selection of her letters in 1978 and then, in 1981, brought out a slim biography, *Rosa Luxemburg: A Revolutionary for Our Times* (University Park: Pennsylvania State University Press, 1997) that is still in print. The essay included here, "Red Dreams and the New Millennium: Notes on the Legacy of Rosa Luxemburg," is critical of her Marxism and many of the assumptions that she made. But its primary intent is to identify what is salient in her thought. Luxemburg remains for me the great symbol of libertarian socialism, and her internationalist values along with her emphasis upon fostering the "creative tension" between movements and organizations still inform my understanding of radical politics.

Luxemburg would probably have had little sympathy for the *Dialectic of Enlightenment* (1947) by Max Horkheimer and Theodor Adorno. Yet this classic work of "critical theory," so powerful in its anthropological and philosophical analysis, so rich in its insights and in its use of new categories like the "culture industry," would exert a profound influence on the young intellectuals of 1968. I was among those inspired by it and my interest in critical theory has never wavered. But this is one of its seminal works that most requires political critique. "The Limits of Metatheory" is indeed part of a more general encounter with this tradition begun in *Of Critical Theory and Its Theorists* (2nd Edition: New York: Routledge, 2002).

"The Limits of Metatheory" contests the unqualified critique of instrumental reason in the name of a supposedly repressed subjectivity; it is skeptical of the refusal to articulate differences between political parties and movements; and it rejects the foundational argument for what have become fashionable interpretations of the Enlightenment as the source of Nazism and the "totally administered society." The essay also calls into question the attempt to render political and historical judgments through metaphysical and anthropological arguments unconcerned with the theory and practice of actual movements and institutions. This contribution to the present volume consequently insists upon the primacy of the political moment for any new philosophical developments in critical theory and, without denigrating the cultural contributions other traditions might offer, the centrality of enlightenment political values for a genuinely progressive political project.

My intellectual work has, in general, stressed the primacy of the political and sought to anchor the socialist project in the enlightenment heritage. These themes would have appealed to Henry Pachter. An activist in both the communist and social democratic movements, an intellectual of the old school whose works ranged from a study of Paracelsus to a history of Soviet foreign policy, he recognized both the practical influence of ideas and the need for speculation. Insistent upon using philosophy to illuminate lived history, as well as the constraints and opportunities offered by practical politics, he was a socialist who never believed that socialism offered a solution to the human condition. Pachter first taught me the classics of Marxism and critical theory at the City College of New York in the late

1960s and early 1970s. The essay included here served as the introduction to my edition of *Socialism in History: Political Essays of Henry Pachter* (New York: Columbia University Press, 1984).

If the realist strain of my thinking derived from the influence of Pachter, however, the more utopian strains derived from a different source. "Remembering Marcuse" was written for a panel commemorating the tenth anniversary of his death. He was one of the most important intellectual influences on the rebels of 1968. Thousands would come to hear him speak at the Sorbonne or the Free University of Berlin or at Berkeley. Unfortunately, however, interest in his writings has waned. And perhaps this is understandable in a more conservative age. Marcuse called upon his readers to engage in the "great refusal" of a "one-dimensional" society. And he knew something about the operational dynamics of institutions. But he was especially sensitive to the catalytic role of marginal groups like women and minorities, and he always privileged the movement over any organization. Marcuse employed the critical method in a unique manner. His thinking indeed highlighted not merely the repressed subjective experience of freedom, but the inquiry into utopia and, by extension, the need for politics to address a new set of existential problems.

Unveiling the sources of these problems is among the aims of Ulrich Beck. His *Risk Society*, which has by now become a classic, highlights the manner in which modernity is not simply engaged in an assault upon subjectivity but rather tends to liberate it. Choices become multiplied, lifestyles change at the drop of a hat, traditional political institutions lose their efficacy, and new social movements evidence a new concern with the quality of life: that is modernity for Beck. No less than many of the most famous critical theorists, to be sure, he is unable to deal with issues of bureaucratic self-interest or institutional power. Beck overestimates the extent to which institutions lost their power in favor of new social movements, the irrelevance of old-fashioned material issues relative to new concerns with the quality of life, and the transcendence of old divisions between left and right. "Ecology, Politics, and Risk: Considerations on the Social Theory of Ulrich Beck" explores some of my disagreements with him. Nevertheless, it also expresses my admiration for his daring thought experiment in which new categories are articulated for making sense of politics in a new era.

"In Pursuit of Progress" is the concluding part of *Imagining the Possible*. Its essays are less concerned with historical events or individuals than with the institutional constraints, the tasks, and the general ideas that the left must confront. The state has not gone away; its reforms are a matter of crucial concern; the right is employing specific rhetorical strategies, and its influence has only grown both ideologically and practically. The essays included here deal with these matters in a critical fashion yet from a positive standpoint. They are fueled by my concern with developing a new critical theory with public aims. Each essay in its own way highlights the connection between principle and interest, movements and institutions, freedom and its constraints, without surrendering to the given or escaping into utopia.

"Transforming the State: Reflections on the Structure of Capitalist Democracy" provides a framework for dealing with some of these issues. It emphasizes the tensions within "capitalist democracy" and existing structural imbalances of power along with their impact on political actors. The essay maintains that bureaucratic institutions remain *the* crucial locus for political change, and not merely that they can be influenced by the organized actions of citizens, but that radical action from below is the precondition for any meaningful introduction of reforms from above. In this same vein, the degree of arbitrary power exercised by capital is still seen as dependent upon the degree of organizational and ideological disunity among working people. Thus, it becomes necessary to consider the need for a "class ideal" capable of identifying interests common to all working people in each of the new social movements without privileging the concerns of any one movement in particular.

Treating class in *political* rather than purely *economic* terms makes it possible to judge any given reform in a strategic rather than merely a functional manner: this becomes clear from "Affirmative Action in Radical Perspective." The essay emphasizes the way in which, from the first, affirmative action served as a moderate response to the call for a more radical set of interlinked programs intent upon achieving full employment. Its point is not to deny the achievements of affirmative action in helping create a level playing field and bring excluded groups into certain mainstream occupations. By narrowing the sense of what was possible, however, the left wound up in the position of defending ameliorative programs that split its own constituency—or, to put it another way, pit "race" against "class." There should be no misunderstanding: defense of existing programs remains necessary given the reactionary assault on the welfare state and the continuing problems associated with racism. Nevertheless, this essay insists upon the importance of imagining a new class-based form of affirmative action that might mitigate existing tensions among exploited groups and serve as an example of what Andre Gorz once termed a "nonreformist reform."

Leftists would be wise to consider, of course, the possible objections of conservatives to such a program. "The Rhetoric of Reaction," which was originally published as a review of a book with the same title by Albert Hirschman, explains some of his important insights into how right-wing thinkers criticize reformist policies and how they rhetorically justify their own positions. He even explores the way in which the assumptions of the left seem to become defined by those they oppose. But what results from the inquiry of this particularly influential political scientist is the vision of a level playing field, a free arena in which various forms of rhetoric engage each other, without reference to differences of interest, conflicting ideals, and structural imbalances of power. Understanding the historical struggle between opposing forces is obscured by employing a metaphysical form of interpretation divorced from any genuine concern with movements and institutions and interests. The situation is no different when political interests and strategies are ignored in favor of the rhetoric used by their partisans: the political is thereby stripped of politics.

When considering contemporary forces of reaction, of course, a person might conclude that the dead do not always stay dead. One might think that a cursory look at the history of the twentieth century would make reflective supporters of nationalism skeptical about the dangers associated with this inherently parochial ideology. Despite the way in which new global economic and environmental issues are dwarfing the problem-solving capacities of even the best governments, however, its attraction has only grown with the demise of the old labor movement and colonial revolutions of the postwar era. "Confronting Nationalism" calls upon progressives to contest this trend. It raises the need for a choice between an old notion of "self-determination" predicated on national sovereignty, which surrenders any serious chance of dealing with pressing planetary problems, and a new internationalism focused upon a burgeoning set of transnational organizations still in need of radical democratic reform. Indeed, while much of the left still vacillates, the new reactionaries have already made their choice.

"Neoconservatism and the New Right in the United States and Abroad," in this vein, refuses to equate the past with the present. The 1930s are over and the offspring is different from the parent. Even conservative elites in the more industrialized nations have made their peace with capitalist democracy; the far right has lost its revolutionary spirit; and imperialist ambitions have, for the most part, withered away. But there is still a residue of the old xenophobia, if in somewhat more tempered form, and the same authoritarian impulses. The modern causes are different: new forms of national competition caused by the global transformation of capitalism; industrial jobs disappearing or appearing threatened by immigration; the assault on the welfare state and the growth of big government. The new ideology of "friendly fascism" and "neoconservatism," which fuses commitment to the free market with know-nothing populism, still speaks to the losers: atavistic sectors of the economy, provincial communities threatened by change, and malcontents on the fringes. In my opinion, however, the more pressing danger derives from those in the conservative mainstream who seek to "integrate" rather than unequivocally condemn their more reactionary associates. They take democracy too much for granted.

But that is perhaps understandable. Liberal constitutionalism ceased being merely the province of Western states in the years between the crumbling of the Berlin Wall in 1989 and the collapse of the Soviet Union in 1992. Just as revolution was breaking out in Eastern Europe, however, the "end of history" became a popular topic of discussion. The political imagination had seemingly culminated in the liberal capitalist state and a global free market. No ideals, new or old, appeared in need of realization. A "sad time" of mediocrity and consumerism loomed, and few anticipated the disillusionment that the attempts at capitalist "shock therapy" and the forces of globalization would bring in their wake.

I concluded *Moments of Decision* with a critical response to the "end of history" thesis that remarked upon the unfulfilled legacy of internationalism while *Ideas in Action: Political Tradition in the Twentieth Century* (Lanham, Maryland: Rowman and Littlefield, 1999) highlighted the emergence of an international civil society and what might be termed a "cosmopolitan sensibility." In the meantime, however, the original thesis concerning "the end of history" became ever more surely identified with the even cruder belief that "there is no alternative" and the idea that we had somehow moved "beyond" left and right had become irrelevant. Thus, I decided to use the opportunity of a speaking engagement at the University of Leipzig in the summer of 2001, following the antiglobalization demonstrations in Seattle and Quebec, to write "The End of History Revisited."

Highlighting the conflict between liberal and illiberal movements and philosophies has become of particular importance in the light of September 11, 2001. The more fanatical partisans of religious fundamentalism have turned terror into an international weapon in attacking not merely global capitalism, but the secular values associated with liberalism, socialism, and internationalism. Modernity does not abolish the pre-modern: one step forward in one direction produces one step back in another. But the real conflict is not between the West and Islam, or the secular and the religious, but between those who privilege liberal notions of tolerance and those would insist upon abolishing all views and life-styles other than their own violence and repression. This conflict has now taken an international form. Initiating a progressive form of planetary politics thus becomes perhaps the most basic task for engaged intellectuals and this, in turn, requires an ability to specify in new ways the intersections between principles and interest, the imagination and the possible, the unrealized possibilities of the past and the constraints of the present.

Imagining the Possible is intended as a small contribution to further such efforts. Its essays were not written to offer policy prescriptions capable of being instantly translated into practice by liberal politicians, they were not particularly useful for building a career in the discipline of political theory, and they were not directed toward the intellectual mainstream. Each after its fashion sought instead to foster the spirit of resistance, create an awareness of rapidly eroding radical traditions, and provoke reflection among those on the outside who, perhaps quixotically, envision a new movement or who, more modestly, remain committed to protesting the inequities and constraints of the existing order. Indeed, if these essays interrogate the past and admit mistakes, they also suggest that sobriety need not dampen idealism or respect for those who sacrificed in the hope of creating a better world.

STEPHEN ERIC BRONNER, NEW YORK CITY

PART I

Radical Impulses

I

THE SOCIALIST PROJECT

In Memory of Rudi Dutschke

THE HISTORY OF SOCIALISM exhibits something profoundly paradoxical: its very success has truncated its potential for liberation. This is as true for the social democratic movement, which can claim the welfare state to its credit, as for the communist movement whose leaders sought to live off the image of a heroic past. It would benefit only sectarians, however, if "socialism" were preserved from history, and were given some purely abstract definition. In reality, the word has been appropriated by the most disparate political and economic formations: state capitalist and neomercantilist governments headed by military elites, reformist parties dedicated to parliamentary democracy, and authoritarian regimes based on the concept of the "dictatorship of the proletariat," as well as states and movements that sought to merge socialism with religion.

Where socialism emerged as a program for revolutionary reconstruction, it originally sought to link particular transitional demands with the overriding goal of an emancipated society based on economic equality and full political participation.[1] What occurred instead, however, is that supposedly "transitional" concerns with industrialization, planning, and nationalization attained the status of ultimate goals. As a consequence, the coherence of the socialist project has been shattered; its truly radical goals—such as the abolition of a stultifying division of labor and the creation of a "free association" of producers—have been suppressed in the name of exigencies ideologically legitimated by a host of repressive institutions.

Of course, real movements and real regimes are imperfect. They never fulfill the goals that require such incredible sacrifices. Yet the rationale for socialism may provide the basis for a critique of those movements and states that employ the term to legitimate repression. Such a critique must reassert the need for coherence between immediate concerns and ultimate goals. It should also illuminate the gap between the progressive gains achieved and the hope of liberation.

This article was first published in *Social Research* 47, no. 1 (spring 1980): 11–35.

THE MEANING OF SOCIALISM

In its Marxist formulation, socialism was conceived as a transitional stage between the overthrow of capitalism and the actualization of communism. As an idea of social and political transformation, it was appropriated by movements whose ideology it became until, finally, it came to stand for the set of institutions that these movements realized in the name of the idea. This idea may rest on a utopian abstraction or a social theory claiming scientific precision, or even simply the demand for a set of social reforms. It may guide the movement in terms of specific policy decisions, or it may serve as nothing more than a mere ideological shibboleth. In turn, the movement may be a tightly organized "vanguard" party of revolutionary intellectuals, or it may be a mass organization with democratic values; its base may vary from peasants to industrial workers to the "new working class" of bureaucrats, professionals, and the like. Finally, with regard to institutions, the achievements of "socialists" may be counted in terms of legislative successes, social or welfare gains, effectiveness in influencing foreign policy, or ways of building class consciousness. Alternatively, the institutions created by a socialist movement may be defined as a "revolutionary" challenge to capitalism or imperialism.[2] In this maze of current definitions, actualizations, and possibilities, the fundamentally radical point is usually obfuscated: Socialism was meant to provide a new form of democratic control over the economy and new humanistic values for directing it. Socialism itself was never the utopian alternative, but its rationale lay in the policies that were pursued and the forces that were unleashed in the pursuit of its ideals.

Of course, the need for certain compromises can be justified even from a revolutionary stance. Antonio Gramsci and others have argued that even after the political break with the past, a revolutionary government must develop a mode of coming to terms with the past. Most had the Russian Revolution specifically in mind, but they make a more general point: the new social forces can never totally obliterate the totality of social relations inherited from the past. If the masses are still only emerging from the past, then the political movement is constrained to compromise precisely for the sake of its own future "hegemony." This compromise involves nothing other than the "revolutionary restoration" of certain older values in order to guarantee the possibility of a more profound transformation in the future.[3]

Socialists often look to the development of capitalism for inspiration. While growing within feudalism, capitalism was already forming the social institutions and economic arrangements that it then proceeded to realize through political revolution. The same process, however, cannot hold for the proletariat.[4] A new socialist set of social relations does not organically arise within capitalism. As Lukács suggested, the reification process penetrates the consciousness of the proletariat[5] and damages its ability to form a liberated set of values. Also, since capitalism cannot completely resolve the contradictions of earlier historical stages, what Bloch termed "nonsynchronous contradictions"[6] find their way into the proletarian consciousness as well. This has implications for what can be expected from modern socialism even as it raises doubts about the orthodox model of revolution for highly industrialized countries.

Most partisans of the First, the Second, and the Third International looked to the French Revolution as the prototype for the future proletarian victory.[7] The partisans of these internationals all sought to build a political understanding of class solidarity while the establishment of new social relations was viewed either as the purpose of a new revolutionary state or presupposed within the achievement of step-by-step reforms. There is a historical justification for this attitude insofar as Marx himself retained the Jacobin notion of revolution, especially in the *Communist Manifesto*. Nowhere did he ever disclose, however, the manner by which the proletariat was to constitute itself or what institutional arrangements it should introduce.[8] The lack of such a discussion indicates more than a mere rejection of utopian speculation; if there were an immanent connection between the dissolution of capitalism and the rise of a new set of proletarian social relations, then the categories for these relations should have been elaborated. Yet, while Marx chose to ignore this issue in a general systematic sense, he saw in practical terms what was at stake. Thus, in the "Critique of the Gotha Programme," Marx criticized the failure of the nascent Social Democratic Party of Germany (SPD) to envision a transitional state that would construct the preconditions for the new communist society.[9]

The question then arises how these preconditions may be conceptualized and what role "actually existing" socialist states play in creating them. The task is made more difficult precisely because the transitional state must be dealt with "not as it has developed on its own foundations, but, on the contrary, just as it emerges from capitalist society, which is thus in every respect, economically, morally, and intellectually, still stamped with the birthmarks of the old society from whose womb it emerges."[10] Caught between the society that is to be overcome and the one that is yet to be created, the transitional state will remain without direction, focus, or even legitimacy, unless the emphasis upon an alternative society to capitalism is retained in the policies that are pursued.

REVOLUTION AND REFORM

The Western social democratic parties and states are currently facing this loss of orientation. Partially in response to the gradualism of dominant trade unions, partially in reaction to the Leninist deployment of the "dictatorship of the proletariat," the major socialist movements long ago abandoned revolutionary Marxism in favor of the reformist path whose theory was formulated by Eduard Bernstein.[11] Since he no longer saw any objective necessity for a capitalist crisis, socialism no longer seemed either "objectively" necessary or historically "inevitable"; instead, it became an "ethical" demand of which other classes and groups within the society had to be persuaded. Consequently, Bernstein viewed socialism as an "evolutionary" development that would unfold within capitalism and find its bedrock in parliamentary democracy. Through electoral activity, guaranteed by the acquisition of civil liberties, the cause of the working class would be promulgated while the stability necessary for increasing affluence would be assured. Because capitalism had stabilized, and through democracy had allowed for the activity of a proletarian party to gain reforms, concern with the revolutionary goal had become useless, if not counterproductive, and it was the movement that had to be stressed. Thus, according to Bernstein, *"the movement is everything, the goal is nothing."*

Bernstein's theoretical position is predicated on a commitment to reform increasingly lacking in contemporary social democratic movements. His concern was not whether class contradictions would continue to exist.[12] He was more preoccupied with legislation that might more equitably distribute income, assure social services, and create a "partnership" between labor and capital. Accepting the thesis that capitalism is learning to deal with crises, prior to the 1990s, mainstream economists of social democracy adopted Keynesian or neo-Keynesian policies of state intervention in the economy, deficit spending, subsidies for desirable production goals, and "direction" of the flow of capital. The twofold aim of modern social democracy was to maintain the stability of the existing apparatus and to gain economic benefits through the involvement of the state. Because they viewed electoral politics as the only arena for change, moreover, social democrats began appealing to the "middle class" and the professional strata. And so, while the bulk of their membership continues to be working-class, social democratic parties long ago ceased to consider themselves as "proletarian." They increasingly sought to present themselves as "national" parties willing to sacrifice the interests of workers for the "national interest" and intent upon allocating "public" goods to "private" individuals.[13]

The electoral success of social democracy is undeniable, though it was built on a belief in compromise that would erode the movement's more radical commitments. Other historical factors, however, prepared the ground for this development. Since the proletariat fought the battles of the bourgeoisie in 1789 and 1848, an "elective affinity" (Weber) resulted between the proletariat and bourgeois democracy where capitalism achieved hegemony. In addition, the trade unions taught the early social democratic parties a reformist tactic that they would transfer from the economic to the political arena. The party and the unions were originally considered the "twin pillars" of the working class.[14] The necessity for a party derived from the idea that the immediate economic demands, with which unions concerned themselves, had to be translated into political ones. But, insofar as no explicit practical relation was ever established between these two workers' organs, it is not surprising that the social democratic theory of revolution should have remained vague at best or that an essentially reformist standpoint should have been prevalent in the movement from the start.[15]

Despite broader discussions at party conventions of internationalism, antimilitarism, and the mass strike, specific reforms were emphasized in the practical arena and the system as a whole was called into question only rhetorically. The electoral path, and the success of that path, helped to create a party bureaucracy.[16] This allowed for the continuation and promulgation of the movement over time, while giving the party organization a stake in maintaining the status quo. The socialist movement thus began to take on the aura of moderation and respectability, particularly after World War I.[17]

Marx recognized the concrete basis for this development when he criticized the old SPD for having "taken over from the bourgeois economists the consideration of distribution as independent of the mode of production and hence the presentation of socialism as turning principally on distribution."[18] Splitting off distribution from production results in more than a tactical adaptation of social democracy to the existing order. With such a view, it is impossible to conceptualize the relation between production and consumption in terms of the reproduction of society as a whole.[19] The state remains inviolate: the notion of workers' councils never enters into the equation. The state becomes the mechanism through which social democracy achieves its gains. In emphasizing distribution to the detriment of production, the social democrats can justify their emphasis upon electoral activity while presupposing the continuous operation and ability of the bourgeois state to meet the needs of modern production.

There is a sense in which, from this perspective, social democrats almost always were willing to serve as "managers of capitalism." For precisely insofar as parliamentary democracy rests upon capitalist social relations, the attempt to transform these social relations stands outside the province of social democratic politics. These social relations range from the continued existence of the law of value to bureaucratic rationalization, resulting in alienation and reification, to "commodity fetishism" and the capitalist division of labor. "Class consciousness" is consequently identified with support of specific reforms, while the need to develop an alternative social structure is disregarded.

To call for a restructuring of these social relations would necessarily question both the bourgeois state and the entire trajectory of modern social democracy. Attempts to introduce fundamental structural changes would obviously impede attempts to gain support from the "middle" classes as well as from the more conservative sectors of the working class—and the price would be paid in electoral losses. Both the French and the German social democrats have resisted attempts by radical factions to turn their policies to the left. Seeking to remain in the movement as long as possible, these factions have traditionally represented the idea of a more profound transformation, and for this reason they have often been driven from the broader party or isolated within it.[20]

Social democrats opposed the Russian Revolution, the uprisings of 1918–1923, and the radical undertakings in France, Greece, and Italy that followed World War II, as well as the more radical tendencies of 1968. Such spontaneous and extraparliamentary movements clearly posed a danger to the electoral paths of social democracy. But the response to them also revealed the looming *identity deficit* of social democracy: for the sake of past achievements, it sacrificed a radical future, and even those past achievements it would ultimately prove willing to compromise in the name of new electoral exigencies. Because social democracy identifies socialism with distribution, and democracy with the existing parliamentary system, a certain finished quality pervades it. Compromise gains a political value in its own right: it is no longer embraced merely as a tactic, but rather as a strategy, and a matter of course.[21] Consequently, social democrats often become myopic when they are faced with radical developments and ideological movements like those associated with the 1960s.

Social democracy confines socialism within the realm of civil society and associates it, almost exclusively, with nationalization, legislation, and social services. But such programs are not unique to socialism. Liberal capitalist governments, theocracies, and even fascist regimes can introduce them. Where social democrats are devoted to civil liberties, often to the point at which it becomes a fetish, democracy becomes circumscribed within the pluralistic political arena of the parliamentary state. The refusal to undertake a critique of the structural relations of capitalism, the dismissal of the need for an alternative, leads social democracy into a position where it can offer its public only greater productivity and more equal distribution as the status quo defines them. The lack of a program intent upon reconstructing work relations or extending democracy into the production process dulls the fundamental difference that should exist between social democratic and other parties. It is consequently differences on specific issues, and not structurally divergent critical outlooks, that provide the basis of choice between parties that compete for support from the center.[22]

Naturally, this cannot be seen in a rigid manner. Specific concerns may retain practical and even radical symbolic value, as in the case of nationalization with regard to the English, French, and Italian workers. Also, in given situations, these specific differences may prove of varying importance; some may involve ephemeral or transitory concerns, while others may involve issues that have already congealed into general policies. Liberal capitalist and social democratic parties, for example, have mostly supported free trade and regionalism, while communist and right-wing parties favored nationalism and protection. Though, by and large, workers have continued to give their electoral support to social democratic regimes in Western Europe, there is a question of how deep this attachment still runs.

A growing apathy among large sections of the young, the rise of what has been called "the new inwardness," and the crass cynicism that greets talk of "socialism" in everyday intercourse are certainly linked to the technocratic stance that the social democratic movement has chosen to take. There are structural reasons for this development. But social democracy has also contributed to the process insofar as it has jettisoned its own radical tradition. Events such as the Paris Commune served as symbols for the young social democrats, and theorists like Rosa Luxemburg, Henriette Roland-Holst, and Anton Pannekoek originally developed their views in the radical current of early social democracy. Their views on the *councils* and the mass strike, "proletarian self-administration" (Selbsttätigkeit), and internationalism arose once again in the 1960s. Even now, they might invigorate what has become a staid, stodgy, and often reactionary social democracy. Disaffection and alienation cannot simply be dismissed. They pose real threats to those very values of social justice and democracy that the social democrats have traditionally sought to pursue.

PARTY AND PROLETARIAT

The reformist critique of revolutionary orthodoxy retained an important truth: Eduard Bernstein called upon social democracy to bring its revolutionary theory in line with its reformist practice and appear as what it actually was. The situation was always very different with respect to the communist movement prior to the collapse of the Soviet Union. Its parties always considered themselves proletarian vanguards and the Soviet Union as the homeland of the revolution. Communism gained its rationale as the revolutionary alternative to social democratic reformism. It can even be argued that when social democracy was becoming ever more tepid, certain ex-communist parties tried to present themselves as a radical alternative by embracing its traditional program and ethos. Such a course made communism appealing to the more militant sectors of the working class. Nevertheless, if this tactic lacked any unique strategic purpose and reveals the bankruptcy of the original theory, the idea that the communist parties of old were actually following a revolutionary course is even more illusory.

Building on the tradition of Lenin and the Russian Revolution, the states of "actually existing socialism" viewed their regimes as dictatorships of the proletariat and transitions to a new society. The socialist ideal was trumpeted along with the theory of inevitable capitalist collapse. The Marxism they employed was crude, but it retained practical benefits. The proletarian masses remained on the side of history, and the vanguard party, as their representative, maintained its "privilege" in interpreting history. It seemingly made little difference that Leninism was far less functional as a theory of rule than as a theory of revolutionary struggle.

Ignoring this difference, ignoring the way in which the radical vision was used as a form of legitimacy, helped produce an ever evolving moral rot.

"What Is to Be Done?" attempted to confront the practical problems facing revolutionaries in Russia. Lenin recognized the lack of a socialist tradition, the lack of a sizable trade union movement, and a small proletariat; under such conditions, in addition to the ferocity of the czarist secret police, a "vanguard party" of disciplined revolutionary intellectuals assumed a certain historical justification.[23] The function of this revolutionary group was to bring consciousness to the workers from outside their ranks. Since the workers themselves can only attain trade union consciousness, in Lenin's view, the party represents the revolutionary conscience of the proletariat. Though Lenin knew that the party must remain "one step, but only one step" ahead of the proletarian masses, ultimately a division between the two occurs in a mechanical fashion. Real discussion of the issues occurs only within the party circle; "democratic centralism" does not allow for a dialogue between the party and the masses, but only for unilateral mobilization campaigns.[24] The ability to maintain discipline, to construct networks of communication, and even to organizationally go underground is greatly facilitated by such a structure. But a price is paid—and not simply in terms of the rise of bureaucratic domination and a terror apparatus.[25] The price is a loss of interaction with the proletariat itself—a central theme in Rosa Luxemburg's criticisms of the Bolsheviks.[26]

The issue is not whether "democratic centralism" actually functioned under Lenin's leadership and then degenerated, or whether Lenin and Stalin are one and the same. The former did not exercise complete control in the manner of the latter. Lenin was overruled by the majority of the party on many critical questions, and, within limits, free speech took place in the party circle. The history of the revolution testifies to the qualitative difference between Lenin's Bolsheviks and Stalin's apparatchiks during their periods of control.[27] But the real issue is that the Bolshevik idea of tutelage would prevent the masses from learning to exercise power themselves. Whether power was exercised by the Bolsheviks in a revolutionary manner or not is immaterial if the masses are prevented from having a say in deciding their destiny.

The refusal to establish any standards of accountability for the vanguard relative to the masses necessarily resulted in curtailing political participation and introducing a dynamic of repression. The public realm would become ever more circumscribed by the party.[28] Apathy on the part of the masses could even be seen as a welcome development: an implicit distrust of the masses emerges from Lenin's theory of the vanguard from the very beginning. Thus, whatever the justifications for Lenin's innovation in terms of Russian social conditions, the mistrust that the mass strike of 1905 initially provoked in him foreshadowed the position that he took when the choice had to be made between the party and the soviets during the civil war.

In abolishing the power of the soviets, and simultaneously banning other socialist parties, Lenin established a dual precedent. On the one hand, he created the identity between the state and the party that was later to result in the identification of the state with the party leader.[29] On the other hand, the party became the sole "revolutionary" organ of a hypostatized proletariat. From this perspective, any spontaneous political action on the part of the working class could be dismissed as "left-wing adventurism" or as "objectively counterrevolutionary" at the party's pleasure. The communist response to the French and Spanish events of 1936, to the postwar uprisings in Italy, and to the strike movement of 1968 testifies to the inherent conservatism of this view.

As the communist party identified itself with the Russian state, it viewed the Communist International as an instrument of Russian foreign policy.[30] If the communist revolution is embodied in a particular state, after all, international communist support for the policies undertaken by this state is the only way to support the revolution. Proletarian internationalism consequently turned into its opposite: support for a particular nation-state. Any interests perceived by the ruling clique in the Soviet Union as detrimental to its own were therefore seen as threatening the foundations of socialism; thus "proletarian internationalism" was invoked to justify the Soviet invasions of Hungary in 1956 and Czechoslovakia in 1968 and condemn any criticism as "objectively" supportive of the imperialist enemy.

More was involved than the metaphysical substitution of the party for the working class as the agent of history. Marxism always insisted upon the need for a party in order to organize the revolution and a state in order to bring the "transition" from socialism to communism. But this only begs the question: what kind of party and what kind of state? In contrast to the social democrats, the communists abolished the "bourgeois" model of pluralistic democracy both in the party and the state. The point was not to elicit the articulation of new interests but to repress any particular interest deemed threatening by the party. Transcending the politics of bourgeois democracy subsequently became the rationale behind the communist "dictatorship of the proletariat."[31] This was perversely, in turn, seen as providing the groundwork for the new society in which, according to Marx, "the free development of each would serve as the condition for the free development of all."

Marxist teleology was understood as guaranteeing this development even though means, ever more surely, became divorced from ends. What resulted, of course, was the arbitrary exercise of power by a bureaucratic party apparatus over the classes it claimed to represent. In spite of the corruption, the existence of a semilegal black market, the return to devices of competition, the privileges given to bureaucrats, and all the inequities, the national welfare system constructed by the communists was far-reaching in its practical effects. All the more is the pity that its accomplishments should now be forgotten. Given the terror unleashed on the populace and the ongoing political repression, however, perhaps such a development only makes sense. Changing the perception of socialism indeed remains among the most important goals of the left and its partisans.

DEMOCRACY ON THE LEFT

Communism was not alone in decimating a generation. The larger historical question is whether it unleashed the hitherto repressed forces and values of an incipient new order. The answer is simple: communism has virtually destroyed the emancipatory perception of socialism and bequeathed a legacy that the nonauthoritarian left still seeks to surmount. Internationally, through the rigidity of its dogma, its continuous refusal to perceive the nature of fascist threats, and its refusal to exploit potentially revolutionary situations, the Comintern relinquished its revolutionary role long before its demise. Domestically, the record is equally bleak. The "heroic years" of the revolution from 1917 to 1921 may have been marked by experimentation, attempts to overcome traditional mores and culture as well as old prejudices. Nevertheless, for the contemporary public, its historical legacy is unambiguous: it is now associated with repression—pure and simple.

As for social democracy, it has been a mainstay of republicanism and policies associated with the pursuit of economic justice. It has changed the standing of workers in the community and introduced the welfare state. In the process, however, it has separated the concerns of its party from the class that still serves as its mass base. Its lack of concern with issues of "alienation" and the prejudices associated with the bourgeois version of everyday life, its technocratic style, and its establishmentarian rhetoric fuel its use of what might be termed an ideology of compromise: the willingness to abandon both principle and interests if the surrender serves the immediate interests of the party apparatus in its electoral campaigns. The liquidation not merely of the socialist "goal" but its basic commitments has gradually liquidated the ability of less moderate socialists to contest the dynamic associated with this ideology of compromise. Social democracy is losing its sense of identity, its appeal to the young, no less than its ability to generate new ideas. Little remains of what was once a movement identified with the protest against injustice.

Conceiving of socialism in terms of centralized planning, nationalizing property, market reforms, or a party apparatus pitted over and against the populace involved a perversion from the beginning. Marx knew that the crucial point in differentiating socialism from capitalism lies not in *what* is produced but rather *how* it is produced. The context within which production takes place necessarily affects production itself; this was recognized by the more radical elements among students and workers in their attempts to introduce *autogestion*, or workers' control, during the great strike wave of 1968. Socialism requires a "third way" that looks back to the Paris Commune, the soviets, the workers' councils, and the thinkers associated with the ideas concerning the "self-administration" of the proletariat.

If socialism is something more than a word, or a slogan, then it must make freedom more visible, more expansive, and more attractive. There are always traces of new tendencies within existing movements that represent the attempt to refashion the old promise. At this time, when radicals stand at the margins, it is not the dogmatic assertion of one interest or party line over another, but rather the willingness to foster these new tendencies— wherever they arise—that alone can invigorate the socialist project.

2

PERSISTENT MEMORIES

Jewish Activists and the German Revolution of 1919

THE YEAR 1919 is extraordinary in German history. It brought the democratic revolution of 1918 abruptly to a close and opened the door for what in 1933 would become the Nazi seizure of power. Paranoia gripped Germany in 1919. Inspired both by the bitter reality of defeat on the battlefield and the radical specter of bolshevism, it produced a subtle shift in the common understanding of anti-Semitism and the fears motivating the anti-Semite. The year saw the preoccupation of the right-wing press with the "Jewification" (*Verjudung*) of German society make way for the vision of a "Jewish-Bolshevik" conspiracy."[1]

The *Protocols of the Learned Elders of Zion*, forged in the aftermath of the Dreyfus Affair, had already been made popular in Russia during the Revolution of 1905.[2] Anti-Semites in Germany learned from the *Protocols*. They continued to bemoan the dominance Jews supposedly held over certain professions including banking, and they still referred to Adolf Bartels, the noted nineteenth-century philologist, and his list of eight hundred Jewish writers who were supposedly displacing German writers from their culture.[3] But the war and subsequent revolutions transformed older concerns. Jews were now considered not merely as religious heretics or profiteers, the worst sorts of capitalists, but also traitors undermining the German nation in the name of democracy while conspiring with the international communist revolution against Christian civilization. This change in the anti-Semitic worldview made it possible to speak of Weimar democracy as a "Jew republic."

Was this new order not the product of defeat on the battlefield, dominated by moneylenders, led by socialists, and willing to accept the provisions of the humiliating Treaty of Versailles? The November Revolution of 1918 had begun with the abdication of the kaiser and the returning troops, disgruntled and without hope for the future, whose plight was so well

The original version of this article appeared in *New Politics* Vol. 5, No. 2 (Winter 1995): 83–94.

described by Erich Maria Remarque in novels like *The Road Back* and *Three Comrades*. A power vacuum arose with the fall of the monarchy, and the German Social Democratic Party (SPD) filled it under the leadership of the prowar "majority" faction led by Friedrich Ebert, Philipp Scheidemann, and Gustav Noske.

Accompanying the rise to power of the SPD were strikes and mass disturbances of which the uprising initiated by a group of sailors in Kiel was the first. The aristocracy and bourgeoisie feared for their status and their property. The military and bureaucracy felt betrayed by the defeat, while peasants and the petite bourgeoisie embraced the legend of the "stab in the back" perpetrated by Jews, pacifists, socialists, and communists on the home front. The situation was perilous, and the possibility of civil war real enough. Social democracy had always held forth the promise of a republic. But it was now in a difficult position.[4] The SPD could either compromise with the antidemocratic and reactionary classes of the Wilhelmine monarchy and introduce a "republic without republicans" or risk civil war and possible invasion at the hands of the victorious allies by taking a more radical approach. This would involve purging the military and state bureaucracy, liquidating the estates of the reactionary aristocracy in the East, and dealing with an insistent minority of the proletariat seeking a genuinely "socialist" republic based on the spontaneously erupting "workers' councils" (*Räte*) or "soviets" if not the more authoritarian tenets of Bolshevik theory. The Social Democrats chose the less dangerous option and turned on the left, whose most important proponents wished to chart the more radical, if somewhat inchoate, course of action.

None of this meant much to the far right. Its ideological attachment to xenophobia, militarism, authoritarianism, and anti-Semitism created the philosophical context in which Jews could appear as the root of the problem. Their inbred lack of principle and national roots supposedly made it possible for them to dominate the liberal bourgeoisie, social democracy, and international communism as well. The "Jews" were thus capitalists and "reds" at the same time: the Jew became a chameleon capable of assuming any guise. Inextricably connected with the forces supposedly dominating the Weimar Republic, or what the Nazis termed "the system," it was not unreasonable to believe that the "Jew republic" should have crushed the uprisings in which any number of Jewish revolutionaries played a highly visible role.

*   *   *

Rosa Luxemburg was clearly the predominant figure among them. Born in 1871 in the city of Zamosc, Poland, to a middle-class Jewish family, Luxemburg became a revolutionary while still in high school. Hunted by the police, she fled to Zurich before making a marriage of convenience in order to enter Germany and work with the jewel in the crown of international social democracy: the SPD. Various writers have emphasized the effect of being a Jew or a woman had on the identity of Rosa Luxemburg.[5] She was always an opponent of bigotry and insisted on equality. Her thinking grudgingly allowed for "national cultural autonomy,"[6] and she saw social democracy as the natural home for the oppressed. But the argument originally made in her dissertation, *The Industrial Development of Poland* (1894), with its critique of Polish nationalism extends by implication to all forms of particularism. Luxemburg would consistently oppose any ideology capable of compromising proletarian unity, the struggle against imperialism, or what she considered the internationalist tenets of Marxism.

Her principles were well known, but her early writings were not. Luxemburg's ascent in the world of international social democracy began with a contribution to what became known as the "revisionist debate" of 1898. Initiated by Eduard Bernstein with a set of articles, which were reworked into a book titled *The Preconditions of Socialism*, orthodox Marxism was charged with ignoring the manner in which capitalism had stabilized and the fact that the "inevitable" proletarian revolution anticipated by Marx was no longer on the agenda. Insisting that "the movement is everything and the goal is nothing," Bernstein called upon social democracy to surrender its "revolutionary phraseology" and foster a policy of compromise with nonproletarian classes to ensure economic reforms so socialism might gradually "evolve."

Social Reform or Revolution (1899) was the liveliest contribution to the debate made by any critic of "revisionism," which included the most famous theoreticians of orthodox Marxism like Karl Kautsky and Georgii Plekhanov. In this pamphlet, Luxemburg noted how crisis was endemic to capitalism and expressed her fears about how an unrestricted politics of class compromise might justify any choice by the party leadership, and shift power to the trade unions. She also argued that there were limits to reform and that it could never transform the production process or eliminate the prospect of imperialism and political crisis. Without a political revolution, she argued, reforms granted under one set of conditions could also be retracted under another. A simple emphasis on economic reforms would thus result only in a "labor of Sisyphus." Indeed, without an articulated socialist "goal," she believed that the SPD would increasingly succumb to capitalist values and surrender its sense of political purpose.

Just as Luxemburg rejected the idea of a democratic mass party run by experts and basically concerned with incremental reforms, however, her *Organizational Questions of Social Democracy* opposed the idea of a "vanguard" party based on blind obedience and dominated by revolutionary intellectuals. Lenin and Bernstein were, for her, flip sides of the same coin. In her view, both sought to erect an "absolute dividing wall" between the leadership and the base. If socialism is to transform workers from "dead machines" into the "free and independent directors" of society as a whole, Luxemburg argued, then they must have the chance to learn and exercise their knowledge. Consequently, it only makes sense that the radically democratic aspects of the Russian Revolution of 1905 should have inspired her finest theoretical work, *Mass Strike, Party, and Trade Unions* (1906).

This pamphlet placed a new emphasis on the innovative talents of the masses in organizing society. It spoke about connecting economic with political concerns. It also articulated her organizational dialectic between party and base, which would gradually build the "self-administrative" capacities of workers by helping them develop new representative institutions and then, at a different stage of the struggle, still newer ones. This radical democratic vision stayed with Rosa Luxemburg during World War I, which she spent in a tiny prison cell. There she wrote various responses to her critics, translated *The History of My Contemporary* of her beloved Korolenko, and—under the pseudonym Junius—produced the great antiwar pamphlet, *The Crisis in the German Social Democracy* (1916), which mercilessly criticized the SPD for its support of the kaiser's war, its obsession with votes, its cowardice in the face of public opinion, and its betrayal of working-class interests.

Also written in jail were her beautiful letters to friends and lovers. They portrayed her diverse interests, her courage, and her deep sense of humanity. Sonja Liebknecht—the wife of Luxemburg's fellow socialist martyr Karl Liebknecht—published a small volume of her more intimate letters in 1922, and another followed a year later edited by Luise Kautsky. Interestingly enough, they served a political purpose. The publication of Luxemburg's letters was meant to build sympathy for the woman who was being castigated both by social democracy and a communist movement undergoing "bolshevization" and attempting to rid itself of what its former leader Ruth Fischer called "the syphilitic Luxemburg bacillus."

There was good reason why this increasingly authoritarian movement should have turned on the first president of the German Communist Party. In jail, while in ill health and with little information other than newspapers, Rosa Luxemburg wrote what was surely her most prophetic and intellectually daring work. *The Russian Revolution* (1918) exposed the compromises that would ultimately undermine the Soviet experiment. Opposed to Lenin's agrarian policy, continuing to reject the use of slogans implying the "right of national self-determination," her analysis is best known for insisting that the revolution extend both formal and substantive democracy, as well as for the justly famous words: "Freedom only for the supporters of the government, only for the members of one party—however numerous they may be—is no freedom at all. Freedom is always and exclusively freedom for the one who thinks differently. . . . Its effectiveness vanishes when 'freedom' becomes a special privilege."

Paul Levi, her lawyer with whom she was intimate toward the end of her life, entreated Luxemburg not to publish the piece for fear of aiding the reaction. She reluctantly agreed. She may not have had the strength to refuse. Alfred Döblin described her in his lengthy novel *Karl und Rosa* (1950) as suffering a nervous breakdown in prison. Following her release in 1918, her hair had turned white and she appeared even more frail and thin. But Luxemburg extended her support to the Spartacus group that would serve as the nucleus for the German Communist Party (KPD) and advocate the creation of "soviets" (or "workers' councils"). In spite of its legendary stature, Spartacus never received the support of a proletarian majority—and Rosa Luxemburg knew it. She warned against setting loose the revolution in Germany and, after initially opposing the idea of a national assembly, ultimately called for participating in the elections of the nascent Weimar Republic. But she was outvoted. The Spartacus Revolt broke out in 1919, and Rosa Luxemburg decided to remain in contact with the masses. Article after article in the bourgeois press implicitly or explicitly called for her death, and even the socialist *Vorwärts* printed the ditty:

> Hundreds of proletarian corpses all in a row—proletarians!
> Karl, Rosa, Radek and company!
> All in a row—proletarians!

Some claim, or like to believe, Luxemburg might have been able to counteract—if ever so briefly—the power of Lenin and the Bolsheviks on the international left.[7] In any event, she warned that a "military dictatorship" would soon supplant the Weimar Republic. But the forces of order got their wish. Rosa Luxemburg and Karl Liebknecht were brutally murdered at the hands of proto-Nazi thugs employed by the socialist government of Ebert and Gustav Noske, and the phony investigation into their deaths caused a sensation.[8] What's more, the murderers of Liebknecht and "bloody Rosa, the Jewish pig" got off easy. They served little jail time, and all became heroes in the Third Reich.

Grimly, for a short time, Leo Jogiches took over the reins of Spartacus. Luxemburg had fallen in love with him during her time in Zurich, and though their affair was now over, he never lost his affection and admiration for her. Jogiches, who was born in 1867, was always her political ally, and while their relationship was difficult, Luxemburg relied upon his advice to the very end. Leo Jogiches was a great and honorable revolutionary. He had spent years underground and in jail. He was not a theorist or a writer, but a man of action who thrived during times of upheaval and used his considerable family fortune to help finance the labor movement in Poland, Russia, and Germany. He participated in virtually every revolutionary uprising during the early years of the century, opposed World War I, and was instrumental in founding Spartacus. He begged Luxemburg and Liebknecht to leave the country when it was clear that defeat was certain. They rejected his advice and moved from one flat to another, without a plan or an idea about what should come next, before they were caught. Ironically, however, Jogiches himself stayed in Berlin. With what must have been a rare smile, he apparently said: "Somebody has to stay, at least to write all our epitaphs."

The death of Rosa Luxemburg left Jogiches a broken man. Obsessed with bringing the murderers to justice, and preserving her papers, his own life lost all meaning in 1919. By all accounts, Leo Jogiches almost purposely left himself open to capture, and while under arrest, he was shot in cold blood.

Paul Levi assumed the leadership of the KPD after the death of Luxemburg and Jogiches.[9] Born on 11 March 1883, he had studied jurisprudence at the University of Berlin and the University of Grenoble and, after receiving his degree, quickly became one of the leading lawyers in the SPD; indeed, it was Levi who defended Rosa Luxemburg in her famous trial for engaging in antimilitarist activity in the months preceding World War I. Opposed to the conflict from the very first, by 1916, Levi had entered the executive committee of Spartacus and represented Lenin's call to transform the conflict between states into a "class war" at the Zimmerwald Conference in 1917.

Levi pressed the investigation into the death of Luxemburg following the defeat of the Spartacus Revolt. He also insisted on drawing lessons from the defeat. This led him into conflict with the Bolshevik leadership in Moscow who supported Béla Kun, the famous Hungarian communist, in maintaining an "offensive" strategy of armed uprising. Levi now argued instead for a "defensive" strategy. He believed that the communist cadres had been devastated, the proletariat exhausted, by the defeats of 1919 and that it was now necessary to begin the task of rebuilding by entering the unions, attracting new members, concentrating on ideological work, and refusing to engage in romantic ultraleftism. The debate came to a head over the March Action of 1921. An uprising that had been called by Moscow against the pleadings of Levi was quickly crushed. In a complicated back-and-forth, Levi essentially demanded that the Moscow leadership take responsibility for the debacle. Lenin was himself initially skeptical about the revolutionary attempt. But when Levi leveled his criticisms publicly, the Russian leader showed no hesitancy in purging him from the Comintern for breach of discipline even while integrating his policy proposals into *Left-wing Communism: An Infantile Disorder*. It was in the aftermath of this controversy during 1922 that Levi released Luxemburg's pamphlet *The Russian Revolution* for publication.

Levi tried to remain active before his death in 1930 in what might have been an attempt at suicide. He ultimately rejoined the SPD. But he remained an outcast without power or influence. The Social Democrats had little use for him or memories of Luxemburg either for that matter. An organized anticommunist witch-hunt had accompanied the birth of the Weimar Republic. It struck hard in Bavaria. This province had remained relatively free from the influence of the Ebert and Noske government in Berlin. Its capital city Munich also witnessed uprisings like so many other cities in Germany. The most famous involved the reformist politician Kurt Eisner—a Kantian pacifist and longtime socialist parliamentarian, a newspaper editor as well as a writer of socialist lyrics and fairy tales[10]—who wound up leading a demonstration of 200,000 people and then, in the aftermath of the kaiser's abdication, heading a minority government that introduced numerous progressive reforms. Eisner was the first of the "five literati" who would dominate the Munich events of 1918–1919. His assassination while on the way to hand in his resignation, coupled with the emergence of a short-lived Hungarian Soviet, generated the desire for a Bavarian Soviet. It was believed by many on the international left that a soviet in Bavaria would induce the Austrians to form one of their own.[11] Thus, the summary declaration of a Bavarian Soviet on 7 April 1919 made a certain degree of political sense even if the material conditions for its success were lacking.

The Bavarian Soviet was initially ruled by independent socialists like Ernst Toller along with a sprinkling of anarchists like Gustav Landauer and Erich Mühsam in coalition with representatives of the SPD. But the independents were organizationally weak, and the majority socialists were increasingly disgraced by the actions of their comrades in Berlin. As a consequence, this regime found itself supplanted by a communist government whose most visible leader was Eugen Leviné. Communist rule, however, lasted only two weeks. It was displaced by a new "dictatorship of the natives" led by Toller and his friends, which lasted only a few days before capitulating to the forces of right-wing reaction.

The Bavarian Soviet never had a chance. It may have had strong support from the working class, but it immediately became the object of intense hatred by the capitalist, the petit bourgeois, and the peasant. The new soviet was also a perfect target for the "philistines." Munich was, after all, a center of the expressionist avant-garde before World War I. Perhaps for this reason, especially at the beginning, the Bavarian Soviet was strongly influenced by representatives of the literati including, among others, Otto Neurath, Lion Feuchtwanger, and Oskar Maria Graf. And these intellectuals did not make the best politicians. The Bavarian Soviet never produced leaders on a par with Luxemburg, Liebknecht, or Levi. The foreign minister of this staunchly Catholic province was, in fact, a certifiable lunatic by the name of Franz Lipp, who—in all seriousness—decided to declare war on the pope. Nevertheless, for better or worse, the Bavarian Soviet was unique in attempting to fuse cultural with political liberation.

Its guiding spirit was undoubtedly Gustav Landauer, who withdrew from active participation when the communists took power. He was a pacifist and an anarchist whose nobility of spirit and commitment was noted by everyone who knew him. Born in 1870 in Karlsruhe, Landauer entered politics very young. "I was an anarchist," he liked to say, "before I became a socialist." And that was true enough. Landauer may have joined the social democratic movement, and he may have edited a journal called *The Socialist* around 1900. But from the start, he had little use for the reformism of the SPD and quickly became a leading figure of an ultraleft faction, known as "the young ones," which was summarily expelled in 1894. Proudhon and

Kropotkin would always play a far greater role in the thinking of Landauer than Marx. His anarchist vision was directed less toward the institutions of the economy and the state than the human condition. He became interested in the "life reform" movement, and, by 1902, his work had already influenced those involved with the journal *New Community*, to which any number of major Jewish intellectuals like Martin Buber would contribute. Indeed, this also was around the time Landauer formed what would become a lasting friendship with Erich Mühsam.

Landauer was more than a political figure or a bohemian. He was also a noted historian of literature, the author of a fine study of Shakespeare, and a novelist whose works brought him a wide measure of acclaim. His world was unbounded, and that was also true of his wife, Hedwig Lachmann, who translated Oscar Wilde and Rabindranath Tagore. Landauer spoke of himself as a German and a Jew in essays like *The Developing Person* (1913). But he deemed the whole of his personality more than the sum of its parts, just as humanity was, for him, more than the various nationalities and ethnic communities making it up. A presumption of human goodness and a striving for a utopian condition of harmony, a respect for the individual and love of community, informed his ethics. These beliefs also played a role in his somewhat less notable political writings like *A Call to Socialism*, which envisioned economic equality along with a new direct form of democracy whose control by a newly educated working class would make violence dispensable.

Marta Feuchtwanger—the wife of the great realist novelist Lion Feuchtwanger—told an interesting story about Landauer. Apparently, after being arrested following the collapse of the Bavarian Soviet, he started talking to the soldiers escorting him to prison about the goodness of humanity when suddenly, tired of walking and weary of his monologue, they summarily beat him to death.[12] He looked to the future without seeing the present. Baron von Gagern, the officer responsible for his murder, was never punished or even brought to trial. This story, which speaks volumes about the judiciary in the Weimar Republic, also provides a deep insight into the moral politics of Landauer. He always considered himself an educator and spoke to the best in people. His concern was less with institutions than the ways people treated one another. He called for a new humanitarian consciousness and a new democratic worldview. And as minister of education in the Bavarian Soviet, Landauer attempted to introduce a set of radical reforms ranging from allowing any eighteen-year-old to become a full-time student at the University of Munich to setting up a "students' soviet" and abolishing examinations. His democratic and bohemian perspective, in fact, becomes abundantly clear from his striking claim: "Every Bavarian child at the age of ten is going to know Walt Whitman by heart. That is the cornerstone of my educational program."

Rimbaud had called upon his generation to "change life." Erich Mühsam heartily agreed. And why not? Mühsam was for Germany, according to another famous anarchist, what Rimbaud was for France.[13] Born in 1878, the son of a Jewish pharmacist in Berlin, he was expelled from high school for socialist agitation. Mühsam felt himself an "outsider" from the beginning and naturally gravitated to the anarchist circles of Berlin and Munich. Max Nomad described him as an inveterate sponger during these early years.[14] But in 1904, *The Desert*, his first collection of poems, was published, and, soon enough, Mühsam began making his name as the author of cabaret songs, anecdotes, and sketches. He riddled social democracy with sarcasm in poems like the untranslatable "*Die Revoluzzer,*" and important journals like *Die Weltbühne* and *Simplicissimus* began publishing his work.

"Let us make room for freedom" was a line in one of Mühsam's poems. And that was what he sought to do when, in 1911, he became the editor of *Kain*, which he described as a "magazine for humanity." It was, of course, nothing of the sort. This journal based in Munich was sophisticated and avant-garde. Mühsam wrote every line, like his Viennese friend and counterpart, Karl Kraus, the editor of *The Torch*. Mühsam advocated pacifism, sexual liberation, and an apocalyptic notion of revolution. He defended his radical friends and castigated the status quo. When World War I broke out, he published a collection titled *Deserts, Craters, and Clouds* in which he made the plea: "drink, soldiers, drink. . . ."

Mühsam refused to serve in the army or register as a conscientious objector. And, for this, he was jailed. He came out against the National Assembly following his release and sought to found an Association of International Revolutionaries in Munich, which came to nothing. The group's program was somewhat unclear, and organizational questions bored Mühsam. Never particularly concerned with the class struggle, in keeping with Landauer, he spoke to the "exploited" and even attempted to proselytize among the lumpenproletariat. Mühsam's vision of socialism, like that of Landauer and Toller, was essentially aesthetic and visionary.

Mühsam was taken alive after the fall of the Bavarian Soviet and condemned to fifteen years at hard labor. The sentence was commuted to five years. He continued his anarchist activities after his release, but grew more sober. His new journal, *Fanal*, no longer criticized social democracy as the main enemy, but the Nazis. Mühsam spoke out against the abuses of the Weimar judicial system and supported organizations like Red Aid, which raised money for political prisoners and sought their liberation. He wrote a play, *Reason of State*, about Sacco and Vanzetti, and an account of the Bavarian Soviet titled *From Eisner to Leviné: A Reckoning*. His own humanistic values and hopes for the Bavarian Soviet are therein made clear along with the stubbornness of the communists. Even in this work, however, Mühsam could not adequately deal with the shortcomings of his own political voluntarism or the institutional and social reasons for the failure of the Bavarian experiment.

Few were hated with the same degree of passion by the nationalist right, and its advocates continued to vilify Mühsam during the years of the Weimar Republic. This anarchist Jew somehow stuck in the craw of the far right. Henry Pachter even suggested that Hitler probably remembered the young bohemian, playing chess in the famous Cafe Megalomania in Munich after the war, and making fun of the future chancellor's drawings.[15] In any event, the philistines had their revenge. Following the Nazi seizure of power, Mühsam was immediately captured and transported to the Oranienburg concentration camp, where he died in 1934 after being slowly and almost systematically beaten to death.

Mühsam was one of the best-loved figures of the Bavarian Soviet, and there are enough reports about workers and soldiers shouting his name and even carrying him on their shoulders. He was a satirist, an ironist, and something of a clown. He never showed favoritism toward any party and acted responsibly as a leading politician of the Bavarian Soviet. Mühsam sought unity, proved willing to compromise with the communists, and even appeared as their spokesperson on one or two occasions. All of this he did without surrendering his principles or his various utopian ideas for reform. He knew who he was and his "identity" was never a problem for him. Thus, Mühsam could write:

> I am a Jew and will remain a Jew so long as I live. I never denied my Judaism and never even walked out of the religious community (because I would still remain a Jew and I am completely indifferent under which rubric I am entered in the state's register). I consider it neither an advantage nor a disadvantage to be a Jew; it simply belongs to my being like my red beard, my weight, or my inclinations.[16]

It wasn't much different for Ernst Toller. The most famous and perhaps prototypical leader of the Bavarian Soviet was born in Posen in 1893, and his autobiography—*I Was a German*—speaks elegantly of anti-Semitism in Germany. But still he joined the military in a mood of "emotional delirium" to fight in World War I. Given his release in 1916, in the wake of a nervous breakdown, he soon became a staunch pacifist and ultimately a socialist. After studying at the universities of Munich and Heidelberg, where he came to know Max Weber and various other distinguished academics, Toller wrote his deeply autobiographical play *Transformation* (1917). Dream sequences, abstract figures, and various other expressionist techniques are employed in this drama whose main character experiences any number of "transformations," each of which liberates him from a prior ideological prej-udice, until finally he finds "redemption" (*Erlösung*) in a utopian vision of "revolution." Based on a fundamental "faith in humanity," concerned less with workers than an image of the oppressed, this "revolution" would neces-sarily prove nonviolent and bring about a change in the very "essence" of "man" beyond all externalities. Toller was—like Eisner—a member of the Independent Social Democratic Party (USPD), which had split from the

SPD in 1916 over the latter's prowar policy. The USPD, small and poorly organized in Munich, had aligned itself with the councilist movement, and Toller quickly became a leading figure in the Bavarian Soviet. His reputedly remarkable oratorical abilities surely didn't hurt; indeed, it was said that "he carried the people by the force of his own convictions . . . They wanted a mission in life; Toller supplied them with one."[17]

The creation of the Bavarian Soviet was accompanied by the planting of freedom trees, the singing of Jacobin songs, and a great deal of libertarian rhetoric. The contemporary German writer Tankred Dorst, in fact, has argued that Toller interpreted the events of 1919 in terms of the expressionist apocalypse his works depicted. Whether that is true or not remains an open question. But it is surely true that Toller knew nothing about economics and not much more about institutions. His grasp of political priorities was also somewhat suspect. While Bavaria was experiencing a food shortage, in the aftermath of the allied blockade, Toller's first speech to the soviet concerned the new forms of architecture, painting, and drama by which humanity might express itself more fully. Administrative services collapsed, and the organization of revolutionary soldiers was a shambles; indeed, with a mixture of affection and sarcasm, Max Weber once remarked: "God in his fury has turned Toller into a politician."

But, in fact, Toller remains a great symbol for socialist libertarians. He was brave and humane. He fought courageously with the defenders of the Bavarian Soviet against the reactionary forces and saved many hostages from the revenge sought by various communist leaders like Rudolf Engelhofer. Toller was captured with the downfall of the Bavarian Soviet and spent five years in prison, part of the time—ironically—in a cell not far from the one occupied by Adolf Hitler. There he wrote his beautiful collection of poems, *The Swallow's Book*, which brought him great popularity, and attempted to unify respect for the individual with solidarity in works like *Man and the Masses* (1924) and *Broken-Brow*, which concerns an impotent war invalid abandoned by society. The pathos in the work of Toller increased along with his despondency. And yet, following his release, he joined the German League for Human Rights and participated in various pacifist organizations. Even while writing for prestigious journals like *Die Weltbühne*, which published his prison writings, and using an innovative expressionist style, he always considered himself a "people's poet" (*Volksdichter*). He was another, like Mühsam, who castigated the criminal justice system for its right-wing bias and *Hooray! We're Alive!* remains among the most trenchant criticisms of the materialistic and chauvinistic underside of the Weimar Republic.

Toller was also, along with Mühsam, one of the very few intellectuals who immediately realized the danger posed by the Nazis and what differentiated them from other "bourgeois" and even "reactionary" parties. Toller fled Germany when they came to power. He went from Switzerland to France, England, and finally to the United States. But he hated exile. He never made it in Hollywood, and while feeling his powers diminishing, he despaired as Hitler won victory after victory. Toller, the pacifist and humanitarian, committed suicide in New York in 1939. He never saw the end of the regime he so despised.

If Toller died too early, however, his communist competitor for power in the Bavarian Soviet—Eugen Leviné—died just in time. He would certainly have perished, perhaps even more cruelly, under Stalin. Leviné was not quite the saint his wife, Rosa Leviné-Meyer, portrayed in her biography. But he incarnated the best of the Bolshevik spirit. He was unyielding and dogmatic, but an honest intellectual and totally committed to the most radical utopian ideals of international revolution. Born on 10 May 1883 in St. Petersburg into a wealthy Jewish family, he was brought up in Germany where as a youth he actually fought a duel against someone who had made an anti-Semitic remark.[18] He returned to Russia in 1904 where he gained revolutionary experience and participated in the Revolution of 1905 before being arrested and severely beaten. After bribery secured his release, he moved back to Germany. There Leviné worked as a propagandist for the SPD and naturally gravitated to the circle around Rosa Luxemburg before joining Spartacus.

Leviné soon enough found himself in disagreement with his mentor. Enthralled by the Russian Revolution of 1917, in contrast to Luxemburg, he took a genuinely ultraleft stance. He was critical of the alliance between Spartacus and the USPD. He also vigorously opposed participating in the National Assembly and ultimately embraced Lenin's new Communist International. Believing the masses would follow an inspired vanguard, in keeping with the Bolshevik example of 1917, he and his close comrade, Max Levien, were instrumental in causing the defeat of the more moderate proposals of Luxemburg and the leadership of Spartacus, thereby paving the way for what would take place in Berlin.

But, for all that, Leviné acquitted himself valiantly during the uprising. The police hunted for him and at the urging of Paul Levi, the new leader of the German Communist Party, Leviné was sent to Munich where he was to put the small and disorganized party cell into order. Leviné's first article warned workers not to engage in any "precipitous" actions, and he opposed forming a Bavarian soviet. When the soviet was proclaimed anyway, appalled by its circuslike character, Leviné was successful in calling upon the KPD to remain in opposition. He still feared working with representatives of the SPD and, perhaps more fully than any other of its prominent figures, recognized the lack of support—especially among the peasants— for the soviet.

The question is why Leviné should have called upon the communists to reverse their position. He knew the soviet was doomed. Perhaps his new stance derived from a desire to take power and use the occasion to make propaganda and identify the communists with the soviet. His policy surely did not find its source in Moscow; indeed, no Bolshevik emissaries were active in Munich. Most likely, following Rosa Luxemburg, Leviné had decided to preserve the soviet ideal and "stay with the masses" in the face of the reaction.

Leviné was, interestingly enough, no less utopian than his opponents. His communists may have introduced censorship, but they too sought to revamp the schools, and proclaimed the famous *Frauenkirche* a "revolutionary temple." All this was a desperate attempt to mimic what has been described as the "heroic period" of war communism in the Soviet Union. Communist workers, however, soon enough turned against the disastrous policy of Leviné, and his heritage is tainted by the useless shooting of hostages and arbitrary confiscations carried out by members of his party. For all that, however, Leviné remained true to his beliefs. He participated in the street fighting, and his defiant death before a firing squad only testified to his courage. Indeed, with his cry of "Long Live the World Revolution!" the tragiccomedy of the Bavarian Soviet came to a close along with the most radical hopes of 1919.

*   *   *

Judaism never figured prominently in the writings or the politics of these activists. All were cosmopolitans and, essentially, assimilationist. But, in keeping with the Old Testament, they considered themselves prophets of justice, equality, and democracy. They were romantics without much sense of the institutions necessary to sustain these values. Each condemned the decadence of the status quo and genuinely identified with those whom, in biblical language, Ernst Bloch liked to call "the lowly and the insulted." Each prized the moment of action and sought to provide the masses with a new sense of their own possibilities. Each also exhibited exceptional bravery and remained true to his or her convictions. Each after his or her fashion challenged an alienation whose source is the story of Adam and Eve. Each dreamed of paradise.

These Jewish revolutionaries spanned the spectrum of radicalism, and seemingly little united them. They were a motley crew. Mühsam and Toller were leading figures of the expressionist avant-garde. But the first was an anarchist and the second a left-wing socialist. It was the same with Landauer and Eisner, though both were influenced by Kant. Leviné was a Bolshevik. As for Luxemburg, Jogiches, and Levi, they had little use for moralism or bohemians and even less for authoritarians. Judaism doesn't help much in explaining their particular form of revolutionary commitment. Viewing the matter in this light, however, is perhaps overly academic. The fascists and anti-Semites certainly didn't feel that way. Judaism has a certain importance when considering the uprisings of 1919, but less with respect to its impact on the revolutionaries themselves than on the activists of the counterrevolution. They used the visibility of these Jews to justify the idea of a "Jewish-Bolshevik" conspiracy intent on destroying Germany and the Aryan race.

Anti-Semitism doesn't disappear simply because Jews don't define themselves as such; 1919 is a case in point. The utopian values embraced by these Jewish revolutionaries, in fact, only heightened the fervor and brutality of those most intent on producing its opposite. And, in a way, they succeeded. All of these remarkable individuals were mostly forgotten long before the collapse of the Soviet Union in 1989 and the emergence of a right-wing cultural climate in its aftermath. The alternative they offered to both the impoverished cultural landscape of capitalism and what increasingly became a gray form of communism is now almost a memory. But this is precisely what makes it important to preserve a sense of their vision and their sacrifice, and contest the dark truth behind the beautiful words of Erich Mühsam:

> Who will remember me when I am dead?
> The sad day has snatched my youth.
> Evening came too soon. Rain fell.
> Happiness passed me by; I remained a stranger.
> My poor heart has its fill of suffering.
> Soon comes the night which has no stars.

3

IN THE SHADOW
OF THE RESISTANCE

Albert Camus and the Paris Intellectuals

WORLD WAR II transformed a generation of intellectuals. This was particularly the case with Albert Camus. The young essayist and novelist discovered a new sense of solidarity during this time in which each, employing a phrase from his play *State of Siege*, "was in the same boat." The defeat of France created a short-lived unity between previously conflicting political tendencies ranging from conservatives like General Charles de Gaulle to communists as well as anarchists like Pascal Pia. Even many who were nonpolitical found themselves drawn into some form of opposition against Hitler and his puppet rulers of Vichy. Intense, if often short-lived, friendships were forged in the cafes, underground cultural events, and countless meetings. The years of defeat were the ones in which Camus came to know Andre Gide, Andre Malraux, and Arthur Koestler, and grew close with figures like Jean-Paul Sartre and Simone de Beauvoir. It was the same with the great love of Camus' life, the wonderful actress Maria Casares, now best remembered for her minor part in the film *Children of Paradise*. Most of these friendships would sour after the war. Nevertheless, the bitterness of defeat generated a new sense of community and a hope for the postwar renewal of France from which the legend of the Resistance was born.

Camus joined the Resistance late. But he quickly made an exceptional contribution both as an activist and as the editor of *Combat*. He moved back to Paris where he lived first in a hotel and then in the flat of André Gide. He performed underground work and saw enough friends like René Leynaud, chief of the Paris sector, fall into the hands of the Gestapo and wind up dead or in concentration camps. All of Paris spoke about his editorials, however, and an aura surrounded him at the time of the liberation. The now famous *Letters to a German Friend*, which were dedicated to Leynaud, only enhanced his image.

The original version of this article appeared in *New Politics* 5, no. 4 (winter 1996): 150–166.

These letters were written as propaganda pieces, and the arguments are emotional rather than reasoned. Saying that France would emerge from the conflict with "clean hands" or that the Resistance killed without "hating," for example, only made sense in the most polemical terms. But, for all that, they evoke stark images and a sense of how a defeated population was forced to live "with humiliations and silences, with prison sentences, with executions at dawn, with desertions and separations, with daily pangs of hunger, with emaciated children, and, above all, with humiliation of our human dignity."[1]

The *Letters to a German Friend* do not simply justify taking up arms against the Nazis. They emphasize the moral cost to the victim of using violence to counter violence. Traces of his former pacifism remain as Camus wonders "if we had the right to kill men, if we were allowed to add to the frightful misery of this world." Questions of this sort, of course, are answered in the affirmative. But within the framework of propaganda, these letters meditate on the motivations for engagement and reflect the change a generation underwent. They admit the illusions of a time seemingly long past as Camus notes how:

> We had to make a long detour, and we are far behind. It is a detour that regard for truth imposes on intelligence, that regard for friendship imposes on the heart. It is a detour that safeguarded justice and put truth on the side of those who questioned themselves. And without a doubt, we paid very dearly for it.[2]

Two traditions are shown in conflict: fascism and humanism, irrationalism and enlightenment, force and what the French call *civilisation*. The ideological reasons for the war become clear in these letters along with what was culturally at stake. They provide a certain self-understanding for what drove young men and women into the Resistance. Indeed, they make plain the preoccupation with solidarity and conscience for which Camus would become known.

*   *   *

Camus was never a great political realist. He had joined the communist movement as a young man just prior to its endorsement of the antifascist Popular Front, which extended from 1936 to 1938,[3] despite his support for the "appeasement" policy advocated by Neville Chamberlain. Even following the German attack on Poland, Camus believed the allies should seek to negotiate with the Nazis.[4] He never really grasped the dynamics of totalitarianism and, whatever his experiences as a poor youth in Algiers,[5] of imperialism either. World War II was initially seen by him as essentially a product of human error and moral blindness.[6]

But, for all that, *The Plague* became one of the most important novels of the age. It soon sold over one hundred thousand copies. The novel was quickly translated into many languages, and turned Camus into an international celebrity. Ironically, however, it was written in the Massif Central where there was no fighting by a man who had never seen tanks rolling. Camus felt the war as an absence, which is precisely why he deals neither with battles nor the singular acts of wartime heroism, but the everyday life of a populace under siege. But, from the very first, everyone understood its purpose. *The Plague* crystallized the experience of a generation sick of war, guilty about its early defeat, and suspicious about the future.

Camus would never again portray as many multidimensional characters with diverse motivations for action. Written in five parts, reminiscent of the structure used in classical tragedy, this novel evidences a complex form of narration as well as a subtle mixture of direct and indirect forms of speech. Its sober prose, its careful construction, its deliberate understatement, all contribute to its enduring success. *The Plague* marks a shift of focus from the isolated individual of *The Stranger* and *The Myth of Sisyphus* to a situation calling for solidarity with others. The novel, according to Camus, "represents the transition from an attitude of solitary revolt to the recognition of a community whose struggles must be shared. If there is an evolution from *The Stranger*, to *The Plague* it is in the direction of solidarity and participation."[7]

This novel is the work in which Camus most clearly pulls together the various themes and images on which his career is built. It most clearly evidences his critique of Christianity, his refusal to love a god who lets the innocent die, and who demands unconditional acceptance of the human condition. It exhibits his humanism and provides perhaps the best understanding of his political worldview. The novel reflects the values of the Popular Front and, like so many other works from the 1930s and 1940s, there is no protagonist. There are no grand words and no grand gestures. There is, in short, "no question of heroism in all of this. It's a matter of common decency. That's an idea which may make some people smile, but the only means of fighting the plague is—common decency."[8]

The Plague portrays the tension between private and public commitments. Each character has his own worldview. Each makes choices and, with the exception of a collaborator named Cottard, assumes responsibility for them. Each has, for this reason, a different version of the events initiated by the plague. According to Camus, however, a "chronicle" is being presented that begins with rats dying in the town of Oran and leaving the plague as their legacy. People start becoming incurably ill and the authorities, after first attempting to downplay these developments, cling to habit and refuse to accept the evidence of an epidemic. Thus, ultimately, they find themselves without any plan for dealing with the emergency.

This is the point at which Tarrou unites a motley group of individuals with very different worldviews into a "sanitation corps" committed to fight the plague. Rieux is a doctor who can no longer heal; Grand is a clerk, who wishes to write a novel but cannot get beyond the first sentence; Rambert is a journalist torn between love for his mistress, whom he wishes to join in another city, and the growing sense of solidarity with the inhabitants of Oran; Paneloux is a priest who, from the pulpit, calls the plague a punishment from God and then witnesses the death of an innocent child; and finally there is Tarrou, a humanist and opponent of the death penalty, who keeps a diary of the plague.

Which of the characters is most "like" the author is an irrelevant question. Rieux illustrates the militant who, like Camus, doesn't subscribe to any particular political creed and quietly engages in the unheralded day-to-day battle with tyranny. Tarrou, like Camus, opposes capital punishment and seeks inner peace through his *morale de compréhension*. Joseph Grand, who could never complete his perfect work of art and reflects the writer's block often experienced by Camus himself, shows his dignity by engaging in the humble task of keeping careful statistics of the plague. Rambert is separated from his lover, just as Camus was separated from his wife by the outbreak of war, and in staying to fight the plague makes perhaps the ultimate personal sacrifice in the name of solidarity.[9] For all his Catholic dogmatism, which Camus experienced while convalescing at a Dominican monastery in 1943, Father Paneloux reflects the courage of his convictions. There is subsequently something in each of these characters with which Camus identifies, and in the solidarity they exhibit as well as the sacrifices they make, he finds "more things in men to admire than to despise."

The novel offers no certainty, however, that the struggle against the epidemic was of any use. Resistance does not defeat the plague, but only bears witness against it. The plague seems to subside on its own and Rieux, who ultimately emerges as the narrator of the novel, ruefully acknowledges to himself "what those jubilant crowds did not know but could have learned from books: that the plague bacillus never dies or disappears for good; ... and that perhaps the day would come when, for the bane and enlightening of men, it would rouse up its rats again and send them forth to die in a happy city."[10]

*   *   *

Roland Barthes called *The Plague* a "refusal of history." And this is obviously the starting point for any criticism. Numerous critics have noted how the real nature of fascism is ignored and the battle against an inhuman plague oversimplifies the matter of commitment. There is no reason for anyone to identify with a disease, and violence carried out against a human enemy is very different from the tactics undertaken in fighting the plague. Sartre was correct, in this regard, when he noted that the conflicts of interest inherent within a concrete "situation" disappear.

But in a way, this critique is external to the novel. It basically attacks Camus for not having written the "realist" or "naturalist" work these critics wanted to read. *The Plague* does not pretend to describe the horrors of totalitarianism in systematic fashion, nor is there a reason why it should. Material and instrumental constraints on action are also less the province of a symbolic tale than the moral conflicts experienced by individuals. Even worse, however, the criticism of Barthes and others like Sartre also obscures what is sociologically important about the work. It ignores the manner in which the novel actually offers a self-understanding of the Resistance.

Participants in the Resistance saw themselves, after all, as engaged in the battle against absolute evil; indeed, men and women of very different creeds united in a common project. Camus glorifies them, and perhaps, in this sense, *The Plague* helped foster what would become the "myth" of the Resistance. But there is also an element of truth in this idealized image. The Manichaean framework of good and evil employed by Camus, in fact, reflects the moral simplicity of choosing between fascism and antifascism. Philosophical excuses for collaborating with the Nazis, in this vein, fall apart. Also, in contrast to the carefully cultivated postwar image of an overwhelmingly popular antifascism, it is important to note how Camus depicts the majority of the populace as apathetic and falling back into a life of habit as the plague runs its course. Indeed, its Christian pessimism concerning the ineradicable character of the plague undercuts the revolutionary optimism in which France found itself enmeshed following the liberation.

Disease as the symbol of evil and as a basic element of the human condition has a long history. It extends from the Bible to the drawings of Albrecht Dürer to the writings of Daniel Defoe to the avant-garde dramatic theory of Antonin Artaud. Symbolically identifying totalitarianism with a plague, of course, obscures the character of a particular political system. Arguably, in fact, it even relativizes Nazism in relation to other forms of tyranny. Naturalizing totalitarianism, however, is a double-edged sword. There is nothing xenophobic about the book, and this was important during a time in which anti-German sentiment was particularly strong. Evil has no name, no race, no sex, and no nationality. Camus may have considered it part of the human condition, but he also knew that it can take many forms. His intention was clear: he would refuse to identify any one form of evil "in order better to strike at them all ... *The Plague* can apply to any resistance against tyranny."[11]

No other work of Camus or of the period so fuses a symbolic rendering of the human condition with the self-understanding of a particular historical experience. *The Plague* reflects the values embodied in a set of articles written for *Combat* in 1946, "Neither Victims nor Executioners." These are the pieces in which Camus rejects not merely fascism, but Stalinism with its perverse belief that a utopian future justifies the use of systematic murder in the present. Such utopianism and lack of respect for the individual are precisely what this novel contests. The infectious character of the disease raises the prospect of contamination, and doctors are warned about taking the necessary precautions in treating the victims lest they themselves become carriers. Thus, in the words of Tarrou, what Camus would consider the basic issue of the age becomes defined:

As time went on I merely learned that even those who were better than the rest could not keep themselves nowadays from killing or letting others kill, because such is the logic by which they live; and that we can't stir a finger in this world without the risk of bringing death to somebody.[12]

This novel is simultaneously an evocation of the Popular Front and a definitive break with the communist party. There is not a single communist among the prominent figures in the novel. Rieux, Tarrou, Grand, and Rambert are all liberal humanists; Paneloux is a Catholic. Communists played a prominent role in the French Resistance and were part of the common fight against fascism. The decision on the part of Camus to omit them was surely purposeful. It was based on what had become a definitive ethical position: "There is no objection to the totalitarian attitude other than the religious or moral objection."[13]

Solidarity would have meaning only insofar as respect for the individual was preserved. Camus had become sick of his age. He was appalled at the thought of untold millions being cynically sacrificed for the utopian dreams of dictatorial regimes. His artistic identification with Tarrou, who wished never to increase the suffering of anyone, now began to take philosophical shape. The idea of a revolutionary transformation would surrender before a concern with "achieving a rule of conduct in secular life."[14]

Rebelling against suffering while seeking to "correct existence" would now define his philosophy. Such was the message of *The Plague* when it appeared in 1947.

*   *   *

With an idealized notion of antifascist solidarity as its theme, however, *The Plague* was already consigned to an age gone by even before its publication. Three interconnected issues led to the dissolution of the Resistance following the defeat of its fascist enemy: the problem of the collaborators, the Communist Party, and the national liberation movement in Algeria. Each would have a profound impact on the career of Albert Camus.

Writing in *Combat* about the collaborators, at first, he advocated a policy of "justice without mercy" as the prelude to a socialist transformation of French society. As the purges proceeded under the jurisdiction of "popular tribunals," however, their arbitrary character became ever more pronounced. Camus grew increasingly disgusted and ultimately agreed in public with the earlier criticisms of his radical position raised by the great Catholic novelist and Nobel Prize winner, Francois Mauriac.[15]Camus learned his lesson. He became ever more concerned with the rule of law, the death penalty, and the sacrifice of individual lives for political purposes.

Camus was, of course, uninterested in "excusing" conservatives and remnants of the old right now gathered around General de Gaulle. He annoyed them by calling for an international boycott of Spain, which was still under the fascist yoke of Generalissimo Franco, and becoming a cofounder in 1948 of the Groupe de Liaison Internationale, which sought to give both moral and financial aid to political refugees regardless of ideological orientation. His opposition to the death penalty and commitment to the politically persecuted, however, also put him directly at odds with the communists who were busily engaged in bloody purges throughout Eastern Europe as well as, once again, in Russia itself.

Understanding postwar Europe is possible only by recognizing the prestige enjoyed by the Soviet Union, particularly in many of the Western countries previously controlled by the Nazis. The USSR was seen, rightly or wrongly, as having supported the Spanish loyalists and opposed the "appeasement" of Hitler. The pact between Stalin and the German dictator, which unleashed World War II and resulted in the dismemberment of Poland in 1939, was perceived as a defensive action caused by the vacillation of the democracies. The Soviet Union gained much sympathy for its enormous losses during the war; its citizens symbolized antifascist heroism during the great Battle of Stalingrad in 1943. Communists also played a valiant role in the European resistance movements, and their organizations commanded the loyalty of a significant number of workers in France, Italy, and elsewhere in the aftermath of World War II. The Soviet Union was also considered the natural ally of all national liberation and the primary opponent of Western imperialism. The future of communism appeared bright, and the inevitability of revolution seemed assured.

Exiles and victims obviously knew about the murderous purges of opponents, the concentration camps, the censorship, the constant lying, the egregious policies of the Stalinist regime. There was a sense among many that the communist utopia had become ever more divorced from the bureaucratic police state intent on economic modernization in the present. But the full horror of the "dictatorship of the proletariat," and its sacrifice of millions for the dreams of an egalitarian society, was not fully grasped. Arthur Koestler, with whom Camus enjoyed a tempestuous friendship, vividly crystallized this reality for a broader public in *Darkness at Noon*.

The novel described a former Bolshevik official's coming to terms with his beliefs and previous actions on behalf of the party while facing death in a Stalinist prison. It created a sensation and was instantly condemned by various communist intellectuals including most notably, a different acquaintance of Camus, the important philosopher Maurice Merleau-Ponty. His rejoinder to Koestler, *Humanism and Terror*, essentially justified the authoritarian brutality of Stalinism in terms of "historical necessity" and the difficulties encountered in the march to a communist utopia. He viewed the individual as subordinate to the collective and intentions as irrelevant to the social consequences of actions. Thus, even if the "subjective" criticisms made by Koestler were true, Merleau-Ponty thought it necessary to oppose them since they "objectively" weakened the Soviet Union and strengthened its Western "imperialist" adversaries in a "cold war" whose potential for heating up could produce nuclear catastrophe.

Camus was caught in the middle. He supported neither the Western imperialist exploitation of colonies ranging from Algeria to Vietnam nor the brutal policies in Eastern Europe practiced by the Soviet Union. Just after the war, in fact, Camus had witnessed the bloody repression of the first Moslem uprising in Algeria against imperialist rule, and his ensuing critical essays were so precise and clear in their demands that he was offered a government position. Camus refused, of course, especially since the army and various conservative cliques in both France and Algeria adamantly opposed liquidating the empire. Governmental cabinet after cabinet was paralyzed, and the intransigence of the right claimed its first victim as the Socialist Party gradually weakened in the face of the Algerian events and its own inability to overcome a mounting set of internal political squabbles. Thus, while the Resistance was fragmenting into communist and Gaullist tendencies, Camus increasingly found himself supporting a form of liberal socialism whose mass base in the proletariat was both numerically and institutionally disintegrating.

Camus refused to make a dogmatic choice between the two sides. His concern about the authoritarian cliques surrounding General de Gaulle caused tensions between himself and Malraux. The communists, for their part, deplored his unwavering commitment to civil rights and republican principles. Camus essentially sought a Scandinavian form of democratic socialism. But this says very little about his own unique idea of "engagement." Camus was increasingly reminded in the postwar era that he had never really articulated a political theory, let alone his fundamental criticisms of the communist worldview and its philosophical foundations.

While working on *The Myth of Sisyphus*, which was an attempt to separate himself from the existentialists by dealing with the question of suicide, Camus began collecting notes for a volume concerning the philosophical legitimacy of murder. *The Just*, a fascinating play about Russian anarchists engaged in plotting an assassination while questioning whether it is ever moral to take a life, was quite successful when it opened in 1949. But he started systematically working on the question of murder only in the aftermath of the Koestler affair. It proved difficult for him. He suffered from writer's block. He questioned his ability to write a treatise with the requisite philosophical, political, and literary depth. Perhaps he even had a presentiment of what would result from its publication. This new book would throw him into a windstorm of controversy, isolate him politically, and even cause the breakup of certain close friendships. *The Rebel* would become his first and last work of political theory.

* * *

The Rebel fused the personal ethic of lucidity and resistance against the inherent meaninglessness of life, which he had elaborated in *The Stranger* and *The Myth of Sisyphus*, with the notion of solidarity developed in *The Plague*. This work of political theory proposed a positive response to an "absurd" existence and a diagnosis of the "pathology" by which the age had come to view mass murder as an acceptable political option. Both aims are encompassed in the title, *L'Homme révolté*, which has a double meaning in French: the rebel and the revolted man.

The Rebel is essentially divided into three parts, dealing respectively with revolutionary transformation, artistic rebellion, and a political ethics based on "Mediterranean thinking." The logic and categories, however, follow directly from *The Myth of Sisyphus*. We live in an "absurd" universe defined by relativism and contingency. Just as suicide is an inadequate response to the human condition, however, so is rebellion opposed to the notion that "everything is possible and nothing has any importance."[16] For if suicide is illegitimate, then human life must assume primary value. The killing of another person is subsequently always wrong unless the murderer is himself or herself prepared to die as well. Herein lies the "limit" to rebellion and the meaning behind the belief that: "murder and suicide are the same thing one must either accept or reject them both."

Rebellion, for Camus, is a product of human nature. It is the practical expression of outrage in the face of injustice by a slave or anyone else who has experienced the transgression of an established limit by the master in any given social situation. Rebellion is based on the desire to be recognized as a person with dignity and certain basic universal rights. Solidarity is, in short, implicit in the notion of rebellion. Thus, Camus can make his famous claim: "I rebel, therefore, we exist."[17]

Too often, however, this concern with reciprocity is forgotten. The legitimate goal of countering exploitation is used to justify tactics directly at odds with it.[18] The rebel must, using the phrase of Nietzsche, "transvalue values." He or she, for this reason, will contest the prejudices of the established order and traditional absolutes incarnated in religion. Particularly in Europe, however, history or "reason" have been turned into new absolutes harboring guarantees of a future utopia in order to compensate for the loss of otherworldly salvation.

> Rebellion is born of the spectacle of irrationality, confronting an unjust and incomprehensible condition. But its blind impulse is to demand order in the midst of chaos and unity in the very heart of the ephemeral. It cries out, it demands, it insists that the scandal cease and that what has, up to now, been built upon shifting sands should henceforth be founded upon rock.[19]

The "absurd" thereby becomes mirrored in the actions of those seeking to abolish it. And so, in this way, a situation occurs in which the rebel can justify the murder of all those who stand in the way of constructing a just world. The end is seen as justifying the means. Therein, for Camus, lies the "pathology" of modern totalitarianism. Formerly "a life is paid for by a life. The reasoning is false but respectable. (A life taken is not worth a life given.) Today, murder by proxy. No one pays."[20] It is necessary to set existential limits. Thus, remembering a conversation with Koestler, Camus can write:

> The end justifies the means only if the relative order of importance is reasonable—ex: I can send Saint-Exupéry [the famous aviator and author of *The Little Prince*] on a fatal mission to save a regiment. But I cannot deport millions of persons and suppress all liberty for an equivalent quantitative result and compute for three or four generations previously sacrificed.[21]

The rebel must assume that life has an intrinsic worth. Otherwise, he or she would not contest injustice in the first place. Commitment to a perfect world must therefore become tempered with compassion. The genuine rebel, for this reason, continually strives to remember what motivated his or her undertaking in the face of political exigencies and the temptation of unethical action against others. "Memory," in this way, becomes the enemy of all totalitarians who, in seeking to break with *all* of history, necessarily destroy any coherent relation between ends and means as they elevate a future utopia beyond the needs of real individuals living in the present. The revolutionary desire to transform the "totality," in short, can only prove disastrous. This is why Camus can write: "It's general ideas that hurt the most."[22]

Art supposedly makes this plain insofar as it seeks to create meaning in a meaningless world. Incoherence is denied precisely because art stamps its own form on the real world. But Camus is, of coruse, talking about a particular type of art. True art must face the absurd without surrendering to it. And insofar as it does that, art mirrors the need for a progressive politics by constantly making reference to the happiness of the individual. When art ignores the conflicts experienced by people in reality, according to Camus, it results in little more than an empty formalism while the preoccupation with *engagement* leads to dogmatism and monotony. Art must take a third path between formalism and realism much as philsophy must reject both subjectivism and historical determinism.

An ability to remember the concrete subject plus a sense of "moderation," born of what Camus calls "Mediterranean thinking," become crucial. These qualities reject the "passion for divinity" lurking behind all utopian experiments. They undermine what turns revolutionaries into tyrants: the desire to transform human nature. These qualities inherently generate a belief in discourse, a certain open-mindedness, and a recognition of human frailty. Mediterranean thinking considers physical life, happiness, and creativity as the purposes of every progressive political action.

Murder and suicide, for better or worse, now become conceptually linked. Denying the possibility for happiness to another through murder is legitimate only by denying to oneself through suicide. A regulative idea, "a principle of reasonable culpability," appears. The rebel now knows himself or herself in the existential limits he or she accepts or, better, the degree of tolerance he or she extends to others in pursuing his or her goals. The point is simple enough. Indeed, even as a young man, Camus could maintain that:

> Politics are made for men, and not men for politics. We do not want to live on fables. In the world of violence and death around us, there is no place for hope. But perhaps there is room for civilization, for real civilization, which puts truth before fables and life before dreams. And this civilization has nothing to do with hope. In it, man lives on his truths.[23]

*   *   *

But what are those truths? Camus could boldly state: "Man is the only creature who refuses to be what he is."[24] But what does this inflated sentence really mean? And is it, either practically or philosophically, the case that because "I rebel, we exist?"

Circular reasoning underpins this claim, which appears all the more arbitrary precisely because Camus refuses to offer a general theory of human nature or society. His defenders might admire his philosophical modesty. But this doesn't change the questionable assertion on which his argument ultimately rests, namely, that "the first and only evidence that is supplied to me, within the terms of the absurdist experience, is rebellion."[25]

Rebellion is seen as an essential element of the human condition; Camus considers it inherently worthy of respect. He knows, however, that not every form of rebellion is justifiable. His aim in linking murder with suicide—the willingness to exchange one life for another—is to place a limit on rebellion, differentiate it from revolution, and "humanize" conflict in the face of the bureaucratic murder of faceless millions by totalitarian regimes. But there are problems with all of this. Neofascists and skinheads also see themselves as engaging in rebellion, but surely Camus cannot consider it necessary to legitimate their initial expression of outrage and, *only then*, condemn the exaggerated form their rebellion takes. Enough Nazis and Communists were also quite willing to risk dying in exchange for the murder of opponents in the brawls and street battles anticipating the rise of Hitler.

Rebellion is ultimately identified with those actions of which Camus approves, and the uncertainty of his argument is reflected in the sprawling structure of the work and its high-flown, often pompous, style. There is no serious historical or political analysis, and ideas are never contextualized within traditions. Baudelaire, Rimbaud, and Sade share the stage with philosophers like Hegel, Marx, and Nietzsche. Differing interpretations of these thinkers are simply ignored and, strangely, their views are dealt with in a completely uninspired fashion. Camus said nothing new about totalitarianism or, for that matter, the importance of civil liberties and republican values. His criticisms of French intellectuals with communist sympathies were also unoriginal. Political commentators like Raymond Aron had already attacked their theories with far more intellectual rigor, while antifascist writers, such as Arthur Koestler or Manès Sperber, depicted the reality of life under communism far more dramatically. Indeed, making matters worse, *The Rebel* lacks any practical referent for its metaphysical judgments.

No antiauthoritarian movement willing to engage in violence, which includes the antifascist resistance, can begin with the idea of equally exchanging the lives of its partisans for those of its enemies; it *must* attempt to maximize costs for the enemy and minimize its own losses. It is not enough simply to note the extreme case in order to justify the rule. Camus is, of course, correct in emphasizing the effect of ideology on action and the manner in which revolutions of the past generated organs of terror. But he never deals with the constraints in which movements operated. He never makes any reference to institutions or interests or possible structural imbalances of power in defining "oppression" or "exploitation." He also never deals with the inherent differences between a theory of revolution and a theory of rule.

All this, however, generally got lost in the emotionally and politically charged climate in which discussion of *The Rebel* took place. Communist hacks blasted it unmercifully. But, somewhat more ominously, conservatives and Catholics applauded Camus for showing how revolutions only produce new hangmen. The extremes met in their criticisms of the book. Camus surely dismissed those of the communists and deplored the "misunderstanding" of his work by the political right. But even liberal critics, who supported his attack on utopianism and identification with democratic values, expressed skepticism about his philosophical claims like the absolute value of rebellion. Raymond Aron snidely complimented Camus only for being less of a romantic than Jean-Paul Sartre.[26] Thus, there were already doubts about *The Rebel* before Camus engaged in his bitter debate with the virtual founder of modern French existentialism.

*   *   *

Camus and Sartre had become friends during the occupation. Both grew famous early in life. Sartre was eight years older than Camus, who was born in 1913. Camus grew up in Belcourt, a working-class neighborhood in Algiers in extreme poverty, while Sartre was part of an upper-middle-class family in Alsace and a cousin of Albert Schweitzer. Camus took his degree at the University of Algiers, while Sartre studied philosophy at the prestigious École Normale Superieure. Sartre was short, ugly, talkative, and a man of the city. He despised religion, liberalism, and everything connected with the bourgeoisie. He was, physically and psychologically, almost the mirror opposite of Camus. But, whatever the differences between them, their work dealt with similar themes: the individual, the absurd, freedom, and responsibility. Both began as bohemians; both were artists and interested in the theater, both were antifascists, and both ultimately formulated their politics only after the war. They associated with the same circle and, following the liberation, contributed to giving the "left bank" of Paris its intellectual glitter.

Much has been written about the relations between these two leading intellectuals of their generation. Their admirers have, in fact, virtually created a competition between them. And for this reason, it is necessary to say a word about their relative standing. Judging them is possible only by evaluating their contributions in different arenas of intellectual work. Camus never produced a philosophical treatise on the scale of *Being and Nothingness* and the much-undervalued *Critique of Dialectical Reason* or a biography with the depth and grandeur of those Sartre wrote about Jean Genet, the famous playwright and novelist, or Gustave Flaubert. Even the essays of Camus exhibited far less range and sheer brilliance than those of Sartre. But Camus was, clearly, the more talented artist. He also exhibited a sense of measure and clarity of ethical purpose lacking in his rival.

And, by 1952, they had become rivals. Sartre and Camus competed for a similar audience, they chose different political paths following the fragmentation of the Resistance, and each became more suspicious about the ambitions of the other. Camus believed his friend was creating an uncritical "mystique" of the working class, while Sartre saw the concern of Camus with democracy and limited revolt as ultimately justifying Western imperialism. Both were right in part. Indeed, while Sartre increasingly turned a blind eye to the repression exercised by revolutionaries, Camus increasingly found himself cast into the despised role of a reactionary anticommunist.

The burgeoning mistrust and misunderstanding broke into the open with a review of *The Rebel* in the legendary journal *Les Temps Modernes*, which Sartre had founded and edited, by François Jeanson. Camus had apparently asked his colleague to arrange a review, without suggesting any reviewer in particular, and Jeanson had volunteered. The result was not what either Camus or Sartre expected. Rather than treating *The Rebel* tactfully, as he had originally implied he would, Jeanson attacked Camus for his superficial philosophical interpretations of Hegel and Marx as well as his willingness to reject revolution without offering any positive or practical content for his vision of rebellion. Camus was furious. Suspecting that Jeanson was merely acting as the front man for Sartre,[27] he wrote a response to Monsieur l'éditeur titled "Revolt and Servitude." Camus essentially dismissed Jeanson, implying he was "unworthy" of reviewing his book, and attacked Sartre along with the rest of the editorial board of *Les Temps Modernes* as bourgeois intellectuals and Stalinists unwilling to condemn the concentration camp universe in the Soviet Union.

Sartre responded to Camus in a singularly biting and trenchant polemic.[28] He charged Camus with exchanging his earlier nonconformism and commitment to revolt for a fashionable anticommunism. He presented the willingness of Camus to condemn the excesses of both sides in the cold war as nothing more than a rejection of genuine political "engagement" and an inability to choose between imperialists and their victims. But there was also a personal attack. And Sartre knew which buttons to push. He castigated Camus for his arrogant treatment of Jeanson, his sensitivity to criticism, his self-professed weariness with politics, and his moral posturing. Indeed, coming from someone who presumably knew Camus well, all this probably carried greater weight with the public than the political arguments.

Each exaggerated the position of the other. Sartre knew that Camus was not some reactionary anticommunist. And for his part, Camus knew that Sartre had steadfastly refused to join the Communist Party and had just recently failed in organizing an alternative movement of the left called the Rassemblement Démocratique Révolutionnaire (RDR) for which Camus himself had campaigned. A *practical* question divided them, however, which has been consistently ignored. The issue was not simply whether to support the communists or oppose them. It was rather how nonaligned intellectuals should act in order to foster a progressive politics when the Communist Party tended to poll about 20 percent of the vote, received support from much of the working class, and a democratic socialist alternative was lacking. Each answered the question differently and, herein, lay the historical source of the existential and political conflicts between them.

Believing "engagement" within a situation always necessary, considering progressive politics impossible without the Communist Party, Sartre felt impelled to give the actions of the Soviet Union a "revolutionary privilege" in the cold war. Seeking to foster militancy among the working class, however, he never specified how an authoritarian communist movement would further this goal. And so, ever more surely, he found himself making one excuse after another for one "dictatorship of the proletariat" after another. The independence and political judgment of a great intellectual were thus increasingly rendered suspect.

Camus stood on principle. He protested against the bloody suppression of the 1953 uprising by workers in East Berlin as surely as he signed petitions calling for the release of the Rosenbergs who had been convicted as Soviet spies and sentenced to death in the United States. Supported by English and American intellectuals in his debate with Sartre, however, Camus wrongly became associated with a conservative anticommunism. He actually longed for a genuinely republican front capable of opposing both Gaullism and communism. But no mass base for such a project existed in

France. Thus, while the "engaged" man ever more surely appeared as an ideologue, the moralist found himself increasingly isolated.

Admirers of both Sartre and Camus still argue about who "won" the debate. But in fact, there was no "winner." Sartre radically underestimated the need for a democratic theory of governmental rule just as Camus lacked a notion of rebellion under colonial conditions in which nonviolence was impractical. Sartre became the great representative of anti-imperialist radicalism, while Camus was content to follow where his conscience led. Neither the revolutionary nor the rebel, however, could offer a coherent theory of "engagement" or an adequate response for *the* practical political problem of their time—perhaps because none was available.

* * *

Camus gave sustained public support to only one individual in postwar France: Pierre Mendès-France. A hero of the antifascist resistance and an intellectual, an anticommunist and a neutralist in the cold war, a liberal and a member of the Socialist Party, Mendès-France had—for a complicated set of reasons—become the leader of a liberal minority government in 1954.[29] He would remain in power less than a year, brought down by the combined effects of his Algeria policy and his call for withdrawal from another colony, Vietnam, following the humiliating defeat of French forces at the Battle of Dienbienphu. And there is a certain connection between these two events. The empire was the heart and soul of the French Republic. Indeed, the military defeat in Vietnam symbolically undercut the ability of any cabinet to extricate the country from the quagmire it had created for itself in North Africa.

The Algeria in which Camus grew to maturity was the jewel in the crown of the French Empire, and, without even making reference to economic matters or the problem of French nationals living in the colony, rightists as well as moderates believed its loss would destroy France as a major power. Mendès-France came under immediate pressure from the followers of de Gaulle to put down the mass-based uprisings of 1954. Thus, while holding out offers of economic reform, he sent in French troops to support the governor of the territory, Jacques Soustelle, who had declared martial law.

European sections, mostly white, were gradually sequestered with troops and barbed wire from the native and nonwhite areas. The Front de Libération Nationale (FLN) meanwhile gained support in the impoverished, Moslem countryside as it became apparent that the reforms were too little and had come too late. Mendès-France tried to negotiate and offered free elections. But his government fell before any attempt was made to realize his promises. A vicious cycle then began in which increased repression brought about new acts of terror.

Malraux stood with de Gaulle, Sartre identified himself with the FLN, and Camus associated himself unequivocally with the policy of Mendès-

France.[30] He had experienced imperialism. But he had also experienced the violence of fanatics personally when his mother and uncle fled to France after an Arab neighbor was stabbed. Camus was torn. He started writing a biweekly column on Algeria for *L'Express*, a liberal magazine owned by Jean-Jacques Servan-Schreiber, which supported Mendès-France. In its pages, Camus condemned the violence on both sides. He called for a cease-fire, negotiations leading to free elections, and the extension of French citizenship to Algerians. He opposed independence for Algeria. Nevertheless, Camus supported immediate autonomy for the colony while keeping it within the French Empire.

Camus was now really betwixt and between. He was seeking, after all, to balance his experience of two cultures. His views were "measured," employing a term from *The Rebel*, and they appear particularly enlightened in retrospect given what would become the authoritarian fate of Algeria. With the fall of the Mendès-France government, however, implementing them became ever more difficult. French and Algerian liberals were invited to Algiers in order to build a new version of the Popular Front, but Camus kept his distance since it would necessarily have included communists.[31] He remained adamant in his hope for a noncommunist republican left, which underpinned his dispute with Sartre, even as he grew increasingly doubtful about the practical feasibility of his Algerian policy.

And for good reason. Camus approached the problem like a moralist rather than a political person aware of existing constraints.[32] He never took account of the basic political issues at stake, and, as a result, his stance proved internally inconsistent. He sought autonomy for Algeria within the confines of the French Empire, but the aims of the FLN were based on the vision of independence. In the same vein, while supporting the anticolonial strivings of the Algerian people, he refused to recognize the FLN as its legitimate representative. He proposed a federal solution beneficial to both French settlers and Algerian natives. While such a policy would cost the colonizers their political privileges, however, it would leave existing economic imbalances of power intact and conflict with the obvious aspirations for self-rule exhibited by the colonized. Neither the French right nor the Algerian revolutionaries were sustained by democratic or cosmopolitan traditions.

Camus may have written that "the only way of eliminating Algerian nationalism is to suppress the injustice of which it was born,"[33] but he never specified the sources of injustice, the interests blocking change, or what it would take to deal with them. Camus wished to identify with the republican legacy of France and the longing for Algerian self-determination at the same time. In keeping with Mendès-France, who resigned in 1955 rather than sacrifice his policy on Algeria or his vision of domestic socialist reform, Camus clung to his views. He had only contempt for those on the far right who were intent on France's keeping Algeria at any cost. But he also feared the authoritarian tendencies of the FLN and stood apart from those, like Sartre, who unequivocally supported Algerian independence. Attitudes only hardened as the violence grew worse. Thus, he found himself advocating an ever more untenable and contradictory position in the political context of the time.

Algeria would only receive its independence in 1962 after General Charles de Gaulle was granted extraordinary presidential power, turned against his far-right-wing supporters, and essentially purged the military of its archreactionary forces. Neither the intellectuals nor the practitioners of the left could have foreseen such a set of developments in 1954. Camus may have more to offer on the question of solidarity and the articulation of the existential prerequisites for a liberal socialism than most of the intellectual luminaries dominant in the postwar era. But in a sense, their failure was also his. An inability to connect principle and practice on the level of theory, whether directly or indirectly, reflected a more general failure to create a linkage on the level of practice. Its consequences are still felt in the conflict between the inheritors of Gaullism and their liberal-socialist opponents even as the next millennium looms on the horizon.

4

THE SICKNESS UNTO DEATH

International Communism before the Deluge

THE CLOSE OF WORLD WAR II left the Soviet Union and its supporters
with a moral capital they had not enjoyed even during the "heroic
years" of the revolution. Stalingrad had clearly been the critical battle of the
war, and no country had suffered losses in lives and resources on a scale
anywhere approaching the USSR. The nature of the concentration camp
universe constructed by Stalin had not yet been fully revealed, and the
Moscow Trials were just a memory. The sectarianism of the twenties and
the deceit of the 1930s were forgotten. The USSR seemed bathed in a heroic
aura that derived from the outstanding services rendered by European
communists in the antifascist resistance.

Following its dissolution of the Comintern in 1943, which helped
assure the formation of a second front, the USSR stood alone. But it
retained the unquestioned loyalty of all communist parties throughout the
world. Many Eastern European nations, like Czechoslovakia, the victim of
betrayal by the Western democracies at the Munich Conference of 1938,
looked with friendly eyes to their larger neighbor. In addition, communist
parties in much of Western Europe emerged as a political force and gained
influence within a trade union movement that had been decimated by the
ravages of World War II. Indeed, with the end of the war, the mentality of
the Popular Front resurfaced and the communists found themselves identified with the new hopes for a radical transformation of bourgeois society
and proletarian unity inspired by new organizations like the World Trade
Union Federation.

These hopes were illusory: the "two camps" doctrine was introduced in
1947 by Andrei Zhdanov, one of Stalin's most despicable henchmen, and a
new set of domestic purges in the USSR would foreshadow what soon

The original version of this paper was written for an international conference in
Budapest marking the tenth anniversary of 1989. It was first published in *Eszmelet*
43 (fall 1999) and then appeared in *After the Fall: 1989 and the Future of Freedom*
ed. George Katsiaficas (New York: Routledge, 2001).

enough would occur in Eastern Europe. Also, while the communists may have been willing to take ministries in bourgeois governments, no communist policy—not even the ill-fated Chinese strategy that led the party into Chiang Kai-shek's Kuomintang in 1928—had ever contemplated blending the organization into some version of a united front. Nor was there any reason why Stalin should have been willing to allow his vassals in France, Italy, and elsewhere to engage in such a tactic. Their independent status rendered them useful in opposing any possible advances of "Western imperialism."

The original interest of Lenin in linking the fight against imperialism with the fight against capitalism had been replaced with a simple emphasis upon "counterimperialism," and international class war had ever more surely made way for a politics predicated on the "national interest" of the USSR. The cold war never really had anything in common with class war, and it is too often forgotten that Stalin's exaggerated political realism was predicated on caution. The dictator was adamant in his refusal to make good on the enormous strike wave that hit Western Europe in 1947 or capitalize on the real possibilities for revolution that existed in France, Italy, and Spain. Even in Eastern Europe, the "revolutions" he initiated all took place from the top down. These revolutions were different from those in Russia, China, and Vietnam. It was also not workers' councils, or the like, that defined them, but rather the immediate emergence of a police state. The revolutionary process evident elsewhere in times past was reversed. The first acquisition of the revolution, its first target, was always the police. The masses may well have played their part, but it was a minor role. Or, putting it another way, the masses did not "become subservient": they were subservient from the beginning. Even later, given the lack of democratic institutions, it was never certain whether the opinions they expressed were pressured by the state or genuinely their own.

In keeping with Machiavelli, when asked whether subservience through fear was preferable to subservience through conviction, Stalin noted that convictions can always change. He was stubborn only where questions pertaining to the security of the Soviet Union were directly at stake. His shortsighted policy of insisting upon the creation of satellite states rather than acceptable allies on the western borders of the USSR was actually inspired by the attempt to insure against any possible future invasion. And so, throughout Eastern Europe, governmental coalitions were constructed with a broad range of representation—though the communists always kept control over the ministries of the interior, or the police, and the army. Each of these countries was obligated, by the particular armistice or through special declarations, to purge its political infrastructure of fascists and ensure the security of the Russian army. This enabled Stalin to deprive the old reactionary ruling classes, along with other democratic or socialist groupings, of institutional expression. The next step, complete communist control, was easy.

Stalin essentially respected the lines drawn where the respective armies of East and West had liberated the various nations subjugated by the Nazis. Even his successors would formally engage the USSR in only two instances of direct armed conflict outside Eastern Europe: the Chinese border and Afghanistan —both of which, arguably, involved areas within the Soviet sphere of influence. Stalin was open to geopolitical diplomacy not only with respect to Western proposals for a United Nations. His acquisition of Eastern Europe can be seen as the price for neutralizing Austria, quitting Iran, and liquidating the revolutionary undertakings led by communists in Italy and Greece.

Ideology played its role: America was condemned as imperialistic and antidemocratic, while the Soviet Union was conceived as the bastion of anti-imperialism and a new form of socialist democracy. It surely played a part in the unsuccessful blockade of West Berlin and the Slansky trials in Czechoslovakia during 1948 that led to the end of coalition governments and the creation of one-party dictatorships in Eastern Europe. These events changed whatever positive memories still remained of communist partici- pation in the war. They created a fear of Soviet imperialism and, in often legitimately equating Stalinism and Nazism under the rubric of totalitari- anism, fueled what would prove a new form of Western anticommunism.

Stalin's fears of the West were no doubt exaggerated. But they were surely intensified by the dreams of fanatics like General George Patton intent on extending the just completed war into an anticommunist crusade. The USSR feared the prospect of nuclear attack, and its leaders were enraged by the Truman Doctrine that sought to make the "defense" of "free peoples" against communist aggression into a universal principle of American foreign policy. It was ultimately the Marshall Plan, however, that sealed the division between East and West. Stalin was never much concerned that the United States would secure control of Western Europe: recognition of divergent spheres of influence was a hallmark of his foreign policy. He was probably also relatively indifferent to the subversion and exclusion of national communist parties by those states willing to accept the Marshall Plan. Stalin had consistently proved more than willing to dispense with their interests when the exigencies of Soviet foreign policy so demanded. But the fear generated by the Marshall Plan was of a different order. Stalin knew that it threatened to explode the entire set of economic, political, and ideological contradictions underpinning the Soviet Union and its relations with client parties and states.

Had he been daring, conceivably, Stalin could have accepted the offer of American aid since, formally, it was directed to Eastern as well as Western Europe. Such a bold move might well have doomed the entire project; with the USSR participating, after all, the Marshall Plan would probably never have gotten through Congress. But the threat that his bluff would be called surely frightened him. Opening the USSR to the West would have been impossible given the new policy combining austerity and terror, ideological rigor and anti-Semitism, which Stalin was intent upon implementing in the postwar period. Accepting the Marshall Plan would have made it necessary to change policies emphasizing heavy industry and ignoring consumer needs in the name of "socialist" construction. The Soviet Union would have had to open not merely its economic but its cultural and intellectual borders. Soviet prestige would have suffered immeasurably and the "revolutionary privilege" accorded the communists would have been suspended.

The Marshall Plan not only made comparison between East and West possible, where a free press was allowed, but also necessary. Attention was drawn to the radical disparities in economic wealth and political freedom between the two blocs. The Marshall Plan, in this vein, reinvigorated the traditional commitment to republicanism on the part of the Western socialist labor movement. Its recipients were also called upon to work with one another in administering the plan. Within the boundaries of established anticommunism, therefore, America's allies were given a degree of political autonomy that the satellites of the USSR simply did not possess. The United States, of course, engaged in the undemocratic subversion of communist and other radical movements. Nevertheless, the Marshall Plan created the economic foundation for a political identification of America with the democratic aspirations of not only bourgeois parties but socialist parties whose leaders also saw in the surrender of laissez-faire capitalism to the New Deal something at least approaching their original vision.

Above all, of course, the Marshall Plan offered Europeans a chance to reconstruct their continent. Stalin was surely right to speak of "Western imperialism," but—just as surely—this was imperialism with a human face. The Marshall Plan would become crucial to the capitalist resurgence of Western Europe in general and "the economic miracle" of West Germany in particular. Perhaps even more than any pattern of centralized mismanagement, the dictator's refusal to allow participation by the satellite nations created the conditions for what would become an ever-widening economic gap between the two blocs. His construction of a rather pitiful Eastern economic community (Comecon) did not help matters. It became clear that the USSR had little to recommend it in terms of either economics or politics, not merely against the United States, but also against democratic socialist experiments undertaken in Scandinavia. With the introduction of the Marshall Plan, few could believe any longer that the Soviet Union was embarked on an alternative path to greater economic affluence that, paraphrasing the later words of Khrushchev, would ultimately "bury" the West.

Without a genuine program of economic recovery for its satellites, even the excitement spurred by the launching of *Sputnik* in 1956 would prove of no avail. The incompetence of Soviet attempts to supplant the market with an inflexible planned economy also did nothing to mitigate the experience of workers who, in the most brutal capitalist fashion, were still being treated as a disposable "factor of production." Memories were still fresh of the more than fourteen million prisoners languishing in concentration camps when Stalin died in 1953. Attempting to regulate an economy with an iron fist was already becoming improbable, and lack of institutional accountability was only worsening a situation in which shortages were actually reinforced by waste. Unfair trade agreements and the introduction of "mixed companies" marked a new form of socialist imperialism, and, to add insult to injury, sub-jugated peoples were made to swallow hypocritical pronouncements that the communist seizure of power in their countries had been undertaken democ-ratically with votes, secret ballots, and the like. The domination of Eastern Europe was accompanied by an arrogance that ever more surely produced resentment and revolt—most prominently—first in East Germany in 1953, then in Hungary in 1956, and finally in Czechoslovakia in 1968.

The "revolutions from above" did not empower the working class, create a new set of emancipated social relations, or modernize the economy. Empowering the working class would have meant surrendering the "leading role" that the communists had assigned themselves and that they employed to repress all critics; thus, the astonishing lack of political purpose and the ensuing ideological stagnation of postwar communism. Extending democratic accountability would have meant criticizing the ongoing bureaucratic stagnation along with the attendant corruption and careerism; thus, the cultural conservatism and inability to further the construction of an emancipated set of social relations under "actually existing socialism." And finally, modernizing rather than merely industrializing threatened to make the entire political-ideological apparatus of Stalinism anachronistic; thus, the cross-purposes at which the state and civil society found them-selves in Eastern Europe.

The refusal to honestly confront these contradictions created a self-fulfilling prophecy. The constant ideological emphasis on "proletarian inter-nationalism" and "national self-determination" by leaders of the Soviet Union produced a mixture of cynicism and resentment among the nations suffering under their rule. Lacking any means to forward their grievances, or assert their demands for accountability outside of direct protest against the regime, working people in the East necessarily looked for inspiration to Western consumer values and repressed national traditions. Enormous domestic spying operations drove people into a preoccupation with private life, underground cultural circles, and religion. The dictatorship of the proletariat generated the very anticommunism it had sworn to defeat.

Abroad no less than at home, then, communism ceased to serve either as an emancipatory political alternative to capitalist democracy or, with its practical perversion, as a transcendent goal to inspire further revolutionary action. Belief in communism increasingly became a matter of faith ever more divorced from practical reality. Loyalty to the USSR, in turn, began to be based increasingly on what was nothing more than prejudice and tradition. Nevertheless, the ideological process that would erode sympathy among Western progressives for the USSR was different from in the East.

Direct economic exploitation and the brutal political repression of nationalist currents by the USSR did not take such dramatic form in the West. Crucial was therefore the knowledge that emerged about the true extent of Stalin's purges and the totalitarian character of the system under his reign. Indeed, from the immediate postwar period through the early 1960s, numerous works appeared that concerned themselves with the structure and ideological effects of "totalitarianism." The vast majority retained an anticommunist thrust. But they were very different in the issues that they raised and fell under a number of fairly distinct rubrics. Clearly there were purely propagandistic works attacking all mass movements and lacking in either theoretical or historical sophistication like *The True Believer* (1948) by Eric Hofer or *Masters of Deceit* (1958) by J. Edgar Hoover. Another set of writings, often of high quality like *The Origins of Totalitarianism* (1951) by Hannah Arendt or *The Rebel* (1951) by Albert Camus, were essentially characterized by attempts to identify the Soviet Union and the Nazis as part of a single overlapping movement-regime with a particular authoritarian mentality. Third, there were the "ultraleft" criticisms like Trotsky's *The Revolution Betrayed* (1937) or the writings of Victor Serge as well as works—generally by ex-communists—that attempted to portray the cynicism and lack of political principle pervading the communist movement under Stalin.

Usually they made little reference to the Nazis, and were not only willing to differentiate Stalin from Marx but also ready to concede the possibility of being a socialist or even a Marxist without subscribing to totalitarian values. These works would include the famous anthology *The God That Failed* (1950) edited by Richard Crossman as well as enormously popular novels like *Darkness at Noon* (1941) by Arthur Koestler, *Animal Farm* (1945) and *1984* (1949) by George Orwell, and the magnificent trilogy entitled *Like a Tear in the Ocean* (1961) by Manès Sperber. Finally, there is the extraordinary literary legacy of those who suffered directly and so shocked the West with their revelations, like Margarete Buber-Neumann, Eugenia Ginsburg, Natalia Mandelstam, Solzhenitsyn, and others.

By and large, the communist responses to this ideological onslaught were pathetic and self-serving organizational justifications. Initially, in keeping with a tendency developed during the 1930s, all criticisms— whether from right or left—were seen as fabrications of "wreckers," "traitors," "spies," and the like; the disillusionment was subsequently all the greater when so many of the criticisms proved valid. Then, of course, there was the denial that Stalinism could be lumped together with Nazism— which is "objectively" legitimate insofar as Germany was already an industrially developed nation when Hitler took power, while the Soviet Union was not when Stalin took the reins. But the obvious similarities of political structure between the two regimes were either disregarded or explained, in the case of Stalinism, as a mere transitional phenomenon of economic underdevelopment. Thus, the communist response never spoke to the suffering—which was "subjectively" just as real as under the Nazis—of the great mass of individuals involved.

Recourse to the demands of historical "progress," which becomes evident in the assault on Koestler's book in *Humanism and Terror* (1946) by Maurice Merleau-Ponty tended to omit the obvious political mistakes and the extraordinary waste of lives and resources. Such arguments presupposed "necessity" to justify communist atrocities in the name of a teleology inscribed into the future. Nowhere were the defenders of Stalin willing to pinpoint the determinate extension of freedom, which the insight into "necessity" was originally meant to forward for Hegel and Marx. The communists and their sympathizers remained content to emphasize the relative character of morality and justify the past from the perspective of the future.

Especially following the various attempts to justify the abdication of personal responsibility under fascism, in fact, Jean-Paul Sartre and Simone de Beauvoir maintained that the very lack of absolute foundations for ethical actions impelled the need for existential "engagement" in the cold war. They and others of goodwill who extended support to the USSR became enmeshed in arguments about whether reports of the camps were a fabrication or grossly exaggerated by the "bourgeois" press. Debate often thereby degenerated into a statistical controversy, which still continues, over the exact number killed by Stalin's regime: as if 20,000,000 or 40,000,000 rather than 60,000,000 corpses should affect the matter at hand.

The faithful abroad were both embarrassed and shocked by Khrushchev's official revelations of Stalin's crimes at the Twentieth Party Congress in 1956. The teleological beliefs of old began to crumble. No longer the homeland of the revolution, the Soviet Union became merely one nation-state among others. Other nations with very different national interests and approaches had already emerged that could legitimately claim to be just as "socialist" and far more revolutionary. Ironically, it was just when Stalin was about to embark on yet another series of purges that the fragmentation he most feared began to take place: Tito's break with the Soviet Union in 1948, the rise of "neutralist" states like India, and—ultimately—the Sino-Soviet split in 1953.

With these developments came the loss of "revolutionary privilege" by the Soviet Union and the increasing difficulty of exacting either the traditional degree of discipline from its working class or the type of ideological unity that would fend off attempts by others to institute their own form of "socialism in one country." It was subsequently no accident that the Twentieth Party Congress should have witnessed the Italian leader Palmiro Togliatti—one of the earliest proponents of the Popular Front—speak about the need for "polycentrism" and the importance of recognizing differences in "objective conditions" for the spread of communism. To be sure, the position of Togliatti was countered with renewed calls for "proletarian internationalism" by the French—whose party was among the most retrograde—until, quickly enough, it was decided to suspend further polemics. Nevertheless, five years later in his report to the Twenty-Second Party Congress, Togliatti reiterated his stance.

And this only made sense. Neither the conditions for Soviet hegemony over the communist movement nor the need for its member parties to maintain their authoritarian internal structure of "democratic centralism" seemed to apply any longer. Previously, the Soviet Union had secured a fundamentally moral support from other communist parties by mixing a revolutionary emphasis on teleology with institutional coercion. With the new talk about "peaceful coexistence" and the increasing inability to ensure "iron discipline," however, differences between communist states began to surface.

But this only begs the question. If the Western communist parties were no longer merely tools of the Soviet Union, then what were they? The Twentieth Party Congress freed Western communist parties from providing unconditional support for Soviet foreign policy initiatives. Taking advantage of the new opportunities, those in Italy, France, and Spain cautiously took the first steps along their own "national roads to socialism." This involved reversing the post-1948 strategy of "opposition" that challenged the legitimacy of the given political order and rejected participating in any coalitions with "bourgeois" parties. The need for such a change was self-evident. The European communist parties were mired in a "left ghetto" that constituted roughly 20 to 25 percent of the voting populace where the communists were strongest. Indeed, though they occasionally received somewhat less, they rarely garnered more.

And so things remained until 1968 when Enrico Berlinguer decided upon a "historic compromise" whereby the Italian Communist Party proclaimed its willingness to enter a coalition of "bourgeois" parties as a junior partner. Too large and with too much invested in the existing order to make a revolution, but too small to rule, European communists now attempted to extricate themselves from the state of limbo. In France, the most Stalinist of all major European parties criticized the barbaric invasion of Czechoslovakia. In Spain, party intellectuals surrendered their commitment to a "dictatorship of the proletariat." Everywhere, the attempt to expand the party base beyond the industrial working class was accompanied by a decrease in the emphasis on "revolutionary" dogma.

Of course, this was precisely the type of thinking that Eduard Bernstein had supported in his call of 1898 for a "revision" of the orthodox Marxism embraced by international social democracy. But that was impossible for communists to admit. They needed a different justification, especially since Khrushchev had tied his critique of Stalin to a "Leninist revival." They could find it only by emphasizing that in placing primacy on the vanguard party as the agent of revolution, Lenin had essentially rendered the empirical character of the organization's class base irrelevant. They also sought to appease Brezhnev, who sought to distance himself from Khrushchev by tilting back toward Stalin, through making reference to the national implications deriving from the idea of "socialism in one country." In this way, a certain legitimacy seemed to exist for their attempts to broaden the party's electoral base and gain support from nonproletarian classes and strata in divergent national contexts. Thus, without reference to its original aims, the Eurocommunists sought to employ the communist legacy.

The hypocrisy of the undertaking was exposed as the ineluctable process of integration took hold. Much like social democratic or even liberal parties, the Eurocommunists began expressing the interests of their predominantly working-class base through institutional forms that neither challenged the reproduction of the capitalist system nor fostered the revolutionary self-administrative capacities of their constituencies. The new commitment to democratic institutions may have invalidated the need for an "underground" organization, a revolutionary ideology, and even support for the USSR, but it also subverted the unique character of the party. Leninist in name, reformist in character, the authoritarian structure seemed to serve no useful purpose. There is indeed a certain irony to the fact that the communists now found themselves in exactly the same situation as the old supporters of the "renegade" Karl Kautsky: they were now members of a "revolutionary party that does not make revolution."

The communists rendered themselves redundant with respect to their social democratic rivals. Probably the voters knew this. Electoral support began to erode. Eurocommunism was no success, and until the rise of Gorbachev, which ushered in a new era, the communist parties of Western Europe vacillated; occasionally reasserting their commitment to the Soviet Union and the old orthodoxy, only to retreat once again. The refusal to follow any sustained, principled, radical policy left the Western communist parties with an identity deficit that became ever more obvious as the second half of the century wore on. The sense of malaise spread. The communist movement found it ever more difficult to attract the young. It had ever less to say, and they had ever less desire to believe.

*   *   *

Kierkegaard was wrong when he wrote that only the Christian knows what is meant by the "sickness unto death." The communists, too, would experience it. The sickness first took hold in Kronstadt in 1921 during the destruction of the soviets and the last real possibility for democratic rule in the USSR. It spread in the 1930s amid delusions about the creation of a utopian society. It deepened in the aftermath of World War II when purges and new horrors greeted the returning troops and the heroic citizenry. It caused convulsions during the Twentieth Party Congress, and it became ever more debilitating during the "period of stagnation" ruled by Brezhnev. With the failed "putsch of fools" in 1991, which sought to reassert authoritarian communist control, the sickness ultimately proved fatal.

Many think that the patient died of malnutrition. But that is a mistake. There had been times of far greater deprivation. The illness had a different cause: moral rot. It explains why so few were crying as the end grew near. Most were tired of being treated as children and told what to read, what to see, and how to think on pain of sometimes the ultimate punishment. The best of them channeled their rage. They organized in loose umbrella organizations. Dissolution at the top combined with resistance from below. Solidarity provided the symbol in Poland, the wall fell in Berlin, the "velvet revolution" introduced the Czech Republic, and finally the USSR disintegrated. Last rites were administered and eulogies prepared.

The remaining priests felt betrayed by their flock: they believed none of it was their fault, and even if they had occasionally fallen into temptation, it was only in response to the machinations of the capitalist enemy. They rambled about the way in which communism had eradicated premodern classes and improved the lives of working people. But they didn't mention how all this had only rendered more anachronistic both the authoritarian institutions and the inflexible forms of planning by which it was achieved. They looked away from the shoddy goods, the bureaucracy, terror, the provincialism, the repression, and the stultifying paternalism created by their church fathers. They expected only gratitude for what had become an ongoing economic downturn justified by ideological principles that no longer bore any serious relation to reality. The priests were oblivious to the pretensions of the old geezer. They had nothing to say about the price of progress or the way in which, time after time, the loyalty and trust of the believers had been betrayed. Indeed, when praising their utopia, they forgot probably the single point on which Machiavelli and Kant agreed: he who wills the end must also will the means thereto.

The funeral didn't last long. Everyone dispersed. There was much to do. New priests had told the people that capitalism would be introduced in "five hundred days," corruption would cease, republican institutions would eradicate the vestiges of arbitrary power, and their nation would once again be recognized as a respected member of the world community. None of it happened that way. Those living in nations previously acquainted with democracy and bourgeois life would fare far better than their more economically underdeveloped neighbors. But most felt the whip of the market. They witnessed the decay of their fledgling civil society and the authoritarian manipulation of their new democratic institutions. For all the grumbling, however, few wished for a return to the past: 1989 gave them the taste of freedom. It was the first time that they could experience the prospect of individual dignity, cultural diversity, and human rights. The lack of respect for these values in the past was something those living in the present could not forgive. The gravestone had already been overturned before the patient was laid to rest. But that, too, only makes sense: when communism was finally buried, paraphrasing the old revolutionary Eugen Leviné, it was nothing more than a "corpse on furlough."

5

LOOKING BACKWARDS

1968 Thirty Years After

JUST BEFORE HE DIED, Abbie Hoffman said that "nostalgia is just another form of repression." When we try to make sense of 1968, it is important to keep in mind that while 1968 epitomizes what we all remember as "the movement," its darker side is often forgotten. Many died in the Vietnam War and some in struggles at home; others had their careers ruined not merely through political repression but by taking romantic and utopian slogans too uncritically, or losing themselves in drugs. It is not as if 1968 offers a single clear picture. Better to view it as a montage: demonstrations at universities across the country; the assassination of Martin Luther King; the slaughter of two thousand students in Mexico; the general strike in Paris; the "days of rage" in Chicago; the Prague Spring; the Tet offensive.

There are other images, and they crowd the mind. Assessing the legacy of that year is no easy matter. But in the first instance, it is useful to recall that no one expected the outbreak of the events. Just a few years earlier, Daniel Bell had spoken about the "end of ideology." And then suddenly, but really not suddenly at all, the civil rights movement was becoming part of something larger; its style of resistance was changing; new concerns with class and identity were emerging. The New Left felt it had a world to win. Everything seemed possible, and politics became imbued with a sense of adventure. That feeling is perhaps what I cherish the most; it is palpably missing today, and it cannot be artificially reinvented.

Times are different, and it is necessary to draw the implications. My point is not that the impact of the "movement" was merely fleeting or transitory. It broke what had been known as the "solid South," brought new constituencies into the political arena, and arguably generated more progressive legislation than the New Deal. It doesn't matter that many gains of the 1960s were ultimately integrated into the commodity structure of

This is the text of a speech given at a panel sponsored by the Caucus for a New Political Science at the 1998 meeting of the American Political Science Association. It appeared in *New Political Science* 20, 4 (1998): 485–88.

capitalism or that its moral claims were later distorted. That would be to ignore both their progressive character and the struggles necessary to bring them about. The ultraleft critique is as blindly sectarian now as it was then: the interventionist state was a critical factor in the successes of the diverse movements constituting the 1960s.

But there is a sense in which legislation takes a backseat to other concerns. The cultures of minorities and non-Western peoples were brought into the public eye during the 1960s. Its music spanned the globe, and its style helped rip the Iron Curtain; its artists were part of every demonstration in the West and, in keeping with their underground popularity in the East, figures like Bob Dylan and Frank Zappa influenced a young playwright named Vaclav Havel whose "Committee for a Merrier World" anticipated the "velvet revolution" of 1989. Anti-intellectual tendencies abounded, of course, spontaneists called for "practice" without regard to theory, and spiritualism was enormously popular. But I can also remember a dynamic intellectual milieu: the concern with revolutionary traditions, the interest in the avant-garde, the debates over strategy and current events, the laughter generated by the hippies and the situationists, the endless discussions following the publication of a new work by Herbert Marcuse or the release of a new movie by Jean-Luc Godard. There was indeed something profoundly exciting and justified about the attempts to free sexuality from provincial norms, transform everyday life, and generate a new sensibility. E. P. Thompson was correct in claiming that the New Left was the first movement to deal with culture as a system of social control and simultaneously employ it to motivate self-activity.

The New Left was often seduced by its passions. It surely romanticized the various movements for national self-determination, dismissed the violence they perpetrated, and ignored their lack of a genuinely republican vision. In the case of the Vietnam War, however, its heart did not stand at odds with reality. The New Left sensed that America did not have the support of the Vietnamese people. They knew that the domino theory made no sense, and they understood that the 58,000 American casualties constituted a fraction of the Vietnamese dead. The official lies and pointless slaughter struck an ethical nerve with young people and minorities on whom the impact of the war was most pronounced. Helping bring this unjust, unnecessary, and ignoble war to a close—while furthering the creation of an anti-imperialist, rather that a mere isolationist, consciousness among a broad segment of the American public—constitutes a lasting legacy of the 1960s.

The New Left was profoundly humanist in character. And when it was Marxist, it was in the sense of the *Paris Manuscripts of 1844* rather than the later works. Most people were content to read Erich Fromm's highly selective edition of Marx's writings, *Marx's Concept of Man*, rather than bother with *Capital*. There was a sense in which this reflected the movement's naivete and its utopian instinct. The New Left was new; it lacked both

ideological and organizational coherence. But that does not justify identifying its legacy with "the days of rage" and the counterattack for the beatings at the Democratic Convention in Chicago of 1968 or the more
exaggerated expressions of what has today become known as "identity politics." I would suggest instead that the genuine and most progressive inher-
itance of the 1960s derives from the radical wing of the civil rights
movement and the Student Nonviolent Coordinating Committee. Nineteen sixty-eight did not deconstruct but rather reconstructed the totality.
The great unrealized possibility presented by Martin Luther King involved
"totalizing" the existing order and creating an organization capable of
linking socioeconomic, political, and foreign policy issues.

The trajectory of King led from exclusively emphasizing civil rights to
opposing the Vietnam War and ultimately calling for the creation of a new
"Poor People's Movement." He considered himself a democratic socialist at
the time of his death, and his politics bridged the gap between the Old and
the New Left, the needs of working people and the concerns of the new
social movements, pragmatism and idealism. There was no ambiguity: the
movements with which he was associated mobilized around universalist
precepts and sought to expand institutional arenas in which freedom was
exercised by all oppressed groups equally. It is indeed striking that the
virtual progenitor of the New Left sought to confront the system by highlighting its most obvious ideological contradictions, its structural imbalances of political power, and ultimately the way in which the economic
power of capital rests on the divisions among working people.

Young people of today are sadly mistaken if they consider the assault
on organization, hierarchy, and discipline the emancipatory legacy of the
1960s. The problem even with the civil rights movement and the Poor
People's Movement was not that they were too centrally organized, as many
like to believe, but that they were not organized enough. It is not a matter
of invoking some outmoded Leninism whose influence on the movement
was always far less than the right would like to believe. Clarity of aims, efficiency of effort, accountability, and discipline are prerequisites for any
successful political organization. Experimentation is still possible. In
considering the Poor People's Movement, which I like to call a "mass association," it hovered between an assemblage of diverse interests and a political party. With its interracial character and its working-class orientation,
the Poor People's Movement offered perhaps the most genuinely radical
threat to the status quo of this century. Nevertheless, when it collapsed,
there was nothing to take its place.

This was when the shift began from "redistribution" to "recognition" by
all the various groups committed to what is called identity politics. Ideological and organizational fragmentation of the original coalition resulted,
along with an increasing inability either to counter what was becoming a
new conservative onslaught or to sustain the old initiatives for economic
and political change. It subsequently became less a matter of changing

institutions than changing people's minds about the ways in which the excluded are perceived. This shift explains how an ever more aggressive roll-back in social and economic legislation could proceed hand in hand with a revolution of everyday life in dealing with grievances ranging from spousal abuse to the Eurocentric character of education. Issues once considered private became open to public debate and redress in this cultural transfor-mation. A displacement of traditional economic and political problems surely took place, but it was still a remarkable achievement of the New Left. And, in this vein, the women's liberation movement prefigured the model for an alternative public sphere with its network of health clinics, rape counseling centers, day care activities, bookstores, institutes, scholarly conferences, and the like.

Developments of this sort were predicated on the ability of new move-ments to create solidarity among particular constituencies by cutting across class lines and highlighting a particular experience of oppression. Hence what would become the positive emphasis upon identity for each specific group and, beyond the subjective political claims of the leaders, the growth of an *interest group mentality*. The result was unfortunate: a certain propa-gandistic radicalism became conjoined with reformist aims. The unfulfilled heritage of the great mass association of the 1960s, the Poor People's Move-ment with its totalizing character and direct challenge to the system, was increasingly forgotten. This skewed the self-understanding of the new social movements even as it tended to preserve them and their interest groups from criticism.

The whole became less than the sum of its parts as these interest groups, which always ultimately separate themselves from the constituen-cies they represent, gained a vested interest in autonomy. Leaders of these interest groups would often agree on the need for specific reforms, of course, and they would even call upon members to work in the Democratic Party for various single-issue coalitions. There is also nothing wrong with any of this. But the ideological sense of purpose can easily become miscon-strued, and even the practical politics can become self-defeating. For, with each new issue and the vision of each new alliance, progressive forces will constantly find themselves reinventing the wheel even as the different coali-tions and member groups wind up competing over increasingly scarce resources. Especially in periods of economic retrenchment, moreover, all coalitions and interest groups are increasingly plagued by the temptation of entering into what might best be termed the moral economy of the sepa-rate deal. Solidarity will then appear more elusive than ever. Indeed, it occurs to me that the unyielding emphasis upon particularism is actually a form of resignation in the face of this partially self-imposed political reality.

And so, finally, it becomes necessary to say it. The 1960s are over. A new movement must speak to the New Left as the New Left spoke to the Old Left. This new movement requires a new style and a new set of cultural motivations to contest the logic of fragmentation that has been unleashed over the last two decades. But the new movement must also integrate the achievements of the 1960s: the challenge to the parochialism of everyday life; the experimental confrontation with the culture industry; the emphasis on participation; and the moral idealism. The new movement of the future must make good on the unrealized organizational possibilities of the past: it should embrace aims by state intervention and reject atavistic concerns with national self-determination; it must call for democratic action within newly emerging transitional institutions and it must recover the hidden internationalism of a movement whose reach extended from Berkeley to Rome, Mexico City to Berlin, New York to Paris, and Prague to Tokyo. Such is the challenge for the next century, and meeting it will surely demand, to paraphrase Rudi Dutschke, a "long march" inside *and* outside prevailing institutions. The path is perhaps no longer quite as clear as it once was. Signposts exist along the way. We can still make them out, but only if we keep our minds alert and our eyes open.

6

CRITICAL INTELLECTUALS, POLITICS, AND SOCIETY

In Memory of Daniel Singer

THERE WAS PERHAPS always a sense in which the intellectual expressed the critical consciousness of society: Socrates not only paid the ultimate price for his philosophical skepticism, but exposed the limits of freedom in ancient Greece. The willingness of critical intellectuals to employ their talents with an eye on common political aims, however, derives from the Enlightenment. The critique of arbitrary power and religious intolerance, which was directed by the philosophes against a crumbling aristocratic order and a stultifying church, would later extend into an assault on other forms of social and economic injustice. Nevertheless, in our postmodern condition, this old sense of political purpose has been called into question and the social position of the critical intellectual has become ever more difficult to comprehend.

The image of the intellectual, which has traditionally informed both liberal and socialist politics, has—to put it bluntly—become an object of mistrust if not derision, and critical intellectuals are left with an identity crisis. Confronting this crisis initially calls for evaluating the insights no less than the limits of earlier interpretations. It also involves thinking about the situational constraints on the critical intellectual who is, in the first instance, both an expression and a response to the modern division of labor: the former insofar as the technocrat and the scientist have assumed preeminence for the functioning of an increasingly specialized society and the latter insofar as the need for coherence, meaning, and logical justification for policies remains in the face of a fragmentation not only of the left, but of the society itself. This essay proposes to cast some light on the divergent roles that critical intellectuals can play, the constraints under which they operate, and some of the tasks they might engage.

This is the revised version of an article originally entitled "Tasks of the Socialist Intellectual" that appeared in *Enclitic* #19 10, no. 1 (1984), 67–86.

THE UNIVERSITY AND TRADITIONAL ROLES

Critical intellectuals can be found in virtually any walk of life. But the university is the institution in which most of them function. The university now plays an expanded role in advanced industrial society. It has grown beyond the confines of the liberal arts and the sciences: accounting, ceramics, public health, and other previously unimaginable disciplines are now accepted parts of a university curriculum. And the reason is simple enough: the university has become a production site of numerous technical skills, innovation, and scientific information for capital, the state, and the military. The university has kept pace with the increasing specialization of the production process as a whole. It is no longer simply a sanctum for the elite.[1] Probably, the university was never the dispassionate and fashion-free institution imagined by its uncritical advocates.[2] But it long ago outstripped the anachronistic fantasies of conservatives. The university now serves a particularly crucial set of functions designed to maintain the broader system. It keeps scores of individuals off the labor market and socializes others. It seeks funds and endowments from the private sector in exchange for patents, research, and the like.[3] The university offers rewards in terms of prestige, money, and access to power. It has become a unique locus of legitimacy for the status quo in both ideological and practical terms.[4]

But the university is not *only* a site of knowledge production for the existing system or what was once called the "military-industrial complex"; it also generates criticism and self-knowledge of that system. The possibilities for research, the diversified courses, and the conflicting standpoints of teachers all allow for a contestation of the status quo. For this reason, whatever its practical constraints, the university still proves the arena most conducive for meaningful discourse in a society whose "consensual" agenda is increasingly being set by the mass media and the forces of reaction. Radicals have employed their academic skills to influence any number of fields requiring technical expertise like ecology, and, under pressure from its own clients, universities have opened their doors to previously excluded groups. The university remains a fundamental site for progressive discourse and action. Continuity clearly exists with the 1960s beyond the obvious changes in the political and social climate.

There are, of course, a host of profoundly reactionary religious universities that openly express the values of intolerance. But, for the most part, the university is distinctly "liberal" in its understanding of the intellectual and his or her political obligation. What is probably the dominant view derives from Julien Benda.[5] Writing during roughly the first third of the twentieth century, Benda witnessed with dismay the increasingly dogmatic partisanship of intellectuals within both the fascist and the communist camps. He believed the political ambitions of such movements would subvert the real function of the intellectual: to safeguard and extend humanist ideals through study of the humanities themselves. Passivity was not his aim, and an abdication of political responsibility was not his purpose.[6] Once humanist ideals come under attack, he considered it incumbent upon intellectuals to demonstrate their political commitments. Benda himself, for this reason, took part in the justly famous International Writers' Conference for the Defense of Culture of 1935 whose purpose was to further what would become the Popular Front.

The situation has, of course, changed from the 1930s. It is no longer a question of fighting the absolute evil of fascism, but a system of capitalist democracy that, for all its failings, retains a commitment to formal democratic procedures and exhibits some degree of intervention in the market. Certain views of Benda, however, are still relevant. It is still incumbent upon the critical intellectual to keep the discourse open against not merely know-nothing reactionaries, but also against those intent upon simply reducing ideas to the dominant or subaltern position of particular groups and the relevance they exhibit for any given "experience" of social identity. The open discourse is still the precondition for both the exercise of criticism and the testing of any particular argument. The issue is still not "who" offers a judgment, but whether institutions exist capable of holding the individual accountable and opening the given argument to criticism.

Maintaining these liberal institutions and the pluralist ethos remains a primary concern for the critical intellectual and, in this vein, it is important to consider the work of Karl Mannheim.[7] Its principal value for present purposes lies in its emphasis upon the importance of ideology—with its utopian components—for political practice. Mannheim noted the manner in which ideology channels energies, informs tactics and allows for only a partial view of the given—socioeconomic, political, and cultural—totality. By contrast, utopia is never complete or finished and it stands in a somewhat tense relation to the closed and legitimating power of ideology. Disagreeing with Georg Lukács, who believed that the unique position of the proletariat in the capitalist accumulation process provided this class with a privileged insight into the "totality,"[8] Mannheim maintained instead that "free-floating" intellectuals have a better understanding of the whole insofar as they transcend the constraints of inherently partial political outlooks and foster some sort of harmonious integration of all viewpoints.

The criticism leveled against Mannheim and his supposedly apolitical view of the intellectual was intense during the 1960s. No less than in the case of Benda, however, there is a sense in which his description of the "free-floating intellectual" explained the position in which most progressive intellectuals of the 1960s found themselves. Arguably the best were concerned with fostering a more encompassing solidarity between particular groups. Few were members of parties with fixed ideologies, and the working class was never their object of primary concern. Even fewer seriously believed in the "privileged" insight into the totality of this or that group. Most identified with particular excluded interests, whether minorities or women, but called for their inclusion in a more liberal society. There is a sense in which the 1960s was characterized by a utopian desire to transform the character of American society by radicalizing its grasp of pluralism. But this concern raised some legitimate criticisms of the ideas associated with Benda and Mannheim. The positions of both papered over the various objective contradictions of society, the power of an increasingly concentrated, corporate-controlled mass media to set the agenda, the ways in which "neutrality" was used by mainstream intellectuals to buttress the status quo, and issues pertaining to structural imbalances of power. To this extent, indeed, a very different view seemed necessary, especially given the experiences generated by the new images of imperialism abroad and masses of people on the march at home.

ENGAGEMENT AND SOLIDARITY

Jean-Paul Sartre has been increasingly, and often legitimately, condemned in the post-communist world of today for his support of the Soviet Union during the 1940s and his identification with various Maoist groups in the 1960s. But usually forgotten is his concern with the Jew suffering anti-Semitism, the homosexual enduring the moral condemnation of society, or the native languishing under imperialism in Algeria and elsewhere. Sartre was the great protector of the outsider, and if only for this reason, it is logical that his views on the intellectual should have so profoundly influenced the radicals of the 1960s.[9] Authenticity demanded "engagement," according to him, and this view was only deepened by the conviction among many that the intellectual should surrender all vestiges of "privilege" with respect to the oppressed he or she wishes to aid.

Many took seriously the belief of Marx that part of the dominant class must "break off" and join the oppressed before a revolution could occur. If the important role played by social democratic intellectuals in the labor movement received scant attention,[10] however, young people in the United States were suspicious about Lenin's notion that "true" consciousness must be injected into the working class "from the outside" by a "vanguard" of professional revolutionary intellectuals. Almost everyone castigated the elitism of a sclerotic soviet-style bureaucracy[11]—if not the seemingly heroic efforts of communists leading various struggles for national self-determination. Even their organizational forms were, however, generally considered irrelevant for progressive action in advanced industrial society. An element of principle was also involved. It was felt that this mode of elitist thinking would separate the "head" from the "body" of the revolutionary movement, thereby paving the way for bureaucratic hierarchy as well as the continued division between manual and mental labor.

Antonio Gramsci had expressed many of these ideas nearly half a century earlier, and he drew the logical conclusions. Gramsci became a major figure in the 1960s and 1970s, even for mainstream social scientists, and his category of "hegemony" along with his notion of the "organic intellectual" were greeted with great acclaim.[12] Bound to the working class through job and lifestyle, a member of the communist movement, this new intellectual would foster "counterhegemonic" values among the oppressed and exploited. That effort would build consciousness, overcome fragmentation, and perhaps even lead to the introduction of new institutions like soviets capable of making a vanguard party unnecessary. Without a "modern prince" or a party tied to the working class, however, the character of the organic intellectual changed radically and the attack on hegemony took on ever more arbitrary and subjective forms. The romantic and anti-intellectual tendencies of the New Left had little use for the difficult forms of pedagogy that Gramsci presupposed. Some attempted to deny the role of the intellectual altogether and engaged in a futile attempt to blend with the truly oppressed, leading to organizationally dangerous forms of self-delusion. Others began to conceive of intellectuals as a distinct social stratum,[13] or even as a "class" intent on separating itself from those "who do the work."[14] The standing of the intellectual relative to the mass became the issue rather than the values he or she embraced.

What Max Weber would have termed an "elective affinity" existed between the populist spirit of the New Left and the American interpretation of the organic intellectual. The assault on hierarchy and rules, the contempt for scholarly work and technocratic expertise, and the romanticism associated with the "street" and the oppressed were all interconnected with the idea—whether perversely interpreted or not—of an organic intellectual. The concept has had an enormous influence. But it stands in need of criticism. With respect to exercising the critical function, in my opinion, the very idea of an "organic intellectual" is both historically misleading and politically misguided. Hardly any critical intellectual beginning with Socrates has probably ever stood in a genuinely "organic" connection to a community. Intellectuals, or those engaged in progressive or socialist politics, are inherently engaged in dispelling prejudices and contesting popular beliefs or, to paraphrase Walter Benjamin, rubbing society and their own allies against the grain. Insofar as intellectuals abandon this challenge they surrender their critical function; insofar as they embrace it, functioning in an "organic" capacity becomes problematic. Thus, while critical intellectuals can serve the public, they can do so with integrity only insofar as they resist compromising the knowledge they offer.

THE CONSERVATIVE ROOTS OF THE POSTMODERN INTELLECTUAL

Political activity involves judgment and for critical intellectuals, most strikingly perhaps, judgments about the extent to which society lives up to the ideals it professes.[15] Universalistic ambitions and a certain "legislative" frame of mind, for all these reasons, inform the thinking of the critical intellectual.[16] By the same token, however, this is what poststructuralist and postmodern intellectuals seek to contest. A number of events were crucial for the development of their views including disgust with the totalitarian hubris of communism and the emergence of new social movements with specific, or particular, ideologies and interests. Caution concerning the validity of all "grand narratives" (Lyotard), skepticism of all universals, hatred of hierarchy, and a quite legitimate preoccupation with previously excluded groups and issues would all become part of the poststructuralist undertaking. Thus, where Gilles Deleuze and Felix Guattari emphasized the need for a new "micro-politics," Michel Foucault sought to substitute the "specific" for the "universal" intellectual of both the bourgeoisie and the working class.[17]

They maintained that critical intellectuals interested in radical politics should now surrender their totalizing ambitions and universal claims in order better to fight "alongside" specific groups battling against "domination" whose forms are primarily constructed in the "binary" terms of black/white, man/woman, gay/straight, and the like. The struggle against one form of domination always generates another and, in this sense, a new twist on the "permanent revolution" presents itself. The implication is clear: critical intellectuals should commit themselves to those groups with whose unique discourses and experiences they, as individuals, are intimately familiar. The practical justification is obvious: it is obviously easier for those intellectuals who share the identity of a subaltern group to work with that group. Nevertheless, the end such activity should serve is left open.

Critical intellectuals can neither view themselves as a vanguard nor simply subordinate themselves to any particular clientele. They should instead walk the line between sectarianism and opportunism by promulgating a creative tension between excluded groups and the organizations that claim to speak for them in the name of a broader unity. In this regard, however, postmodern intellectuals are less concerned with furthering a more inclusive form of solidarity than highlighting the way in which the universal is an artificial social construct and each subaltern group must retain its own "intellectuals" in order to voice demands ignored by organizations with more universal aspirations. Genuine interaction is seen as taking place less between strangers confronting one another in a public sphere than between "brothers" or "sisters" or any group whose members share a common experience.[18] Criticism from the "outsider" thereby loses its value and questions concerning the adjudication of differences between groups are never faced: experiential "authenticity" and "rootedness" become the hallmarks of the postmodern intellectual.

Just this stance, however, has traditionally marked the ideology of the right. It was the proto-fascist Maurice Barrès, after all, who derided "intellectuals" for their critical rationalism and universalistic inclinations during the Dreyfus affair.[19] And, in a way, his critique was legitimate. Intellectuals like Emile Zola and Jean Jaurès could decry the injustice accorded Dreyfus—the Jew—precisely because they placed reason above experience, evidentiary truth above tradition, and human rights above the French national "community." Their opponents like Barrès and his friends Paul Bourget and Charles Maurras, by way of contrast, viewed themselves in very different terms. They denied they were intellectuals in the name of their more "authentic" and rooted connection with the people of France. Their argument was simple enough. Their rejection of universal reason in favor of intuition and the logic of the particular supposedly enabled them to remain "rooted" in their community and stand in a more genuine experiential, or "organic," relation to the "people." These right-wing intellectuals, of course, actually stood in no closer connection to the "people" than their Dreyfusard opponents—and probably less so. Nevertheless, by effectively popularizing their conception, an elitist stigma soon became attached to the left-wing "intellectual."

Too many left intellectuals have bought into this peculiarly reactionary mode of thinking. Instead of priding themselves on their connection with the heritage of the Enlightenment and the French Revolution, instead of emphasizing their commitment to cosmopolitanism and rationalism, too many have gone on the defensive. They uncritically identify with the voices of the oppressed and it becomes more a matter of "who" says what than what is actually being said. They privilege "intuition" over discursive reason,[20] base their judgments on the unreflective encounter with reality, and employ their "experience" as a defense against criticism. The self-denying intellectual of today is not far removed from the anti-intellectual intellectual of yesterday. Both place engagement before thought and, whatever the differing political intentions, their legacy is the same. Its implications are, indeed, what the critical intellectual must contest.

CRITICAL THINKING, EXPERTISE, AND POWER

Bureaucracy involves the "rational" delimitation of authority in a hierarchy predicated on the existence of given rules.[21] Its justification lies in its efficiency or, better, its ability to transform complex problems into routine and calculable tasks. Bureaucratic thinking, in this way, tends to identify intellectual activity with the creation of operational hypotheses and prize normative forms of interdisciplinary knowledge less than narrow expertise in a particular subject area. Any inquiry into the role of the critical intellectual must consequently make reference to the division of labor and the impact of instrumental rationality. Administrative rationality is, for better or worse, the form through which struggles between different groups with different normative orientations are channeled into grievances capable of institutional redress. Thus, the ability of the critical intellectual to intervene in any given policy debate will—at least partially—depend upon having an expertise denied to the broader public.

Knowledge is both a force and a relation of production: it can even be argued that intellectual cognition rather than industrial labor, to pick up a possibility first raised by Marx, has become primary for the "postindustrial" form of modern life.[22] Expertise relevant to a sophisticated scientific or bureaucratic endeavor is, of course, not the same kind of knowledge suitable for informing normative judgments about the value of a particular scientific pursuit. But it remains important. Unfortunately, however, the New Left has often underestimated the value of such knowledge along with the need for radical intellectuals with policy skills and the ability immanently to confront the arguments of reactionary opponents in any number of highly specialized fields. This is all the more damaging since real battles are being waged in highly specialized areas, and those engaged in fighting them are no less important than intellectuals with broader interdisciplinary interests who reach a larger public. To ignore the need for critical disciplinary intellectuals with various forms of scientific expertise is to abdicate responsibility for engaging a host of issues ranging from international trade and genetics to computer programming and waste disposal. There must be a place on the left for the scientist, the technocrat, and the bureaucrat with a political conscience.

Evaluating a given method immanently always presupposes knowledge of the techniques and disciplinary arguments employed whereas external critique speaks to the validity of the particular research undertaken and its potential implications for the broader community. Admittedly, scientific methodology and political commitment often overlap. But it is dangerous to conflate them. Fascists with their notions of "Jewish science" and communists who, in the 1930s, liked to denounce Einstein's theory of relativity as "un-dialectical" and an example of "petit bourgeois idealism" were both ultimately forced to acknowledge the validity in practice of what they despised in theory. By the same token, however, any serious notion of democracy must involve keeping the purposive goals of knowledge and its priorities open to external criticism. Neither ethics nor interests, however, have anything to say about the logic or the usefulness of a given scientific method. Drawing a distinction between what is immanent and what is external to an inquiry, in this vein, need not result in a dry positivism unconcerned with ethical issues. It might illuminate the interplay between inquiry and interests, combat positivist dogma, and perhaps even generate a meaningful exchange between the public and its experts. Insisting upon the difference between form and content, method and application, knowledge and interest, consequently itself becomes a form of critical intellectual activism.

Knowledge is power: but within limits. It is true enough that "lumpenintellectuals"—toadies of the fascist and communist states who surrendered their independence and critical standpoint—were important in legitimating totalitarian regimes.[23] It is also possible to criticize the similar role played by those whom Noam Chomsky called "the new mandarins" of the liberal capitalist state with imperialist aims.[24] But this is far removed from the claims of those concerned with the "legislative" ambitions supposedly harbored by critical intellectuals, who draw upon humanistic and enlightenment traditions, and their connection with the triumph of authoritarianism. This kind of fashionable criticism is actually little more than a sectarian justification for the intellectual who can "speak truth to power" only insofar as he or she remains completely marginal.[25] It lacks any serious political or historical justification.

Just when did critical intellectuals with humanistic or enlightenment political values ever hold power? Was it really they who brought about the dark time? If so then what was the ideological complexion of those groups committed to republican values *and* economic justice while opposed to both fascism *and* communism? Better to note how critical intellectuals were held in contempt by the forces of totalitarianism. Better to understand how fascism emphasized the intuitive over the reflective and communism stripped the expert of his conscience. Better to highlight masses on the march, mobilized by neo-romantic myths and populist sophistry, and organized by a technocracy whose members were intent on obeying orders and keeping their mouths shut.

None of this had anything to do with the critical intellectual intent upon engaging issues seemingly beyond his or her particular "experience" or expertise. Sartre was correct when he noted that the critical intellectual will always "meddle in what is not his business."[26] This is the legacy of Voltaire and the critics of the *ancien regime*, of the Dreyfusards, and the students who went to protest segregation in the American South or the atrocities of the Vietnam War. Most were neither intimately associated with the oppression they witnessed nor experts in legal, military, or political affairs. These critical intellectuals could involve themselves precisely because they felt unrestricted by their particular "experiences" or fields of expertise. They would ultimately be faced with ethical and practical choices that profoundly influenced the future of progressive politics.

Arguments claiming that intellectuals must simply remain content to "interpret" misunderstandings between groups, rather than "legislate" conclusions,[27] exhibit the type of warmed-over populism, petit bourgeois guilt, and reactionary notions of equality associated with the worst elements of the New Left. A dictatorship of the intellectuals is an appalling notion, of course, but it has never been tried. Furthermore, the belief that critical intellectuals with universal values can "legislate" anything, especially in a modern capitalist democracy dominated by the mass media, is absurd. Their progressive function is inherently critical and their positive impact is always indirect. Talk about the "legislative" dangers posed by critical intellectuals is actually just another mode of avoiding political responsibility— as if *reaching conclusions* on matters of policy or organization were somehow better left to uncritical technocrats or the shifting popular determinations of the moment.

THE CRITICAL INTELLECTUAL AT WORK

Every intellectual seeks to make an impact and reach as wide an audience as possible. But what does having an impact really mean? Does it mean affecting policy in the manner of—interestingly enough—those having expertise in a given field? Or does it require "reaching the masses"? Academics and experimental artists are widely regarded as writing only for themselves; the techniques and high discursive level they employ are seen as making already obscure matters even more opaque. There is surely an overabundance of jargon and mystification, and Russell Jacoby is correct in calling for a new sensitivity to the vernacular.[28] But it is also the case that complex issues sometimes require complex language, and often for good reasons, fields generate their own vocabularies. A judgment is undoubtedly necessary with respect to whether the language employed in a work is necessary for illuminating the issue under investigation: that judgment, however, can never be made in advance.

The ivory tower is an easy target, and it is even easier to condemn as useless those ideas separated from the "masses." Insisting that the intellectual become what Nietzsche termed the "terrible simplifier," however, is both self-defeating and dangerous. It is precisely the possession of complex knowledge that justifies the intellectual in the first place. Besides, just how many sales or how much exposure does it take to qualify as a "public intellectual"? It is always amusing to hear an author whose books sell about 20,000 copies pompously lecture other authors of less "popular" stature about the need to "reach" the masses. Such critics of work that is engaged but specialized and sophisticated, whether consciously or unconsciously, make the mistake of overestimating an author's freedom in determining the popularity of his or her efforts. The outcome of an intellectual's struggle for recognition is never simply decided by the person or the work in the abstract. Other more powerful factors are involved. There is the object of analysis and the level of difficulty with which it is engaged. There is also the political climate of the time, the publishing company, the advertising, the distribution, the contacts, and—perhaps above all—plain luck.

Publics vary in their makeup and their concerns. But whether the audience is mass market, general interest, or scholarly, latent conflicts fester beneath what often appears as a seamless uniformity. The political importance of one "public" over another will change according to circumstances and the topic under discussion. The real issue is therefore neither the decline of some idealized "public intellectual" nor whether most contemporary intellectuals work within the university, seek tenure, and attempt to carve out a secure life. It is instead the political commitment that different intellectuals bring to the specific projects in which they are engaged. The point is no longer one of placing priority on one mode of discourse over another by fiat, but linking the efforts of different intellectuals engaged in different arenas of combat. The moral overlap in their efforts is what deserves consideration. But this should not occur at the expense of their divergent interests. And so, precisely because no cohesive political movement now exists in the United States, a "multi-frontal" strategy with respect to the work of critical intellectuals is the only reasonable one to pursue. That is the simple political reality.

Ernst Bloch once said that no story is ever read to its end. There is similarly an unfinished quality to all intellectual endeavors. Knowledge like power is not a quantum capable of being divided and subdivided. The will to know does not stop at the boundary between the sciences and the humanities. It merely changes form with the knowledge gleaned. The "small world" of the self does not stand apart from what Goethe called the "great world" or society. That is why any attempt to circumscribe the role of the intellectuals, whether from the standpoint of the tribune or the expert or those with a specific experience, constrains the will to know.

Above all, perhaps, the search for the new is the task of critical intellectual inquiry. But the new never exists in the abstract; it always makes reference to the past. History in its unexplored possibilities stands open before those willing to appropriate it. Every movement of the oppressed has projected anticipatory ideals into the future. Dealing with them is no longer a luxury, since given the failure of older teleological enterprises, critical intellectuals will have to uncover new sources of hope. The commitment to learn is now, more than ever, the product of an ethical decision: Sir Karl Popper was surely correct when he claimed that those in Germany who did not know about the concentration camps did not "want to know." Expanding the range of knowledge and experience should consequently assume a value in its own right. The new must be seen as taking unexpected forms, and if only for this reason, critical intellectual activity has nothing in common with producing a road map. There is no simple "line" to follow. There is only the striving to comprehend reality, give it meaning, and change it in a more progressive direction. Thus, ironically, the work of the critical intellectual ultimately rests on ethical impulses that transcend intelligence: honesty, tolerance, and the will to know.

PART II

Words and Deeds

7

GANDHI

Nonviolence
and the Violence of our Times

I never saw Gandhi. I do not know his language. I never set foot in
his country, and yet I feel the same sorrow as if I had lost someone
near and dear.

—Leon Blum (1948)

Thank you for inviting me on this occasion for celebrating the birthday,
and reinvigorating the ideal of service, of the Mahatma: the great soul.
I remember images of Gandhi from when I was a child. Cartoons produced
by the Disney Corporation used to depict him, as a grotesque spindly creature with huge glasses and a loincloth looking something like an octopus.
Only later, when I entered my teenage years, did I read the short biography,
Gandhi: His Life and Message for the World (1954) by Louis Fischer that gave
me a sense of his true stature: the beatings he withstood, the imprisonments
to which he was subjected, the kindness and the generosity of his bearing.
Over the years I would read many more books about him with wonder and
admiration. The question today involves Gandhi's legacy following the
attack on the World Trade Center.

Intoxication with the drama of revolutionary violence beginning in the
cold war years made it easy to forget that the great modern struggle of the
colonized for national self-determination following World War II began
with the emancipation of India under the leadership of Mohandas K.
Gandhi (1869–1948). His youth was undistinguished. In England, while
training for the law, he sought to ape the styles of the colonizer with little
success. Following his return to India, he failed in his pursuit if his chosen
profession. Only upon moving to South Africa, and being tossed out of a
first-class train compartment because of his skin color, did his political

---

This talk was given on 5 October 2001, the day before the military bombing of
Afghanistan began, for the National Gandhi Day of Service at Rutgers University.
It was published in the online journal, *Logos* Vol. 1, No.1 (November, 2001). See
http://logosonline.home.igc.org

commitment become manifest. It was in South Africa, where he remained from 1893–1914 and where the young Nelson Mandela later heard him speak, that he developed the doctrine of passive resistance.

The roots of his doctrine were ultimately religious: Hinduism, the *Bhagavad-Gita*, and the Sermon on the Mount. Others like Martin Luther King, Jr. and Nelson Mandela would also employ nonviolence in order to confront rampant discrimination in the name of a liberal rule of law. But none understood *ahisma*, or "non-harming" in quite so radical a way as Gandhi. He connected nonviolence with *satya*, truth and love, and *agraha*, or the discipline of the soul. Thus, the emergence of a movement grounded in *satyagraha*: the personal fused with the political, the individual with the community, religion with secular aims, and a new conception of mass action took shape. *Satyagraha* touched the world in 1930 when, opposing the hated salt tax imposed by the British, and in a remarkable display of solidarity among the lowly and the impoverished. Gandhi and seventy-eight of his coworkers began their famous "march to the sea" that, twenty days later, had swelled into thousands upon thousands, thereby beginning a new phase in the struggle against British colonial rule that would culminate in an independent India.

Nonviolence was, for Gandhi, not simply a political tactic, but an element in forging a moral way of life. The relation between oppressor and oppressed changed. Militant passive disobedience was meant both to instill discipline upon its practitioner and provide an example of moral rectitude in the face of a brutal enemy. The point was not merely to achieve solidarity among the oppressed, but to change the oppressor. Nonviolence, in this sense, retains a universal dimension. Gandhi was more than the national leader of an independence movement or a fundamentalist fanatic who termed members of rival religions "pigs" and "monkeys." Still less did he divide the world into believers and infidels. Gandhi did not dehumanize people, but rather highlighted a common sense of decency. His notion of *ahisma* points to the unity of all beings or, what in secular terms, we might consider as the harmony between humanity and nature. Gandhi was willing to let a hundred blowers bloom. The nationalism that became the hallmark of his influential journal *Young India* was never parochial, xenophobic, or intolerant, but rather, linked to internationalism and a sense of planetary responsibility. Gandhi indeed provides a sterling rebuke to those like Frantz Fanon or Jean-Paul Sartre who would suggest that only violence is an appropriate response to imperialism.

Gandhi had his contradictions, as Manfred Steger noted in his fine book: *Gandhi's Dilemma* (St. Martin's Press: New York, 2001). A tension existed between the humanitarianism of the *mahatma* and his nationalism. He embraced liberal western values, but he rejected the western life-style. He also had his weaknesses. He knew little about economics and his use of the spinning wheel as a call for economic self-sufficiency, for all Indians to spin their own textiles rather than buy them from the British, can be seen less as an insistence upon what is now called "appropriate technologies" for economically underdeveloped nations than an implicit acceptance of Indian economic underdevelopment. In this same vein, intent upon personal purification, his renunciation of comfort verged on romanticizing poverty and turning it into what his contemporary Hugo von Hoffmansthal, called an "inner glow."

But, for me, these failings only render Gandhi more human and his ultimate ideal more powerful precisely because it could not always be translated into practice. He was a politician, albeit, a politician driven by ethical imperatives. He knew that not the rhetoric of radicalism and power, but the language of peace and persuasion, the language of common humanity, would provide his movement with the moral high ground. But he also knew that principles divorced from interests are simply words. Gandhi's power derived from the way in which he connected his principles with his interests, and his means with the ends he wished to achieve: equality for people of color and the liberation of India.

Perhaps the attack on the World Trade Center and the Pentagon was an example of what Chalmers Johnson has called "blowback" or the unintended consequences of the policies pursued by the United States in the Middle East. Its refusal to support democratic forces in the Middle East is as appalling as its alliances with many of the most reactionary forces in the Arab world. There is even a perverse irony in that the *Mujahedeen* received aid from the Carter administration and Osama bin Laden was supported in his subversive activities in Afghanistan against the Soviet Union by President George Bush, Sr. But it would be absurd to place responsibility for this crime against American citizens on the misguided policies of its government rather than on those who committed the crime. Seeing the attack on the World Trade Center as simply another occasion to expose American imperialism without privileging the need for a response to the attack is an insult to the victims: it is like going to a wake and then spitting in the coffin.

Simply invoking the oppression suffered by the perpetrators of this action, or those whom these perpetrators claim to represent, does not help matters. Every fascist movement was generated by the experience of real suffering on the part of its mass constituency. Each targeted the evils of capitalism and most castigated the imperialist ambitions of their opponents. It is time to consider that the determinate response to imperialism—rather than the indeterminate causes for it—is what requires political evaluation and judgment. The point for those with progressive politics is really very simple. There exists a moment of personal responsibility for political action, beyond the oppressive policies that may inspire it, which we ignore at our peril. Forgetting that those who perpetrated this crime are not our comrades, or simply dismissing the question of punishment and retribution, is both a moral and a political abdication of responsibility.

Especially on this day commemorating Gandhi, perhaps, it is useful to contrast him and his followers with the terrorists. He, and King, and Mandela were not only men of peace, but freedom fighters who brought out the best in their people. The means they employed were related to the achievement of realizable ends and they were not aimed at imposing their beliefs on others through coercion. Those whom Richard Falk has appropriately termed "apocalyptic terrorists," by contrast, filled the heads of their followers with the most atavistic and intolerant interpretations of Islam, killed 5,000 and were willing to kill ten times as many people in their symbolic attack on capitalism. No group has claimed responsibility for the attack on the World Trade Center. And the demands by Osama bin Laden concerning Palestine and the withdrawal of American troops from Saudi Arabia and the Middle East, while they have a long history, were relayed after the event. There is indeed no reason to believe that these terrorists would cease and desist even if their demands were met. Osama bin Laden and the Taliban have indicated in word and deed that they despise the most basic values any progressive holds dear and that they feel themselves engaged in an ongoing religious assault against modernity and "the great Satan."

I never had much sympathy for the "just war" doctrine, which reaches back to St. Augustine, because every war breeds acts of injustice. Even when considering what has been called "the good war," the Second World War, any decent person must shudder at the thought of the devastation wreaked upon Dresden and Hiroshima. The idea of the "just war" should be turned on its head. War always evidences injustice, which should always make it the tactic of last recourse, but some wars are less unjust than others. It is foolish, of course, to equate reasons with consequences. A moral judgment on whether military action is appropriate depends on the evaluation of the convictions and interests of the enemy no less than the harm done and the threat posed. In this vein, considering these apocalyptic terrorists as anything more than religious gangsters would be a travesty, and perhaps there is even something wrong with dignifying their attack as an act of war rather than a spectacular crime. Enough supporters of the Islamic faith have condemned them for claiming to speak in their name. These people, too, understand the value of liberty.

We should be clear: that different communities have different customs and beliefs is a truism. This does not abrogate the need to make normative judgments about the conflicts between *and also* within these diverse communities. As far as I am concerned, the left should not put itself in the position of accepting the validity of traditions simply because they exist or embracing abstract notions of "community." Otherwise the left will become tolerant of intolerance. Progressives should instead distinguish between repressive and progressive traditions and identify with those living within the "community" who resist its authoritarian and parochial constraints. The issue here is not religion or some "clash of civilizations," but a clash over

what is politically acceptable in the pursuit of interests—whether spiritu-
ally or materially defined—and what is not.

Terrorism is unacceptable. If it should go unpunished when undertaken
by imperialist states in one set of circumstances, this does not excuse its
employment or justify ignoring it in another. Terrorism is always totalitarian: it obliterates the difference between guilt and innocence, citizen and
solider, and it intensifies the difference between "us" and "them." Terrorism
leaves no room for discourse and it denies any sense of common humanity
or decency. The terrorists who attacked the World Trade Center and the
Pentagon are totalitarians in Islamic guise: they deserve to be treated the
same way as other totalitarians. Too often in the past, partisans of the left
found ways to excuse or mitigate the severity of terror in the name of
"historical necessity" or the suffering of the oppressed. That is no longer
possible. It has become evident that what is sown in the struggle against
oppression is reaped in the new society that is created.

If freedom is the standard of judgment then few political figures
demand respect or, better, a sense of reverence like Gandhi, the *mahatma*
"the great soul." It is to him we look when emphasizing the responsibility
of political actors for the politics they choose and their ability to choose
responsibly even in an immoral environment. But there is a profound
difference between Gandhi insisting upon the employment of nonviolence
by a movement out of power and those who today insist upon a strategy of
paralysis by a sovereign state whose citizens were attacked without warning.
I do not believe that the United States can simply withdraw, or turn inward,
in response to this provocation. It would be best, of course, if any military
action were undertaken by the United Nations and this is a golden opportunity for the United States to endorse an international court of justice.
Extraditing bin Laden would probably also require the use of force,
however, and most of those opposed to military intervention in
Afghanistan were equally opposed when bombing received international
sanction in Kosovo. The bulk of military hardware and personnel would still
come from the United States, even if support may diminish in a long war,
eighty nations including the Palestinian Authority and various Arab
nations have extended support for a military response.

This is understandable. The assault on the World Trade Center and the
Pentagon was different than the terror exercised by national liberation organizations in Algeria, Northern Ireland, and even Palestine. There was little
doubt in any of these cases that the simple withdrawal of the imperialist
aggressor or the introduction of certain policies would end the conflict. But
that is not self-evident in the present instance when the goal has little to do
with national self-determination, and when religious motivations are para-
mount. The new terrorists are internationalists, but they are unlike the best
of those discussed by Michael Forman in his study *Nationalism and the
International Labor Movement* (Penn State University Press: University
Park, PA: 1998). These terrorists demonstrate a commitment to stamping

out not just democracy, but even republicanism, and their most secure base of support can be found in an anti-liberal and often violent "Islamic Brotherhood" whose influence extends from Algeria and Egypt to Turkey. There is no justification whatsoever for suggesting that a policy of passivity—not passive resistance, because the term has no meaning in this context, but passivity—will in any way mitigate the likelihood of further terrorist actions in the future. The strategy of *provoking* an over-reaction is not dependent upon any action that the victims of terror might take.

No counter-terrorist strategy can assure the capture of all those responsible for planning and abetting the attack on the World Trade Center. Bombing will not abolish terror and, as the terrorists use non combatants to shield themselves, civilian casualties will prove a growing concern. There is also the possibility that this new "propaganda of the deed" undertaken by the terrorists will ignite a chain reaction of conflict between secular governments and fundamentalist movements throughout the Arab world. Tensions are high in many nations including Indonesia and Pakistan. Should the latter explode, then India might invade Kashmir, which might result in a war with Pakistan, and perhaps even draw China into the conflict. But that there are real risks attendant upon military action, does not justify embracing a new version of the old domino theory. Bombing by the United States and Britain might not be confined to one nation. That is why political people on the left should urge a combination of vigilance and caution. It would ultimately be both irresponsible and self-defeating for progressive actors to beat the drums of war or endorse the stirrings of a disquieting new nationalism that harbors its own threats to tolerance and civil liberties in the United States. We must we wary of the rising tide of domestic militarism and the growing preoccupation with enforcing conformity in the name of patriotism. This is a time for uncertainty and tentative decisions.

Nothing requires abandoning a critical standpoint on the imbalances of power in the United States in the interest of presenting a united front. Down the road, should obviously unacceptable consequences result from a widening military action, progressives must be prepared for going into the opposition. But then is not now. We should be guided by what Albert Camus termed a "principle of reasonable culpability." To strike at the bases of the terrorists, to seize the assets of their supporters, to pressure governments in supporting anti-terrorist measures, offers at least a chance that the activities of the terrorists will be hampered, that a measure of security will be gained, and that a minimum of retribution will be exacted. Perhaps the atavistic and authoritarian Taliban regime might fall; its demise would certainly be no great loss.

Gandhi knew that revenge is not politics or justice. The possibility is real of retaliatory bombing in Afghanistan turning into the first phase for an all-out conflict with the Islamic world in which any semblance of a connection between means and ends would be lost. The argument that the end—even the elimination of the terrorist international—justifies the means only begs the question: what justifies the end? There is really only one answer to that: the means used to achieve it. This was the answer Gandhi gave. And he gave it in absolute terms. Louis Fischer was correct when he wrote that: "Gandhi's means were actually a means to a better means, a better man." The "new man" was an integral part of his political vision. There is even a sense in which the image of the "new man" lies at the source of all revolutionary action. That vision motivated Benito Mussolini and Adolf Hitler as surely as Joseph Stalin, Che Guevara, and Mao Tse-tung. But the result was usually less a new man than a new monster. Only Gandhi did not betray the old utopian belief in the "new man."

Gandhi was indeed the *mahatma*, "the great soul." His politics evidenced the nobility and power of the human spirit. Purity was the end he sought. But that is not the goal for most of who are engaged in politics and, sadly, I think we must prove a bit more modest in our ambitions. The new man is a mirage and it has become necessary to admit the obvious: a secular rule of ethical conduct must rest with establishing a plausible, rather than an absolute, connection between means and ends. Especially we on the left must recognize that in this imperfect world a perfect symmetry between them is impossible to achieve. And the same can be said of violence. It is what all progressive people hope to mitigate, try to abrogate, even if reality requires surrendering the belief that it can be completely abolished. That is indeed the most sobering thought of all.

8

RED DREAMS
AND THE NEW MILLENNIUM

Notes on the Legacy of Rosa Luxemburg

ROSA LUXEMBURG always seemed larger than life. An intellectual and a social activist, possessed of enormous charisma, she exacted tremendous loyalty from her friends and often a grudging admiration from her enemies. She struggled both as a woman and a Jew in the socialist labor movement, and she suffered a martyr's death at the hands of the *Freikorps* during the Spartacus Revolt of 1919. Her letters published following these events, and the castigation of her legacy during the "bolshevization" of the KPD during the 1920s, provide abundant evidence of her courage, her sensitivity, and her humanism. None of this, however, gives her any particular salience for the present. Luxemburg disliked turning personal issues into political ones. She would probably have noted that there were many less heralded men and women—just as sensitive and just as brave—who died just as tragically. Luxemburg would have said: "Look to my work."

Especially in our neoliberal culture, however, her form of political commitment is as unfashionable as the values she held dear. Luxemburg was consistent in criticizing a strategy based purely on the quest for economic reform and unwavering in her contempt for authoritarianism. She was a Marxist with a romantic vision of revolution and an economistic belief in the ultimate "breakdown" of capitalism. She remains the most important representative of a libertarian socialist tradition inspired by internationalism, economic justice, and a radical belief in democracy.

Appropriating her legacy, however, involves more than regurgitating her old slogans or finding the appropriate citations from her pamphlets and speeches. Luxemburg knew things had changed from the time of Marx, and she worried publicly over the "stagnation of Marxism": the outmoded claims about political events inherited by the party regulars, including the

---

This is the text of a lecture given at the Rosa Luxemburg Foundation in Berlin on 19 June 2000; it was translated and published in the German journal *Utopie-Kreativ*, no. 123 (January 2001): 9–16.

independence of Poland, no less than the unresolved questions about the workings of capitalism. Since her death, even more profound changes have taken place. And what is good for the goose is good for the gander. The same critical method Luxemburg employed against Marx must now be turned against what appears inadequate about her own views. It is indeed a matter of freeing her thinking from an outmoded teleology and drawing the political consequences. Perhaps the following will offer some steps in the right direction.

* * *

Luxemburg was no slave of Marx. But she too believed that capitalism would create its own gravediggers. And if she liked to quote the famous line from Engels that the future hinged on the choice of "socialism or barbarism," no less than most of her contemporaries, she felt confident about which would ultimately prove victorious. Everything about her politics derived from her dialectical understanding of capitalism and the revolutionary mission of the proletariat. Indeed, from the very beginning, she intuited that the political power of capital rested on the degree of organizational and ideological disunity among workers.

Luxemburg's concern with internationalism followed from this insight and her dissertation written at the University of Zurich, *The Industrial Development of Poland* (1898), already provided the outline for her distinctive critique of "national self-determination." Polish independence had been a demand of the left for generations. In this work, however, Luxemburg argued that Polish independence would only slow the progress of capitalist development and thus the growth of the proletariat within the Russian empire as a whole. Unqualified support for Polish nationalism would privilege symbolism over the need for a constitutional republic to replace the imperial regime. The arguments of Marx and his followers, she maintained, were actually anti-Marxist and self-defeating.

Luxemburg saw any endorsement of nationalism as a breach of proletarian principle. Her work highlighted the way this ideology strengthens capitalism by dividing workers, justifies the wars in which they will fight, and inhibits their ability to deal with what she correctly considered an international economic system. She would develop these themes further in her major economic work: *The Accumulation of Capital* (1911). It, too, would prove critical of views taken for granted in the labor movement. Marx had claimed that capitalism is based on investment and without it the system will collapse. Given his insistence that production always outstrips demand, however, no logical reason exists why capitalists should continue to invest and reinvest. Something within the very structure of capitalism must, Luxemburg reasoned, allow for the consumption of its surplus and thereby offer an incentive for ongoing investment. Imperialism was her answer.

New markets and cheap resources, the prospect of modernizing precapitalist territories both within the nation-state and abroad, seemed to provide the safety valve for capitalism. She indeed viewed the existence of such territories as the precondition for the survival of capitalism. Should they ever become capitalist in their own right, which the dynamics of economic production guaranteed, then the international system would suffer an immediate "breakdown." But that remained for the future. In the meantime, spurred by their own self-interest, capitalist states would have no other choice than to compete with one another frantically for a steadily diminishing set of colonies. Militarism and nationalism subsequently become intrinsic elements of imperialist strategies generated by capitalism: war is built into the system and incapable of reform. Thus, Luxemburg called for revolution.

* * *

No less than most social democrats of her generation, she longed for a republic. Such was, in fact, the way in which the "dictatorship of the proletariat" was generally understood in the decades between the fall of the Paris Commune in 1871 and the triumph of the Bolsheviks in 1917. The European labor movement prior to World War I functioned on a continent still dominated by monarchies, and the commitment to a republic was the political dividing line between right and left. Conservative programs everywhere called for authoritarian institutions and restraints on "the masses." Social democracy alone provided the alternative vision. With the insistence that the working class would expand as capitalism expanded—its parties embodied the proletarian class interest—it only made sense to call for the creation of political institutions in which the labor movement could organize freely and ultimately rule as the majority. Therein lies the connection between Marxism and republicanism.

Luxemburg was a romantic, but never fully a utopian: the new socialist society was always identified with a certain institutional arrangement for the practice of politics. Her critique of "revisionism" in *Reform or Revolution* (1899), which made her famous throughout the labor movement, was far less based upon contempt for reform *tout court* than on her contention that an unqualified "economism" undermined the revolutionary commitment necessary for instituting a republic. Luxemburg herself supported "revisionists" in various electoral campaigns and fought for numerous reforms including the forty-hour week. She did not reject reform out of hand but only insisted that it should be employed to whet the appetite of the masses for more radical political demands. Luxemburg was no different from Kautsky or Lenin or most other members of the socialist left regarding the connection between reform and revolution. She was unique only in her understanding of what was necessary to bring the revolution about and the radical democratic purpose it should serve. This was what she sought to articulate in *Mass Strike, Party, and Trade Unions* (1906).

The Russian Revolution of 1905, what Trotsky called the "dress rehearsal" for 1917, was the pamphlet's inspiration. A series of spontaneous strikes beginning in Baku in 1902 gradually engulfed the Russian Empire. These seemingly spontaneous actions were, of course, indirectly influenced by years of underground party activity. Luxemburg extrapolated from these events in order to develop her general political theory. She believed that the party should now preoccupy itself less with immediate organizational interests than with forming the perquisite consciousness required for the political struggle. Thus, committed radicals should foster a certain "creative tension" between party and base in order to mitigate the bureaucratic tendencies of the former and the adventurist experiments of the latter.

This tension was exemplified, according to Luxemburg, in the mass strike. Here is the core of her notion regarding the "self-administration" of the working class. Drawing upon a tradition reaching back over the Paris Commune to Rousseau, she understood democracy in terms not merely of securing civil liberties but also of its practical exercise. Socialism must therefore logically involve the extension of democracy rather than its constriction. The purpose of the labor movement was not merely the introduction of reformist legislation but also the creation of an institutional arrangement wherein workers might administer their own affairs without alienation or the impediments of bureaucracy. Her beautiful letters, written amid the factory takeovers in Warsaw during 1905, evidence her enthusiasm for the burgeoning "soviet" or "council" movement and the introduction of democracy into everyday life.

But this new enthusiasm never fully supplanted her original goal. Luxemburg intuited that only a republic could guarantee the maintenance of civil liberties. Genuine democracy is not simply equivalent with the will of the majority, she realized, but also with the ability to protect the minority. Her famous line from *The Russian Revolution* (1918) was not merely an aperçu. There is a sense in which her entire political project rested on the belief that "freedom is only and exclusively freedom for the one who thinks differently." Luxemburg foresaw how the communist suppression of bourgeois democracy in 1917 would unleash a dynamic of terror ultimately paralyzing the soviets and undermining public life in the nation as a whole. Even in 1919, while the Spartacus Revolt was brewing in Germany, Luxemburg vacillated between her traditional commitment to a republic and the new popularity of workers' councils. Only when she was outvoted would she completely identify with the "soviet republic" (*Räterepublik*) and the policy of her less sober followers intent on emulating the events in Russia.

The Russian Revolution indeed inspired revolutions all over Europe and the formation of communist parties around the world. Luxemburg was skeptical about the plans for a Communist International. She was fearful about its domination by the fledgling USSR and the identification of socialism with its national interests. Neither authoritarianism nor nationalism was understood by her as some historical "deviation" demanded by the present that the dialectic would somehow set right in the future. She instead considered both as infringements upon that future. In the same vein, neither the party nor the revolution should serve as an end unto itself. It was the freedom of working people with which Rosa Luxemburg was concerned. This ultimately made her a rebel in both major camps of the labor movement. It is also what makes her salient for the present.

* * *

Rosa Luxemburg lived during what has appropriately been called the "golden age of Marxism." The years between 1889 and 1914 witnessed a growing labor movement with a thriving public sphere whose political parties were everywhere making ever greater claims to power. It was a time when each could see the socialist future appearing as present. That time is over. Marxism can no longer be construed as a "science"; the industrial proletariat is on the wane; and the labor movement is obviously no longer what it once was.

"Actually existing socialism" had its chance, and little from history suggests that workers' councils can either deal with a complex economy or guarantee civil liberties. New utopian speculations, moreover, cannot compensate for the lack of any serious alternative to the liberal republican state. The institutional goal of the revolution initially sought by Luxemburg has, in short, been realized. Presenting socialism as the *other*, the emancipated society, no longer makes sense. It is necessary to approach the matter in a different way.

Modern capitalism is no longer the system described by Charles Dickens. Its liberal state has been used to improve the economic lives of workers, foster participation, and provide the *realistic* hope for a redress of basic grievances. Luxemburg was wrong: the choice is not between socialism and barbarism. Not only has history shown that the two are not mutually exclusive, it has also shown there is much room in between. The issue is no longer "capitalism" in the abstract, or the future erection of "socialism," but the pressing need for a response to neoliberal elites intent upon rolling back the gains made by the labor movement in the name of market imperatives. Or putting it another way: the contemporary problem is not the prevalent commitment to reform, which concerned Rosa Luxemburg, but the *lack of such a commitment*. Revolution is no longer the issue in the Western democracies. This, in turn, has general implications for the meaning of socialism under modern conditions: whatever else the term might imply, it must initially be understood as a practice intent upon mitigating the whip of the market *through* the state and abolishing the exercise of arbitrary power *by* the state.

Such an economic and political enterprise is now, furthermore, predicated on little more than an ethical commitment. Teleology, if not ideology, has lost its allure. Capitalism can survive, and, more important, most people believe it will. But, ironically, there is a sense in which the very success of neoliberalism may attest to the validity of Luxemburg's claim that the fight for economic reform is a "labor of Sisyphus." Without an articulated alternative and a meaningful form of revolutionary agency, it is still necessary to roll the rock of reform back up the hill. This cannot be left in the hands of social democratic or ex-communist parties, intoxicated by neoliberalism and the unprincipled compromises associated with the "third way" or what is now being called "progressive governance." Indeed, without forgetting the institutional arrangements in which real politics takes place, those with a more radical commitment to social justice should now increasingly seek new forms of alliance between workers and members of the new social movements.

Justice is a river with many tributaries. Most women and gays, minorities and environmentalists, have a stake in protecting the gains made by labor in the past as surely as labor has a stake in furthering many of their concerns in the future. The mass demonstrations contesting the inequalities and devastation generated by global capitalism, which began in 1999 in Seattle and triggered other mass demonstrations elsewhere, provide a case in point: they not only exerted real pressure on the Democratic Party and momentarily united competing groups in a spirit of internationalism, but also raised precisely those calls for international labor standards and environmental protection repressed in the mainstream discourse.

The genuinely progressive response to globalization still requires formulation. But nothing so demeans the internationalist spirit cherished by Rosa Luxemburg like the current insistence of some leftists upon the primacy of ethnic aspirations or national sovereignty over the international obligations of states to the planetary community. The proletarian internationals of the past have collapsed. The only institutions capable of furthering internationalism are now intertwined with capitalist interests, and they tend to privilege strong states over their weaker brethren. But I think Luxemburg would have realized that the choice between furthering relatively progressive ends through imperfect institutions and simply opposing their empowerment is no choice at all. She was never fooled into believing that insistence upon national sovereignty would align her with the masses of the formerly colonized world rather than the corrupt elites who still rule them in the most brutal fashion.

Luxemburg may not have anticipated the rise of national liberation movements. She was surely mistaken in believing that World War I had put an end to purely national conflicts, and she ignored questions concerning the right to resist invasion. But there was a way in which she understood nationalism far better than her opponents. Luxemburg realized that nationalism like authoritarianism has its own dynamic and that it cannot simply be manipulated for socialist purposes or by the prospect of economic gain. Instead of relying upon historical "laws," or dialectical sophistry, Luxemburg always correctly insisted on establishing a plausible relation between means and ends.

Diseases like cholera, dysentery, and AIDS are ravaging continents. Entire species are disappearing, global warming is taking place, pollution is intensifying, garbage is littering the planet. All this while a global society is taking shape in which wealth and resources are ever more inequitably distributed, political power is ever more surely devolving into the hands of transnational corporations, and petty ideologues are ever more confidently whipping up atavistic passions with the most barbaric consequences. The nation-state is incapable of dealing with most of these developments, and the usual invocations of national sovereignty or the disclaimer on any form of international intervention under any circumstances is simply an abdication of responsibility.

No less than Machiavelli and Kant, in this vein, Luxemburg would have agreed with the dictum "He who wills the end also wills the means thereto." Either planetary issues of this sort will have the *possibility* of being dealt with in the international arena through existing international institutions with the powers of sanctioning transgressors or they will *assuredly* not be dealt with at all. Human rights and new forms of transnational welfare policy constitute the only concrete *prospects* for a livable planet. The slogan of "the worse the better" has always been a losing proposition: the belief that intensified repression or exploitation will somehow automatically produce a progressive response is an illusion. The question facing the left is whether to embrace outmoded forms of thinking or provide new meaning for an old vision. Make no mistake: internationalist, socialist, and democratic values are in danger of petrifying. They must be adapted to meet new historical conditions without surrendering their bite. This is no easy undertaking, and the possibilities for opportunism are enormous. But, then, Rosa Luxemburg never walked away from a challenge. I don't think she would walk away from this one either.

9

THE LIMITS OF METATHEORY

Political Reflections
on the Dialectic of Enlightenment

DIALECTIC OF ENLIGHTENMENT by Max Horkheimer and Theodor Adorno was perhaps the first great critical encounter with the philosophical legacy of modernity undertaken from the left. Completed in 1944, published in 1947, this is surely the most influential work of the Frankfurt School and perhaps the most representative of what would become the philosophical project of its Institute for Social Research. Its critique of the "culture industry" would profoundly influence an entire discourse. It provided one of the earliest attempts to link Marx not only with Freud but also with Nietzsche, and it frankly surrendered those optimistic assumptions about "civilization" which, in an era of totalitarianism and war, it was no longer possible to sustain. *Dialectic of Enlightenment* contested dialectical orthodoxy by claiming that the price demanded by all teleological notions of progress is too high and, above all, placed the resurrection of an increasingly threatened subjectivity at the center of the radical discourse. Horkheimer and Adorno point to the "nonidentity" between subject and object, highlight a radical understanding of reification, and introduce a new anthropological perspective for understanding history and an explicitly "negative" basis for dialectical analysis.

Especially from a political perspective however, *Dialectic of Enlightenment* remains a flawed masterpiece. There should be no understanding: the purpose of this paper is not to discredit this remarkable work by two of the most important thinkers of our time. It is instead a call to begin the political critique of critical theory. Commitment to the ongoing struggles of the oppressed, and the specification of institutional constraints, has been lost. *Dialectic of Enlightenment* evinces all of these problems. The book may have attempted to confront the limits of enlightenment from within the enlightenment project. But it sought to

This is the text of a lecture given at an international conference on critical theory sponsored by the University of Tel Aviv in 1998. It was originally published in Hebrew in *Mikarev: Journal of Literature and Society*, no. 3 (summer 2000): 92–98.

understand historical events through anthropology, politics through metaphysics, and it offered only the glimmer of an indeterminate freedom. The analysis of Enlightenment, no less than its unintentional transformation into the source of fascism, strips theory from any connection with practice. Anticipating the later claim of Adorno that "the whole is false," *Dialectic of Enlightenment* robs advanced industrial society of its mediations and qualitative distinctions. Its refusal to look at institutions, movements, and struggles indeed results in precisely the form of political disorientation and hyperintellectualized sectarianism that, I believe, new forms of critical theory must seek to overcome.

Enlightenment takes on two meanings in the thinking of Max Horkheimer and Theodor Adorno. It comprises both a historically specific scientific "theory of knowledge," which was developed in Europe during the seventeenth and eighteenth centuries in contesting theological dogma, and an anthropological struggle with error and superstition.[1] The two come together, and, in this way, a genuine critique of the one implies a critique of the other. Thus, the radicalism of their undertaking: the critique of the historical Enlightenment becomes the lever for an anthropological critique of human history. Scientific rationality is seen as defining the philosophical method of enlightenment insofar as its "objective" or instrumental character can best undermine the dogmas of religion and myth in the name of normative concerns like freedom and tolerance. But this rationality is also seen as having its own dynamic and, gradually, as turning its power against all nonscientific precepts including those emancipatory values that inspired the scientific project in the first place. Just to this extent, however, the ability of "reason" to contest repression diminishes, and it becomes, in keeping with the prediction of David Hume, a "slave of the passions."

Deluded by assumptions of unilinear progress, intoxicated by scientific rationality, arrogant in their attempts to dominate nature, the proponents of enlightenment are seen as engendering that very revolt of the irrational that they wished to suppress. Or, as Adorno put the matter later, "in the innermost recesses of humanism, as its very soul, there rages a frantic prisoner who, as a Fascist, turns the world into a prison."[2] Horkheimer and Adorno saw enlightenment rationality as becoming increasingly inseparable from a "rationality of domination" and claimed that the irrational beliefs it originally sought to destroy reappeared as its own product. The weaving of all realms into a seamless web of bureaucratic domination is subsequently seen as an outgrowth of the enlightenment legacy. Or, to put it another way, fascism must be interpreted as the product of "the conditions that prevailed before its coming to power, not in a negative sense, but rather in their positive continuation."[3]

Myth had originally sought to control nature and now, in the age of fascism, enlightenment simply makes room for it. Such is the real—if unacknowledged—legacy of the Enlightenment that, according to the authors, extends from Kant over Sade to Nietzsche. For, if Kant undercut the truth claims of theology and all forms of metaphysics in the name of scientific objectivity, Sade took the next logical step and considered all subjects as instrumental means for *his* personal gratification even as Nietzsche, ruthless in the critical application of his skepticism, rendered history subordinate to the arbitrary preoccupation with furthering the "life instincts." Commodity production is seen by Horkheimer and Adorno as "objectively" sustaining this development, and, insofar as exchange value transforms qualitative differences into quantitative ones, it necessarily turns technical rationality against all forms of metaphysics and normative concerns. Enlightenment thereby undercuts the possibility of reflexivity, which originally inspired it. Humans now "pay for the increase of their power with alienation from that over which they exercise their power. Enlightenment behaves towards things as a dictator toward men. He knows them insofar as he can manipulate them."[4]

The exercise of arbitrary power complements a process that ever more surely subordinates individual wants and desires to the mercy of objective market criteria and strips people of the capacity to make anything other than arbitrary or technical judgments. More than that, it frees the irrational and the instinctive from what is commonly called conscience. This dynamic of reification is thereby seen as evident in capitalism from the start, and it fuels the conformist and profit-driven "culture industry," which seeks the "lowest common denominator" for its products, and subverts critical reflection. But its apogee lies in anti-Semitism and the gas chambers. Thus Horkheimer and Adorno can write:

> Antisemitic behavior is generated in situations where blinded men robbed of their subjectivity are set loose as subjects. For those involved, their actions are murderous and therefore senseless reflexes, as behaviorists note—without providing an interpretation. Antisemitism is a deeply imprinted schema, a ritual of civilization; the pogroms are the true ritual murders. They demonstrate the impotence of sense, significance, and ultimately of truth—which might hold them within bounds. . . . Action becomes an autonomous end in itself and disguises its own purposelessness.[5]

Horkheimer and Adorno essentially identified "enlightenment" with a debunking of what stands beyond instrumental rationality, or what Kant called "pure reason." They treated it primarily in philosophical terms or as an ideology that, following Karl Korsch, serves as a form of "lived experience." In the process, however, they ultimately wound up engaging in the very form of dogmatic and ahistorical inquiry that critical theory *initially* wished to oppose. There is not a word about the political genius of Locke and Montesquieu, the battles against injustice and dogmatism undertaken by Lessing and Voltaire, the democratic radicalism of Rousseau and the cosmopolitanism of Simón Bolívar, or the influence of enlightenment ideals upon "the age of democratic revolution."

This is all somehow secondary, or even irrelevant, to the heritage of the enlightenment and its "dialectic" as interpreted by Horkheimer and Adorno. The fact of the matter is that they simply never took into account the actual movements with which enlightenment ideas, as against the critics of those ideals, were connected. It is also worth considering that there is nothing even remotely approaching a sustained discussion of the "counter-enlightenment," let alone its political impact. *Dialectic of Enlightenment* evidences a deeply indeterminate and abstract quality from the start: the whole becomes false and the critique subsequently incorporates the reification it sought to contest. Indeed, its authors never really took to heart the insight from Nietzsche that Adorno liked to quote: "to perceive resemblances everywhere, making everything alike, is a sign of weak eyesight."[6]

Horkheimer and Adorno, of course, recognized the differences between republican and fascist regimes in their everyday political intercourse and intervention against the increasing threats to liberal norms was even deemed possible in *The Authoritarian Personality*. None of this, however, received genuine political, philosophical, or anthropological grounding. Their claim in *Dialectic of Enlightenment*, after all, was not the truism that fascism grows in liberal societies. It was rather that fascism is the logical extension of a particular form of bureaucratic, instrumental thinking generated by anthropological enlightenment and a direct continuation of the "Enlightenment." According to either definition they provided, however, their stance is misguided.

Fascism was not the product of some philosophical dialectic, but rather the self-conscious ideological response to the Revolutions of 1848, whose democratic values derived from the international community of philosophes associated with the Enlightenment, as well as the two great political offspring of modernity: liberalism and socialism. The mass base of the Nazis primarily lay in precapitalist classes like the peasantry and the petite bourgeoisie whose interests felt threatened by the capitalist production process and its two dominant classes. Much of the bourgeoisie and a great majority of the proletariat, moreover, identified with an impotent set of parties embracing a continental form of liberalism and a social democratic party still formally embracing orthodox Marxism or its communist rival. All except the communists were supporters of the Weimar Republic, and all were enemies of the Nazis who made war on them in word and deed.

Dialectic of Enlightenment casts these real historical conflicts into an anthropological fog: the metapolitical obliterates the political. Its famous interpretation of Odysseus, wherein the destruction of subjectivity becomes the only way of preserving the subject, offers a case in point. The story is useful in highlighting a reifying dynamic reaching back into the beginnings of civilization whose culmination is seen as the concentration camp victim with a number on his or her arm. But the sweep of the argument, the impression it leaves, is predicated on belief in a form of false concreteness and misplaced causality. Instrumental reason did not bring about Nazism or even destroy the ability of individuals to make normative judgments. The Nazi victory was rather the product of a clash between real movements whose members were quite capable of making diverse judgments concerning both their interests and their values. The attempt to unify *qualitatively* different phenomena under a single rubric can only produce historical disorientation and political confusion.

As regards the dialectic, it is not at all strange that Horkheimer and Adorno should write that "liberal theory is true as an idea. It contains the image of a society in which irrational anger no longer exists and seeks for outlets. But since the liberal theory assumes that unity among men is already in principle established, it serves as an apologia for existing circumstances."[7] That this "apologia" could inform a critique of the status quo never occurred to them, though, obviously, it did to any number of progressive philosophers as well as figures like Martin Luther King Jr. In the same vein, the decision of Horkheimer and Adorno to broaden the Enlightenment to include its greatest and most self-conscious critics—Sade, Schopenhauer, Bergson, and Nietzsche[8]—reflects an absence of political judgment in their reading of history.

None of these thinkers had the least identification with the principles of enlightenment *political* theory or the practice associated with it. They were antiliberal, antisocialist, antidemocratic and antiegalitarian, antirationalist and antihistorical: most important, they prized the very exercise of arbitrary power that enlightenment political theory sought to curb. There is indeed something provocative about the later insistence of Adorno that "not least among the tasks now confronting thought is that of placing all the reactionary arguments against Western culture in the service of progressive enlightenment."[9] As usual, however, he left the "progressive" character of this imperative hanging in the abstract. Obviously, there are important insights to be gained from conservative thinkers. But that is not the point. Adorno never thought to consider the contradictions generated by the attempt to merge right-wing ideology with left-wing practice.

Horkheimer and Adorno intended to write a sequel to the "fragments" known as *Dialectic of Enlightenment*. Its deconstructive pessimism was to have later made way for what Horkheimer termed a "rescue of enlightenment."[10] He, in particular, recognized that what counts is "the development of a positive dialectical doctrine which has not yet been written."[11] But this positive work never came to fruition. There is much debate regarding why not. Some look to the fragmentary nature of *Dialectic of Enlightenment* as the cause, but other works like Marx's "Eleven Theses on Feuerbach" or Nietzsche's aphorisms adequately inspired the creation of a positive worldview; others highlight the dismissal of Marxian concepts like class, but differentiating between regimes and movements is not dependent upon class analysis. I would like to offer a different view. The reason why no "positive dialectical doctrine" was forged, putting the matter crudely, is because the authors did not have anything "positive" to say.

Their metapolitical and metahistorical form of analyzing events, the reifying character of their approach, was as all-encompassing as the seamless administrative form of advanced industrial society they envisioned. There was no place for mediations or qualifications: each institution suffered equally from the impact of instrumental reason; there was never a sense that some institutions could expand the range of free experience for citizens in ways others could not. Bureaucracy became the problem, the "commodity form" the culprit, and the state the enemy. *Dialectic of Enlightenment* directed itself against a reality in which, seemingly, the whole was false. Its logic obliterated the possibility either for deriving categories useful in making distinctions between regimes or for building solidarity. The only logical outcome of this book is an uncompromising commitment to what Adorno termed "negative dialectic," which is predicated on the "non-identity" between subject and object, the individual and his world, as well as what Horkheimer termed, in a different and more religious venue, "the search for the totally other."

But this "other" desired by Horkheimer and Adorno somehow always tended to manifest itself as the "other" they feared. Viewing the enlightenment as the source for suppressing subjectivity, and thereby creating the inevitable "return of the repressed" not merely in the form of fascism but also later in the form of a student movement, naturally made them anxious. It is unsurprising that in their more hysterical moments the students of 1968 should have repelled them as much as fascism had and, through another example of misplaced concreteness, for many of the same reasons. No less than the critique they offered, the resistance they sought was purely metapolitical: the repressed moment of subjectivity, like fireworks, is denied all forms of objectification. Thus, if *Dialectic of Enlightenment* inspired "the movement" of 1968 in its spontaneous character and its assault upon hierarchy, brutality, and the consumer culture of everyday life under capitalism, the unqualified rejection of instrumental reason underlined in this intellectual project not only subverted any organizational attempts to channel the energy of the insurgents, but also informed many of their more irrational tendencies.

The excessive pessimism of Horkheimer and Adorno is, in this vein, merely the flip side of the exaggerated optimism inspiring their ultraleft followers: the "whole" is what counts. Attempts to transform it are never radical enough since either revolution or reform must, in some degree, have recourse to instrumental rationality. The choice is between the retreat into the private realm or the infatuation with utopia. But that choice is no longer viable. The critique of instrumental reason itself stands in need of political critique. The metapolitical must make way for politics, and the metahistorical for history. Without categories capable of illuminating the qualitative differences between institutions, movements, and policies, the attempt to preserve subjectivity from the incursions of advanced industrial society turns into little more than an abstract exercise grounded in what Thomas Mann first called a "power-protected inwardness." If critical theory is really to assert its "positive dialectical" character then it must highlight its institutional purposes and its political ideals. It goes without saying that the ideal of emancipation can and should be enriched by the insights and contributions of different cultures and traditions. Nevertheless, when speaking politically, in my opinion it is the institutional purposes and ideals deriving from the much-castigated Enlightenment that will ultimately serve as the precondition for any genuinely progressive movement or liberated society in the future.

10

A Teacher and a Friend

Henry Pachter

WHEN HENRY PACHTER died in 1980, a luminous intellect was lost. There were few who could boast of his enormous scholarly range, probably fewer still who could make equal claim to his intellectual rigor or his disdain for passing academic fads. The posthumous publication of his beautiful *Weimer Etudes* brought him a measure of renown that he never really experienced in his lifetime. Before then, some knew him only as the author of *Paracelsus: Magic into Science* (1951), others as the contemporary European historian who had written *Modern Germany* (1978), still others as a publicist or a teacher.

In America, he was primarily regarded as an essayist. This pleased him too, for there was no form he loved as much as the essay—the political essay. The essay form allowed him to act as the gadfly and confront the specific thinker, issue, theme, or idea with which he, always a restless intellect, was concerned at the moment. His essays often appeared cantankerous, and often they advanced positions opposed to the values of the left in the United States. But each of his essays was intent upon exploding a myth, expanding an outlook, and provoking the reader into confronting what he or she took for granted. The essays collected in *Socialism in History* were originally written as separate pieces; nevertheless, they rest upon an interconnected set of values and a certain tradition of inquiry. In this sense, they form a coherent worldview that can only benefit the socialist cause to which Henry Pachter dedicated his life.

He was born in 1907 to a bourgeois Jewish family in Berlin, and he grew up in a rigid, stuffy, and thoroughly Victorian atmosphere. It was surely in response that, as an adolescent, Pachter joined Der schwarze Haufen, one of the many groups which composed the German youth movement. This movement, commonly known as the Wandervogel, lacked

---

All articles mentioned are included in the volume—introduced by this essay— *Socialism in History: Political Essays of Henry Pachter*, ed. Stephen Eric Bronner (New York: Columbia University Press, 1984).

a direct political purpose. There, however, Pachter received his first taste of community, rebellion, and the possibilities of individual expression. The songs, the hikes, and the élan of a countercultural lifestyle had a pronounced effect. But the adult world could not be avoided forever, and it ultimately became impossible to ignore the movement's ideological reliance on neoromanticism, elitism, and irrationalism.

When the youth movement split in 1926, Pachter, at the urging of his friend Karl August Wittfogel, who would later write the classic *Oriental Despotism*, joined the youth league of the German Communist Party. Later, in Freiburg, he took courses with Husserl and met his lifelong friend Hannah Arendt. There he also studied with a conservative professor of history named Georg von Below, who made Pachter's ideological transition to Marxism easier by emphasizing the romantic roots and the speculative character of that theory, which the old Junker despised. It was also von Below who advised Pachter, in the friendliest terms, to shift his scholarly focus from medieval history and concentrate on another area—medieval history was tacitly closed to Jews.

By the end of 1926, Pachter had returned to Berlin where he met Karl Korsch—author of the influential *Marxism and Philosophy* (1923), minister of justice in the short-lived revolutionary government of Thuringia, Reichstag representative for the KPD, and editor of the party journal *Die Internationale*—who would become the major intellectual influence on his life. Along with Georg Lukács and Antonio Gramsci, whom Pachter discussed in two essays included in *Socialism in History*, Korsch would also emerge as one of the major contributors to the development of what would be called "critical" or "Western" Marxism.

Although Pachter never completed the essay on Korsch that he always wanted to write, it was from him that the student learned firsthand what was common to all three of these thinkers. None of them viewed Marxism as a fixed "system" or an objective "science" based on a causal notion of economic determinism. They instead interpreted Marxism as a method of sociohistorical inquiry that can question even its own specific usage from a critical standpoint. Their personal political beliefs aside, from their method, it becomes impossible simply to identify the working class and its aims with any party or movement. For Korsch, and then for Pachter, there could be no evasions and no pseudo-"dialectical" sophistry. Socialism and the extension of democracy were inextricably bound; the goal of Marxism could only rest upon working-class control—and not mere national ownership—of the means of production.

There was no way for Pachter to hide these heretical views from his communist comrades. Trouble had been brewing for some time when he found himself expelled from the Communist Youth in 1928 over the question of "socialism in one country." In the meantime, however, he witnessed the degeneration of the KPD. This experience informs Pachter's essay on Gramsci; it is the reason for his critical detachment, his emphasis on

Gramsci's political role and mistakes, beyond any admiration for this Italian thinker's theoretical contributions. Pachter could never forget the "bolshevization" of the German party under Zinoviev's henchmen Ruth Fischer and Arkadij Maslow, who later would themselves be dismissed and vilified in favor of the dull-witted Ernst Thälmann once Stalin's star had risen in the homeland of the revolution. A dynamic of intraparty repression had allowed the ruthless persecution and expulsion of the KPD's finest members, including Korsch himself. Indeed, the mid-1920s also witnessed the transformation of Marxism into the codified dogma of "Marxism-Leninism"; the rise of the apparatchik mentality; the reliance on outright lies that were—sometimes cynically, sometimes naively—accepted as truth; and the concerted efforts of the Stalinists and the Nazis alike to bring the Weimar Republic to its knees.

After his expulsion, Pachter frequented the bohemian cafes in Berlin. There he came into contact with the expressionist avant-garde and the cultural intelligentsia. He also got in touch with such splinter groups as the Communist Worker's Party (KAPD) and the Socialist Worker's Party (SAP), a group for which he always felt great sympathy and through which he first became friendly with Paul Frölich, the pupil and later the biographer of Rosa Luxemburg. This was also a time of great intellectual activity. Under the supervision of two renowned liberal historians, Hermann Oncken and Friedrich Meinecke, Pachter wrote his dissertation, *Das Proletariat des Vormärz* (1932), which dealt with the creation of the German working class before 1848. That knowledge would also be put to good use later in "Marx and the Jews" (1979), which is a small masterpiece in the sociology of knowledge. But Pachter didn't confine himself to scholarly pursuits; he also began to teach economic history in one of the workers' schools that flourished in the "red" districts of Berlin.

It didn't last long. Following Hitler's rise to power, Pachter led a shadowy existence. In concert with his wife, Hedwig, and Richard Löwenthal, whom he had first met in the Communist Youth, Pachter put out what was probably the first resistance journal, a little paper called *Proletarische Aktion*. That didn't last long either. By the end of 1933, Pachter had been forced to flee to Paris. There he took odd jobs, taught at the Université Populaire, agitated for creating a "popular front" of all antifascist forces, and ultimately served as a publicist for the POUM, a mixed group of Trotskyists and socialists that served the loyalist cause during the Spanish Civil War.

The collapse of Spain left a void. By the late 1930s the grand vision that the Russian Revolution initially projected had become a nightmare, while the fascist barbarians had conquered much of Europe and sought to rule the rest. Gérard Sandoz (Gustave Stern), formerly a companion of Pachter's during their Paris exile, inscribed his *La Gauche Allemande* to his friend in 1970 with the words: *"En souvenir de nos espoirs et désillusions."* Henry Pachter found the inscription "fitting."

Throughout this time, Pachter still considered himself a revolutionary Marxist. That becomes clear from his first substantive work, *Wirtschaft unterm Rutenbündel* (1932), which constituted a critique of Mussolini's economic policies. The pamphlet highlighted the sophistry of the fascists and their reliance on cartels; it is still valuable, however, insofar as it retains the flavor of those agitational writings which flooded the left in that period. It is a work of transition. The ultraleft sentiments are there along with a somewhat mechanistic quality, reflecting a bit of the KPD style. Yet the brochure closes with the following: "No political miracle can save the proletariat; no god, no dictator, no tribune. Only the workers themselves can achieve their liberation through the social revolution."

Despite the emphasis on proletarian self-organization, however, there is a clear opening to the Social Democratic Party of Germany (SPD), which served as the bulwark for the Weimar Republic. After all, Pachter's call for a "social revolution" was unmistakable in the context. The concept had received its popular connotation in Karl Kautsky's *The Social Revolution*, which appeared in 1902 and which argued that the attempt to build the socioeconomic power of the working class could not be divorced from a support for democratic political forms. The same year the brochure was printed, Pachter formally joined the SPD. Few illusions remained about its revolutionary potential. The SPD had supported the kaiser in the First World War, opposed the revolutionary upsurges in Russia and Europe during the years that followed, and become a stalwart of the status quo in the new parliamentary regime. But it retained a working-class base, forced the passing of numerous pieces of very progressive welfare legislation, and emerged as a clear-cut opponent to the Nazis. Besides, the old aura of the past still had an effect.

In *Weimar Etudes,* Pachter described some of his experiences in this socialist party that had grown bureaucratically petrified with its own success. But the flavor of the movement before its "great betrayal" in 1914, its contradictory commitment to orthodox Marxist theory and reformist practice, its belief in democracy, and its relation to contemporary developments are all explored in "The Ambiguous Legacy of Eduard Bernstein" (1981). In a way, it makes sense that this should have been Pachter's last published essay. "The movement is everything, the goal is nothing" was the phrase most associated with Bernstein, and Pachter liked its antimetaphysical implications as well as its emphasis on concrete politics. Also, aside from Pachter's own long-standing commitment to pluralism, parliamentarism, and reform, the figure of Eduard Bernstein provided him with an example of intellectual courage, decency, and an honest willingness to exert the critical faculty, even if it meant clashing with the dominant dogma.

In any event, the young ex-communist's political decision to join the SPD demanded a philosophical confrontation with his recent past. Despite the forced, and sometimes over-complicated style, the first step was perhaps his finest article of the period, "Communism and Class." This essay appeared in the prestigious *Die Gesellschaft*, a journal edited by Pachter's SPD patron, Rudolf Hilferding, author of the classic *Finanzkapital* and twice minister of finance in the Weimar Republic. The essay was first published in 1932, after Stalin's "left turn" of 1929. This change of line instituted what came to be known as the "social-fascist thesis," which equated the Social Democrats with the Nazis. Insofar as both groups were hostile to the Communists, and so "twin brothers," any support for a KPD alliance with the SPD against Hitler could be seen as a "right-wing deviation"— even though this division of the working class would ultimately help the Nazis gain power.

In Pachter's view, a fundamentally different worldview had provoked the break between these two competing organizations of the working class at a critical historical juncture. As far as the KPD was concerned, its revolutionary ideology had become split from what was essentially an opportunist practice. This situation is seen as deriving from the "substitution" (Trotsky) of the party—which, by definition, incarnates the "true" revolutionary consciousness of the proletariat—for the actual working class as the agent of revolution. But, following the theoretical lead of his friend and teacher Arthur Rosenberg, Pachter saw that such a substitution does not lead to a revolutionary identification between the party and the interests of this specific class. Quite the opposite: replacing class with party creates a vacuum that can be filled by any mass base.

Through its adherence to "democratic centralism," lacking any check from below, the party can choose any means to pursue that revolutionary goal which legitimizes it in the first place. It can also change the goal at will. Any tactic can be decreed a "revolutionary" necessity so long as it meets the immediate needs of the organization. Moreover, just as any mass can fill the vacuum at the base from the standpoint of the revolutionary vanguard, any party capable of exercising discipline and instilling commitment to chiliastic goals can assume primacy from the standpoint of the radical masses. This is precisely what allowed the "vanguard party" to be employed by a variety of movements with ideas ranging across the political spectrum.

In this respect, Pachter provides one of the most interesting analyses of the ideological degeneration of the communist movement as well as the crossover in membership between the Nazis and Communists that was so striking toward the end of the Weimar Republic. Actually, however, Pachter probably overemphasized the implications of this overriding ideological moment for the KPD position on the "United Front" with the SPD. If means really take the place of ends, and if any tactic can be viewed as a revolutionary necessity, then there is no reason why the Communists should have ideologically excluded a "United Front" policy per se. Such a policy could have been propagandistically justified just as easily as the separatist course—and it would be proclaimed only a few years later in the "Popular Front" period.

What Pachter underplayed in this essay was the ideological subordination of the KPD to the Soviet Union, and so the actual concerns that determined the party line. In fact, Moscow's "left turn" was anything but "left" insofar as it assumed that capitalism had "stabilized" and that all Comintern efforts should be directed toward supporting the industrialization campaign that would construct "socialism in one country." As a consequence, the Soviet Union moved away from Lenin's emphasis on exploiting international class contradictions to intensifying the conflicts between bourgeois states. From this new standpoint, Hitler's success could appear useful to the Soviet Union in disrupting the West, and Stalin's suicidal German policy would at least retain a certain deranged logic. But then, it would also follow that the "revolutionary" line accompanying the "left turn" was pure fluff. The Communist claim that the Nazi state would last only five years at the most—under the slogan "After Hitler, Us!"—would then be nothing more than the ideological veil for a defeatist policy.

Basically neither the orthodox Communists, despite the efforts of Togliatti and Dimitroff, nor the Social Democrats were able to develop a coherent understanding of fascism. In his broad and insightful essay "Fascist Propaganda and the Conquest of Power," which was written for the UNESCO-sponsored volume *The Third Reich*, Pachter attempted to make his contribution. Through his analysis of the Nazi propaganda effort, it becomes clear that the Nazi purpose was neither to persuade nor simply to deceive. Both persuasion and deception occur within a discourse that, at least potentially, allows for an opponent's response. The Nazi vision was much more radical: the very possibility of rational discourse had to be destroyed, arbitrary power had to prove decisive, and the audience had to be directly subjugated to the speaker's will.

Following the work of Franz Neumann and Hannah Arendt, Pachter argues that terror, symbols, and organizational details are all manipulated to prepare the psychological condition in which individuals become atomized into an amorphous mass to ensure an immediate identification with the "leader." Real communication is subordinated to the creation of a spectacle in which the entire society will participate. Through mass meetings, torchlight parades, and ideological bombardment, "an artfully contrived mass regression into the age of tribal magic" occurs in which the human condition will be portrayed as one of perpetual combat readiness. Nevertheless, the question remains: combat against whom?

According to Pachter, the choice of enemy was as contingent as the conflicting promises that Hitler made to conflicting classes and groups. Although he did not ground Hitler's mass support in a sociological analysis of the precapitalist groupings within German society, the image of the "little man" is useful. It explicitly refers to the title of the best-seller by Hans Fallada entitled *Little Man What Now?* This "little man"—the peasant, the clerk, the small businessman, the petty aristocrat, the disillusioned army veteran, the civil servant—felt his traditions, position, and possibilities being extinguished by the modern industrial classes of society, their political parties, and their institutions no less than by the values they affirmed. Indeed, Pachter beautifully shows how the cultural climate of the time militated against Enlightenment traditions in favor of irrationalist, vitalist, and neoromantic ideologies.

The Nazis were, according to Pachter, able to harness the resentment, the moral indignation, and the frustration of the "little man" through the call for harmony, through the fanatical insistence on an abstract apocalypse, and through the demand for revenge on the representatives of modernity: the "bosses," the "Communists," the "democrats," liberals, intellectuals, and Jews. In this orgy of resentment, sadism took the place of a revolutionary impulse and became socially ennobled. Callousness, hatred, fanaticism, violence took on positive connotations. Intuition replaced reason as the criterion of truth; empty abstractions such as "destiny" gave primacy to myth as a form of social cohesion and dynamism. Intensity became its own end. Fanaticism rather than any specific goal is seen as defining fascist propaganda. Such fanaticism, however, must be perpetually fueled. Fascist propaganda will subsequently always portray the world as being on the brink of war—and there is a sense in which the prophecy becomes self-fulfilling. Only in this way is it possible to ensure a perpetual dynamism—a dynamism without purpose or rational justification—which becomes the vitalistic, existential compensation for what Erich Fromm called "the escape from freedom."

But there were those in the 1930s who were not willing to hand over their freedom quite so easily. In France, the newly formed "Popular Front" sought to defend democracy against the fascist tide in the name of a progressive attempt to "reform the structure," while 1936 also saw the great experiment with revolutionary democracy and antifascist resistance in the Spanish Civil War. In that year, the military, the church, the aristocracy, and other reactionary classes unified behind Franco's leadership in a revolt against the Spanish Republic. Liberals, socialists, Communists, Trotskyists, and anarchists rose to defend it. While Hitler and Mussolini sent massive military aid and personnel to Franco, the Western democracies—despite the underground shipment of some arms and the enthusiasms of volunteer regiments—remained rigidly neutral. The only real defender of the republic appeared to be the Soviet Union, whose "Popular Front" line was transported to Spain.

This reformist strategy, soon enough, came into open conflict with the revolutionary aims of the anarchist movement. That contradiction on the Spanish left would be tragically resolved in 1937 when communist forces, with socialist support, slaughtered the revolutionary front of anarchists, syndicalists, Trotskyists, and their partisans in the battle of Barcelona. During the intervening year and a half, Pachter wrote *The Spanish Crucible*, which would remain his favorite work. A testament to the anticommunist revolutionary left and the struggle of the antifascist cause, when it was republished in Spanish in 1965, Pachter wrote a new introduction. The revisions are startling and the criticisms are balanced. Critical of those liberal historians who in retrospect argued for compromise on the left, Pachter maintains that "the Civil War was inevitable precisely because the revolution was inevitable." Nor should the tragedy of Spain be simply seen as a prefiguration of World War II or a situation in which the international proletariat stood ready to defend the republic. Casting aside the vestiges of nostalgia, Pachter is unafraid to question whether the war should actually have been prolonged after late 1937 when it was known to have been lost; ruefully he points out how the zealous antifascists of the time "owed it to the militants to sacrifice them to the cause." That cause itself was the splendid mixture of solidarity and individual dignity that has become the transcendent symbol of the Spanish ordeal. To this cause, Pachter would remain committed. His book is indeed still remembered by many on the radical left: at the urging of the famous anarchist Daniel Guérin, it was last translated into French as *Espagne 1936–1937: La guerre dévore la révolution* (1986).

By 1941 Henry Pachter's second exile had begun in America. Through the influence of Otto Kirchheimer and Franz Neumann, the important theorists of law and the state, he became a consultant for the Institute of World Affairs and the Office of War Information. He also become a research associate for the Office of European Economic Research, which was a branch of the Office of Strategic Services, and it was for this organization that he wrote his little book on Nazi rhetoric, *Nazi-Deutsch*. Afterward, Pachter taught at the New School for Social Research, the City College of New York, and Rutgers University.

As the 1950s turned into the 1960s, Pachter became known as one of many cold warriors, an impression that grew through the impact of certain articles he published in *Dissent*, of which he was a cofounder and editor, as well as through his exaggerated criticisms of leading American revisionist historians like William Appleman Williams and Gabriel Kolko. He, too, participated in the American Committee for Cultural Freedom along with other organizations covertly supported by the CIA. But the truth is that Henry Pachter was not a mandarin, or a McCarthyite demagogue, or a reactionary. He felt a certain intellectual affinity for those like Maurice Merleau-Ponty who tried to distance themselves from both superpowers in the name of what may be called "a-communism." But, for better or worse, Pachter fundamentally believed that such a stance was an evasion of the concrete political choice that had to be made. Just as certain leftists like Jean-Paul Sartre provided the Soviet Union with a special "privilege" in foreign affairs, whatever their own reservations about its regime, Pachter did the same with the United States. His criterion of judgment was clear: he would always "prefer the most inefficient democracy over the most efficient dictatorship."

When the cold war began, Pachter maintained his commitment to social democracy. At the same time, however, any past traces of solidarity with the Soviet Union from the common front against Hitler had vanished. In this regard, Pachter was no different from many of his friends—such as Franz Borkenau, Richard Lowenthal, and Fritz Sternberg—who suffered what Brecht called "the Stalin trauma." It is nothing more than fashionable nonsense, however, to suggest that these thinkers somehow created the foundations of modern neoconservatism. All of them contributed to the development of what might be considered a political realist approach to Soviet foreign policy. *Weltmacht Russland* (1968) fit into this general enterprise. Pachter suggested that Soviet foreign policy is less a set of discrete strategies reflective of shifts in the leadership than a function of aims and ambitions connected with the emergence of Russia as a modern nation-state under Peter the Great. These ambitions would include barriers to possible invasion from the West, warm water ports to the South, and hegemony over the Baltic, as well as secure borders against China to the East. Pachter indeed considered the USSR neither inherently expansionist nor inherently peaceful but rather as a superpower intent upon responding to given circumstances as its national interests dictated whether at the expense of its "socialist allies" in the East or its "imperialist enemies" in the West.

This view informs his understanding of "socialist imperialism" in particular and imperialism in general. His essay "The Problem of Imperialism" (1970) interprets the phenomenon as neither intrinsic to capitalist development nor even necessarily as economically profitable for the capitalist class as a whole. Pachter instead highlights its contingent character and views imperialism as fundamentally political in character rather than as a reflex of economic processes. Opposition to the Soviet Union consequently should be in tactical terms, and the tactics should not be confused with the strategic purpose: peace. Even Pachter's *Collision Course: The Cuban Missile Crisis and Coexistence* (1963), which is certainly not the most evenhanded study, made a plea for coexistence as the only realistic response to the possibilities of nuclear war. He believed that the question of nuclear arms should be severed from all other foreign policy issues and, just a few months before his death, he even drafted an essay on unilateral disarmament titled "A Suggestion for Surrender."

Internationalism was perhaps the value Pachter held most dear, and it profoundly informs his major work of the postwar era, *The Fall and Rise of Europe* (1975), which he dedicated to Willy Brandt and Jean Monnet. Whatever its inadequacies, in Pachter's view, the United Nations, along with its many international agencies, as well as regional organizations such as the European Economic Community, needs to be strengthened, which naturally does not preclude reform. This position is also what set Pachter at odds with leftists who uncritically supported Third World dictatorships and the movements of "national liberation." He was always, fundamentally, a cosmopolitan with an innately skeptical view of tradition. Nevertheless, he did not simply dismiss the legitimate grievances of oppressed communities and the tragedy of their plight.

The point becomes particularly clear in his essay "Who Are the Palestinians?" (1975). As an editor of *Dissent*, Pachter noted with alarm the increasing Israeli bias of the magazine and many of its contributors, such as Bernard Avishai, Gordon Levin, Irving Howe, and others. It should be remembered that this article appeared long before the barbarous slaughter of Lebanese civilians in 1982, which jolted many on the left into reconsidering their positions on the Mideast. Still, Pachter did not fall into the common mistake of those who, in criticizing the role of the oppressor, cast a romantic aura over the representatives of the oppressed. He was suspicious not merely of the terrorism but of the authoritarianism of Arafat and the Palestinian Liberation Organization, and he deplored the way in which neighboring Arab states have used the Palestinians as a political pawn rather than allow inmates of the refugee camps to settle on their territories.

Whatever the importance of realism to his way of thinking, in any event, normative questions always played a decisive role. Pachter never underestimated the role of ideology when dealing with movements or the speculative moment underpinning a genuine critique of the status quo. In keeping with Karl Korsch, he sought to understand socialism in terms of the normative purposes it originally was meant to achieve. Only by raising the epistemological question "what is socialism?" could Pachter consider it possible to connect tactics and strategy, or means and ends, in a plausible manner. Thus, he refused to identify socialism with either the economic reformism of mainstream social democrats or the political authoritarianism of the communists.

"Three Economic Models" (1964) is one of Pachter's best-known essays. It seeks to explain the epistemological assumptions that underpin the workings of "pure" capitalism, the welfare state, and socialism. Considering these systems as ideal types, according to Pachter, both laissez-faire capitalism and the welfare state presuppose the existence of private property as well as a mathematically based notion of efficiency that will judge the value of production solely in terms of its profitability. An iron rule therefore applies: New production methods must produce savings in excess of the capital they make obsolete. Both forms, moreover, tie ownership of capital to decisions over investment, identify labor as a commodity, and seek to maintain a consistent flow of profits for the capitalist class. Given that capitalism always requires a degree of state intervention, whatever its goal of enabling the individual to maximize profits, it is not seen as inimical to a welfare state. Underestimating the struggle between those committed to the "free" market and those committed to state intervention, which was somewhat understandable in the context of the time, Pachter views the differences between pure capitalism and its welfare variant as matters of degree rather than kind.

But the iron rule remains, along with the market and the insecurity caused by private control over investment decisions, no less than the lack of control by the ultimate consumers. The crucial issue for socialism is consequently neither wages nor the simple "expropriation of the expropriators" (Marx) under the guise of ownership of the means of production. Its partisans must focus instead, according to Pachter, upon democratic control over the means of production and how investment might be directed toward projects that might not bring an immediately calculable profit but will make life easier and better. It is, for him, a question of priorities: socialism as against any form of capitalism must "provide different answers to the same questions." Thus, socialism should not be identified with a new era of unrivaled productivity in terms of those criteria usually associated with the capitalist labor process.

And, if that is the case, the entire notion of what constitutes "progress" under capitalism must be reformulated. At the time of his death, Pachter was still collecting notes for a philosophico-historical work on a problem that had passionately intrigued him for many years: the concept of time. This work was never completed, but he did finish what would have constituted a chapter, "The Idea of Progress in Marxism" (1974). Pachter shows himself as critical of economic determinism as of sophistic attempts to identify the interests of communist states with those of a liberating world spirit. Progress is instead understood in normative terms: it projects bringing the alienated forms of bureaucratic action under democratic control with a view to the extension of humanistic, universal, participatory ends. And discussing how this *might* be achieved becomes the aim of "Freedom, Authority, and Participation" (1978). Aside from its many economic suggestions, usually of a speculative sort, there are practical political insights as well. Thus, while socialists are a minority, they can only press for reforms. Only when real inroads or majorities have been achieved can demands be made for fundamental changes, while a substantial majority is necessary for any structural transformation that assumes "the symbolism of revolution."

Although his description of actual possibilities at any particular stage might well prove accurate, Pachter ignored the way in which emphasizing a strategy of instrumental reform might preclude the possibility of thinking about a more radical transformation. He shows little sensitivity for the problems of moving from one position to the next. He also ignores the way in which "capitalist democracy" tends to transform long-term political goals into short-term economic ones. This not only places socialists on the defensive but also, I think, changes socialism itself into little more than a regulative ideal predicated less on workers' control than on mitigating the whip of the market and furthering the fight for time.

There is a way in which Pachter anticipates this in what is my favorite of his essays: the humorous and prophetic "The Right to Be Lazy" (1956). Building on the earlier pamphlet of the same name by Marx's son-in-law, Paul Lafargue, Pachter envisages socialism as stepping back from the single-minded emphasis on production and capitalist notions of efficiency that have dominated the mass organizations of the left. He calls for new criteria for a newly planned and democratically controlled economy no less than a shift from industries that may be profitable in the short term to the construction of hospitals, parks, and other projects that would provide benefits for the community as a whole over a longer period of time. Whether the new society is as "productive" as capitalism is, for him, ultimately not the point. The value of socialism, again, lies in the priorities it will set; the manner in which people will be freed from the drudgery of labor; the way in which their capacities for participation, leisure, and creativity will be fostered.

"What is socialism?" Henry Pachter was willing, for better or worse, to provide an answer: it is the process of emancipation whose realization remains always unfinished. He believed that peace can never exist between humanity and its creations. Ironically, in his view, the person who demands the realization of socialism cannot be a socialist. Socialism is not merely the expansion of wealth or democracy: it is rather the ongoing struggle for intelligence and experience. Thus, for Henry Pachter, socialism can be nothing other than "the highest stage of individualism—its fruition for all."

11

Remembering Marcuse

Herbert Marcuse was 81 when he died in July of 1979. I never met him. But I heard him lecture often, and I was among those who were profoundly affected by his thought. Even now, roughly two decades after the events of 1968, it is difficult to describe the character of his influence. His background was so different from what was familiar to American radicals. Even his critics recognized the erudition of this man, so steeped in classical European culture, who seemed to possess the key to the dialectic. The most tumultuous events of the century seemed etched on his face: World War I, the Russian Revolution, the German Revolution of 1918, Weimar, Nazism, Stalinism, World War II. Marcuse had participated in the Berlin Workers Council of 1919, he had studied with Martin Heidegger, and had become part of the "inner circle" in what we then only vaguely knew as the "Frankfurt School." He was a product of what Stefan Zweig termed "the world of yesterday."

Marcuse, in contrast to what the popular media trumpeted, was never a "guru" of the New Left. His thought was too esoteric, and also too radical, for a movement whose worldview depended upon a vague conglomeration of welfare liberalism, populism, romanticism, and anarchism. Few of us knew anything about philosophical idealism or "Western Marxism," let alone phenomenology and the modernist avant-garde. Most of us, in spirit, were far closer to Paul Goodman. But Marcuse struck a cord in a way no one else did. He offered an intellectual challenge. He called upon people to think beyond what they had been taught. He gave "alienation" a palpable meaning and made young people confront the "system" in which they were reaching maturity. Above all, perhaps, he gave us an image. *One-Dimensional Man*: he was the central character in a hundred rock songs and a

This is the text of a speech given in at the CUNY Graduate Center in 1989 marking the tenth anniversary of Herbert Marcuse's death. It was published in the first edition of *Of Critical Theory and Its Theorists* (Oxford: Blackwell, 1994), 234–237.

thousand poems, and he nauseated the cultural strain of the movement. Marcuse's most famous work seemed to expose the mechanisms of integration and constraint that cloaked the contradictions operating within advanced industrial society. No matter that others had already shown how the revolutionary consciousness of the working class had been defused, or the pervasive power of the "culture industry." It was Marcuse who, whatever the difficulty of his prose, gave the young an image they could grasp.

The rebellion sought an alternative to this one-dimensional being through what Marcuse, following André Breton, termed "the great refusal." Revolution would now transform the everyday life of the "establishment." Our generation on the left was composed of people who hated the stultifying sexual relations, the vapid music, and the style of success extolled during the 1950s. Marcuse seemed to expand our horizon in an age championing "the end of ideology." Marcuse taught us otherwise by employing utopian speculation mixed with *Ideologiekritik* to attack the prevailing "operationalist" mentality and suggest that political repression existed within the supposedly value-free rationality of scientific discourse. He fostered the belief that current modes of production were historically mutable. He demanded that we envision a "new technology" and a "new science"; indeed, no matter how naive this may sound, his thinking provided us with a new respect for nature and helped generate what would become a new environmental consciousness. But, even more than that, Marcuse's thinking inflamed our hopes. *Eros and Civilization* taught us about utopia, and, whatever the problems with this work, it almost single-handedly gave a new dignity to this complex concept so alien to American pragmatism.

Marcuse made us consider what Stendhal called "*la promesse de bonheur.*" He turned aesthetics into an issue for social theory. And again, whatever the problems with his theory, this was an intellectual achievement of the first magnitude. His work spawned discussion and gave a new cultural connotation to the notion of revolution. It was rarified. Perhaps too much so. His thinking had no place for sexual promiscuity, drugs, rock and roll, or pornography. In fact, it is almost laughable to reread the charges of Marcuse's numerous mainstream critics who claimed that, like Socrates, he was undermining the morals of the young.

Nothing could have been further from the truth. Marcuse, no less than Camus, was a moralist par excellence. He envisioned new ways of individuals' treating one another, loving one another. He envisioned new emancipated forms of social and personal interaction; indeed, he would accept nothing less. His heroes were not Herman Hesse, Castenada, or others fashionable at the time; they were Schiller, Hegel, Marx, and Freud. Marcuse was as disgusted with the anti-intellectual, mystical, and irrationalist strands of the movement as any of the New Left's more conservative critics. But in the criticism he made, there was one difference everyone except the worst dogmatists recognized: Marcuse always spoke as a friend. Whatever the parallels that existed between Marcuse's ideas and those of his former comrades at the Institute for Social Research, his criticisms were always seen as those of a partisan. They were understood as coming from a revolutionary of the past to a movement half-conscious of its goals while groping with new organizational possibilities in the midst of bitter sectarian squabbles. His thinking gave a new place of importance to what were then the excluded "marginal groups" of advanced industrial society: bohemians, students, minorities, and women. Marcuse provided an impetus for a host of thinkers who would concern themselves with the "new social movements." But if the students served as catalysts for the French working class, which is what he suggested in *An Essay on Liberation*, Marcuse nonetheless overestimated their revolutionary character. He did not anticipate that the new social movements would ultimately generate interest groups seeking to extend the unfulfilled ideals of the bourgeois state to their own constituencies. Institutional analysis was not really Marcuse's strong suit. Indeed, if he exposed how hegemony is practiced under the guise of free speech in "Repressive Tolerance," his conclusion concerning the need to repress the proponents of repression was vague and bureaucratically ill conceived.

Marcuse had a certain neo-Leninist streak. Still, the partisans of orthodoxy despised him. His *Soviet Marxism* was a devastating critique from the left of the petrification that the "fatherland of the revolution" had undergone. He showed how the revolution had turned against itself and the terrible effects of authoritarian control on the life and culture of the Soviet citizenry. Marcuse earned the unmitigated hatred of the Old Left long before the rise of the student movement. Few philosophers, in fact, have received such abuse. Marcuse even went into hiding for a time during the 1960s after threats were made against his life. It was disgusting by any standard. Marcuse was called an "intellectual termite," a "cretin," and worse.

Most of his critics, of course, probably never read his remarkable essays from the 1930s or knew that his *Reason and Revolution: Hegel and the Rise of Social Theory* had become one of the seminal interpretations of the great idealist philosopher. It is still easy to forget how Marcuse held up a mirror to advanced industrial society, challenged its notion of progress, and brought the quest for happiness back into the political vocabulary. His work is an enduring commitment to the most radical, speculative, and concrete impulses of critical theory. A pacified existence defined his utopia, but his dialectic never came to a halt. That is why, wherever the revolt against oppression surfaces, someone will remember the legacy of Herbert Marcuse.

12

ECOLOGY, POLITICS, AND RISK

The Social Theory of Ulrich Beck

1. INTRODUCTION

EVERY WRITER wishes to present the world in a new light. Ulrich Beck is one of the few who have succeeded. Over the last decade, he has become one of the most controversial intellectuals in Europe. He is among the founders of modern ecological theory and a leading sociologist with a new theory of modernity. He is also a public intellectual whose essays have been published in popular magazines like *Der Spiegel* and a thinker whose categories "risk society" and "reflexive modernization" have become part of the sociological vocabulary.

Beck is one of the very few thinkers capable of envisioning a different world on the horizon. He is unconcerned with the failed radical undertakings of the past. His environmental and sociological enterprise evidences a profound enthusiasm for the *novum*. A new "risk society" is seen as emerging, in large part due to the problems, not least of which is environmental devastation, wrought by its predecessor.[1] Assumptions carried over from industrial capitalism are now, according to Beck, being abolished. Revolution is being incorporated into the system.[2] A new "reflexive" form of modernization is rationalizing issues ignored in the past. Ecology and other "postmaterialist" concerns of the new social movements have become intimately connected with a new period of previously unimagined technological change. The environment, individual needs, and the quality of life are the pillars of Beck's theory of the risk society. None of these concerns, however, is mechanically juxtaposed against technology, bureaucracy, and the corporations. The thinking of Beck is unique insofar as its critique of modernity rests on an embrace of its most radical possibilities; Beck is contemptuous of the ecological Luddites. He has little use for anti-technological preju-

This essay was originally published in *Capitalism, Nature, Socialism* 6, no. 1 (March 1995): 67–86.

dices or other conservative assumptions inherited from an antiquated industrial capitalism. The risk society is capable of generating new scientific possibilities as well as ecological dangers.

There is nothing traditional about his thinking. His ecological social theory, for want of a better description, is a fusion of anti-institutional liberalism and cosmopolitan communitarianism. Ecology is linked with modernization, everyday life with a new notion of politics and a cosmopolitan sense of multiplicity, including an assault on racism. Beck occupies a peculiar niche in contemporary intellectual discourse. His work stands somewhere between the discourse theory of Jürgen Habermas, the institutionalism of Niklas Luhmann, and the postmodern skepticism of Jacques Derrida. Beck is an eclectic, the master of many traditions and the servant of none. Influences upon him range from Zygmunt Bauman and Anthony Giddens to Hannah Arendt, Karl Popper, and the thinkers of the Frankfurt School. He employs the insights of poets and painters such as Gottfried Benn and Wassily Kandinsky, as surely as arguments from Marx and Weber. Beck uses a pinch of this and a dash of that and then, like a good cook, gives the meal a decidedly unique taste.

All of this gives his work a certain verve. His thinking is somehow always provisional and, mirroring the ambivalent character of the world it describes, rife with tensions. His orientation is decidedly subjective, yet it builds on the Enlightenment project. It privileges the new social movements but emphasizes the importance of private industry. It illuminates the experience of a new society but is informed neither by existentialism nor phenomenology. It analyzes a new phase of history but is unconcerned with actual interests. It deals with the radical implications of scientific progress on the environment but ignores matters of scientific methodology. There is, however, one point on which this self-critical sociology is completely unambivalent: it is committed to contest all forms of theoretical and practical authoritarianism in the name of an always unfulfilled set of possibilities for individual happiness and a new "global" dialogue.

Modernity makes it possible, according to Beck, for people to "create" their own biographies.[3] His is a case in point. Beck's cosmopolitanism and contempt for dogmatism surely derives from his self-conscious attempt to deal with the legacy of fascism. Born in 1944 in Pomerania, part of what is now Poland, his mother with her five children made her way to the West. They wandered about before finally settling in Hannover, Germany, where Beck went to public school. Then, with aid from the American Field Services, he spent 1962 attending high school in Springfield, Massachusetts. In America, Beck saw a different society and he was impressed with its lack of status consciousness and spirit of technological progress. Nevertheless, he went back to Germany, finished gymnasium, and then attended the University of Munich.

There he met Elisabeth Gernsheim, who would interest him in questions concerning women, the family, and the social implications of gene technology.[4] They married and studied sociology together. It was a popular discipline among members of the New Left, and Beck finished his dissertation in 1972. The work dealt with objective and normative elements in the debates over the relationship between theory and practice in modern variants of German and American sociology. Jürgen Habermas and Niklas Luhmann, Alvin Gouldner and Paul Lazersfeld, along with any number of other thinkers, make their appearance in Beck's study. The views of each are presented as inadequate, however; Beck is clearly already engaged with developing an approach of his own. The dissertation was published by Rowohlt and, soon enough, Beck became an assistant at the Institute for Sociological Research in Munich. He remained there until 1979 when he took a post at the University of Münster, followed by one at the University of Bamberg. This was the year he finished his habilitation, *Reality as the Product of Social Labor.*

Later Beck would argue that the "risk society" and ecological threats to the planet had undercut the importance of class contradictions relative to the new social movements and the middle strata of experts and professionals. But his habilitation was profoundly influenced by Marx. It extended the interpretation of the "commodity form" in *Capital* to the content of various needs or goal orientations, and it analyzed how different dimensions of social life are constituted by different forms of work. Preoccupation with content would increasingly dominate the Marxian concern with form, and given Beck's growing interest in ecological matters, he also began to place less emphasis on institutions and the production process in favor of movements from below and their ability to express unfulfilled subjective needs. Nevertheless, in keeping with Marx, Beck would continue to consider nature less as an "objective" given than as a social product.[5]

How much the early studies prepared the way for his future works, which would make his reputation and provide him with a chair of sociology at the University of Munich, is open to question. Certain themes, however, remain constant: the preoccupation with the quality of life; the meaning of social experience; and the consequences deriving from particular forms of human interaction with nature. These are reflected in the three core dynamics of the risk society: the individualization of politics; the "reflexive" urge toward modernization; and, perhaps most important, the new ecological threats to the environment.

2. NATURE AND POLITICS IN THE RISK SOCIETY

We live in a world, according to Beck, different from the one in which we think. Risk society is more than a catchphrase or a sound bite. This form of modernity explodes the very values and categories it created. The risk society describes a new social formation in which experience and the environment are transformed in particular ways. Instrumental rationality, market mechanisms, bureaucratic divisions of labor, and class conflict no longer define its dynamics. A totally new logic of unintentional consequences informs the risk society and its process of "reflexive modernization."[6] Debate will now concern itself with latent and potential risks rather than manifest and calculable options.

Industrial society was predicated on binary oppositions of the latter sort. Its logic was based on the proposition "either/or." Mutually exclusive claims are often generated, and emphasis is always given to one of two antinomies: subject *or* object, benefit *or* cost, proletarian *or* bourgeois, left *or* right. Chernobyl exploded oppositions of this kind by illustrating the manner in which incalculable risks are created through traditional bureaucratic or calculable forms of decision making. Risk society contests the logic of industrial society by ever more surely generating multiplicity along with ambivalence:[7] the "and" contests the "either/or." Nature is no longer comprehensible as a calculable object for human use, and its mechanical opposition to society breaks down.[8] Subject *and* object, bourgeois *and* proletarian, are now embedded in a situation where local environmental policy choices in a relatively unimportant nation like Ukraine can produce planetary disaster.

The "globalization of unintended consequences" undercuts the difference between "friend *or* foe," by substituting a conception of "you *and* me." Once unimaginable technologies now create radical benefits *and* equally radical costs. Economics is no longer capable of mechanically separating one from the other. Technology has turned the world into an experiment, and the risks undercut the authority as well as the stability of every institution legitimating itself through the guarantee of security.[9] Nature takes revenge on those who would administer it in the risk society. The source of physical existence invalidates the more mechanical assumptions of decision making derived from industrial capitalism. If the smallest mistake can produce the most monumental disaster, such as the Alaskan oil spill, traditional notions of causality and legal liability obviously become anachronistic.[10] Furthermore, to the extent that broader forms of ecological risk accompany all forms of productive activity, dealing with its implications must assume increasing importance. The latent "risk content" of any action serves as a stimulus for progress.[11] Modernization ever more surely manifests the meaning of the phrase "to theorize about nature is to create it."

The "ecological question" is to the risk society what the "social question" was to industrial society.[12] Modernization raises the ecological problem, and it spurs change in turn. Progress is no longer driven, according to Beck, by concerns over profit or class contradictions. Modernization is now seen as creating wealth while essentially abolishing classes, and, for this reason, progress is generated by conflicts between experts of different "scientific" interests competing with one another. Resignation concerning the "certainty" of planetary destruction, however, has as little place in a risk society as does hope. Both rest on precisely the type of binary assumptions that the risk society is rendering irrelevant. This new phase is defined by a profound "ambivalence."[13] It is necessary to move "beyond" resignation and hope.

Technology possesses the potential for redeeming what it has destroyed. There is, however, no guarantee that it will. Disciplinary boundaries are becoming blurry as those engaged in an increasing division of labor must now confront the implications of specialized decisions on the totality. Problems are no longer discrete, and administrators, according to Beck, will avoid making choices and taking responsibility. Bureaucracies will increasingly manifest what Hannah Arendt called "the rule of nobody" given the manner in which incalculable risk ever more surely accompanies every calculable policy option. Alienation thus takes new forms as institutional paralysis threatens to leave the most dangerous ecological trends in place.[14]

The risk society reaches into everyday life. Nature ceases to exist "outside" us. New choices appear involving matters ranging from cloning and programming intelligence to changing one's appearance and extending life.[15] There is an irreversible quality to technology, and this makes progress on the ecological front impossible to predict. Seeking to "take back" the new choices or expel nature from our subjectivity is as senseless as the attempt by Leverkuhn, the main character in Thomas Mann's *Doctor Faustus*, to "take back" the Ninth Symphony of Beethoven. Its social ramifications would prove disastrous. The expansion of choice only renders more anachronistic the religious and political ideologies of the past. Thus, "the goal is not a return [to the premodern], but a different modernity."[16]

Modernization in the risk society is unique. It engages in a continuous "self-abolition" of the past,[17] but less by building on what has been made rational than by recognizing what has previously remained closed to reflection. Environmental danger is a case in point. It was essentially ignored by the organized parties, state institutions, and ideologies of industrial society. The lesson learned is, of course, that politics must change in the risk society. Inherited prejudices must fall by the wayside. Politics should now harness the processes of risk society in order to further autonomy and decrease alienation rather than flee its implications by embracing reactionary values.

The ecological conflict retains a moral and social structure, which derives from the desire to survive, and profoundly affects the individual.[18] The environmental merges with the existential. The globalization of risk and new possibilities for increasingly individuated forms of action emerge concomitantly. The system generates a new "individualization process,"[19] driven by the unintended and latent consequences of bureaucratic decisions, to which an entire range of new social movements have responded. In this vein, *The Normal Chaos of Love*, by Beck and his wife, Elisabeth Gernsheim, is a remarkably insightful analysis of the ways personal relations have changed, as well as how new forms of decision making are being liberated from an increasingly paralyzed bureaucratic political apparatus committed to universal forms of rationality.

Just like nature and the self, the larger issues and the smaller ones converge in the risk society.[20] Institutions must now face the decentralizing demands of the new social movements with their new set of "postmaterialist" issues. Thus, in a new version of the dialectic, ecological threats to the planet actually intensify the self-critical tendencies within every facet of the risk society. These transform an industrial modernity founded upon instrumental reason and naive assumptions concerning progress into a new form of "reflexive" modernity wherein the freeing of individual needs is the ultimate object of emancipatory concern.

Ideological and organizational remnants of industrial society constrain the new "reflexive modernity" with its individualization of interests. The old continues to exist. But that does not make the "risk society" any the less new. Reflexivity, in fact, presupposes vestiges of the past in need of change. The past is no longer demarcated from the present in some form of binary opposition; it is instead an ongoing referent for the new. There is no "end" for modernity and nothing beyond it. This indeed is what makes Beck so critical of the assumptions underpinning "post" modernism and "post" industrialism.[21]

Modernity is always, according to Beck, "half-finished" (*halbiert*). This is a logical consequence of its substitution of the *and* for the *either/or* and multivariant forms of systemic "self-transformation" for more traditional linear models of technological or rational development. Action capable of dealing with the manner in which unintended consequences undermine purposive rational action must simultaneously, or "ambivalently," foster both "autonomy" and "coordination." This is possible, according to Beck, only through a "reinvention of the political."

Everyday people are becoming increasingly cynical about an organized or institutional form of politics incapable of expressing their real interests. Their lack of interest in politics makes sense even for those who are unaware of the new risk society in which they now live. The risk society is not merely an existential invention; it retains objective dynamics, and its implications for subjectivity are not arbitrary. The individualization process of the risk society, coupled with its universal ecological threats, have rendered traditional binary oppositions between "left" and "right" irrelevant.

A new division between the "secure" and the "insecure" will determine the fate of risk society.[22] Commitment to old concepts like "class," in this vein, undermines our ability to understand a society in which the threat of ecological devastation has produced an "equality of risk" and various forms of gene technology have generated radically new problems. Even the uncritical acceptance of liberal republican beliefs can, in similar fashion, blind us to the new institutional condition of "organized irresponsibility" in which bureaucracies are becoming ever more anonymous, the law is no longer fulfilling its protective functions, and criticism is being democratized through social movements. The "reinvention" of politics envisioned by Beck must consequently prove less concerned with extending the rule of law, parliamentarianism, and state institutions than transforming them.

A new politics is necessary in the risk society precisely because the type of reflexivity driving its modernizing processes highlights what prior forms of modernity ignored. Industrial society was, according to Beck, created by two opposing yet interconnected processes for organizing social change: republicanism, with its various political forms of democratic legitimation, and technology, with its unpolitical and nondemocratic aspects, justified by progress and rationalization. The risk society with its individualizing process, however, now enables new social movements to face what were previously extra-institutional and unpolitical issues like the environment and the family. It ushers a new "sub-politics" into existence,[23] which is essentially opposed to the "politics" usually identified with worn-out parties and decrepit state systems.

A "double theater" continues to exist.[24] Conflicts between institutional actors and interests are still taking place. Even if the real possibilities for political activity have multiplied,[25] however, the real action occurs less in the institutions of the state than in the initiatives undertaken by the new social movements through "coalitions" and the "traffic jams" or "political standoffs" resulting from the use of various techniques for "blocking" legislation. The "political" system thereby loses its function.[26] What was once political now becomes unpolitical and vice versa. A "reinvented politics" must make use of this insight. Just as technology uncouples itself from the market in order to further its experimental possibilities, which Beck views as a modern equivalent of "art for art's sake," [27] politics divorces itself from concerns identified with the market and the state. It concentrates less on "the politics of politicians" and "power politics" than a (somewhat vaguely defined) "creative politics" or "art of politics."[28]

No one standpoint or party can any longer make universal identity claims within a world increasingly defined by difference and individuation. Unified by a new ecological morality or "red-cross consciousness," according to Beck, the new social movements alone can liberate subjectivity from its stultifying institutional definitions and further multiplicity by calling into question the binary oppositions of a bygone age. These movements offer new forms of identity and challenge individuals to create their own biography. Multiplicity, in this way, assumes a value in its own right. The *and* embraces the cosmopolitan, the multifaceted, the complex; it confronts the *or* on which xenophobic, sexist, and racist worldviews are constructed. The tolerance of the *and*, the skepticism it evidences against all Manichaean claims, opposes the dogmatism of the *or*.

Certainty underpinned the various worldviews of industrial society. But faith in religion, science, and philosophy has now been undercut. Uncertainty is our lot in the risk society, and, according to Beck, we must make the most of it. Xenophobia, intolerance, and violence offer no solutions. They merely try to preserve a sense of certainty, which can only prove illusory.[29] Those committed to liberating subjectivity must consequently embrace a new skepticism.

Beck looks to Montaigne.[30] Only skepticism can confront a reality in which every institution and definition, procedure, and prejudice is losing stability. It alone can preserve autonomy, tolerance, and a spirit of cosmopolitanism. A willingness to engage the new, paradoxically, rests on skepticism, and in this way, according to Beck, it is less a purely philosophical attitude than a basic element of any political theory appropriate to the risk society. Even skepticism, however, needs cultivation. It thus becomes incumbent upon the new social movements and a reinvented politics to nourish the "art of doubting." Indeed, according to Beck, only this can make reflexivity worthy of its emancipatory possibilities in the risk society.

3. TWO MODERNITIES: A CRITICAL ENCOUNTER

Risk society is the product of what Beck calls a "dialectic of the modern and the counter-modern:"[31] the multivariant and the linear, unintended consequences and purposive rationality, individualism and collectivism, symbiosis and mechanical opposition. The idea of the new being generated by contradictions of the old has deep roots in the past. Hegel is perhaps the most famous proponent of this view. A number of important contemporary thinkers, however, have also embraced it. Joseph Schumpeter saw capitalist rationality, for example, as engaged in an ongoing battle with the ideological holdovers from a "warrior" past fueled by expansionist concerns.[32] Rosa Luxemburg, in the same vein, believed that capitalist economic development depended upon precapitalist territories whose existence created the likelihood of future investment and the necessity of imperialism.[33] The interplay between contemporary class contradictions and those carried over from earlier stages of development is also central to the social and historical theory of Ernst Bloch.[34] With the exception of Bloch, of course, nature was never a basic category or concern of their theorizing. Nevertheless, each of these thinkers sought to highlight a given set of practical problems and conflicting interests for a particular normative political enterprise.

This is where the problems with Beck's approach initially become apparent. His substitution of nature for capitalism, of course, is a radical philosophical move. But there is some question regarding how well the categories of his dialectic render social change "concrete" with respect to institutions, interests, and the conflicts over particular issues. His theory is lacking in derivative categories, and those provided are overly general and imprecise: the conflict between the "secure" and the "insecure" is a case in point. Problems with indeterminacy result, and these have profound implications for his theory as a whole. His categories become defined by what they oppose and, for this reason, lose their critical edge. The binary relation between "friend" and "enemy," for example, never provided a basis for speci-ficity. Every state may presuppose those categories, according to Carl Schmitt, but not every (counter-modern) state engages in "ethnic cleansing" like the Serbs in Yugoslavia. The *quality* rather than the bare fact of antagonism is decisive, along with the particular organized economic and political interests involved. Beck, however, offers no new categories capable of illuminating any of this. Even ideologically, the events in Yugoslavia are probably best explained as responses to traditional liberal and socialist ideals associated with industrialism rather than as "provocations of reflexive modernization."[35]

Juxtaposing the *and* against the *either/or* also employs precisely the type of "binary" coding which Beck seeks to explode. Clarity is subverted by his refusal to distinguish the manner in which his categories, whose meanings constantly shift, apply to diverse spheres of action. The countermodern, for example, is seen as opposing tolerance, democracy, and the experiential liberation of the individual. But, if this is obvious in some cases, it is more difficult to discern in others. Is the continuing commitment to the welfare state given the new concern with "deregulation" in the West, and free market "reforms" in the East, "counter-modern" or "modern?" Isn't it also the case that the "counter-modern" played a liberating or even "reflexively modern" role in the art of the European vanguards during the turn of the twentieth century?

Concepts lose their abstract quality only when they are related to insti-tutions or determinate forms of practice; claims that conceptually distinct branches of activity are losing their specificity don't help matters. Making sense of politics, for example, calls for identifying its dynamics and core con-cepts even if only heuristically. Harold Lasswell, in this vein, once defined politics as "who gets what, when, where, and how." Perhaps his view was too narrow. Lasswell ignored the reflexive moment. The definition of what is "political" is, after all, itself a political act. Arguably, new values, notions of power, or forms of organization have also come into existence. But none of this justifies a political worldview essentially intent on ignoring questions dealing with structural imbalances of power or the systematic ways in which interests are organized, wealth is distributed, and grievances are adjudicated.

Simply claiming that what was once political is now unpolitical, and vice versa, is inadequate. Sovereignty remains the locus of international politics and even internationalism needs an institutional referent. Less the new awareness of risk generated by Chernobyl than the traditional concern with finances proved decisive when, in 1993, Ukraine decided to keep open its twelve defective nuclear plants and then shut a few of them down a year later. Nor have the structures for political action, and its constraints and possibilities, qualitatively changed in the advanced industrial societies. Profits still dictate the investment decisions on which workers are depen-dent for their jobs and the state for its taxes and programs. A "capacity for self-organization" may define the new politics. But it is illusory to claim that the "prevailing objective constraints have begun to crumble."[36] Indeed, this becomes particularly evident with the tactics of "coalition-building" and "blocking" employed by the new social movements.

There is an obvious difference that becomes apparent between the capacity to "block" a given individual or proposal and the ability to determine the agenda. A "political standoff," putting the matter bluntly, cannot go on forever. Coalitions also have their problems. They are dictated by practical concerns and organized interest groups rather than "movements" that are engaged in them. Putting coalitions together is especially costly and time-consuming for representatives of the disempowered and exploited; they are immediately placed at a disadvantage since competing coalitions dealing with competing single issues are simultaneously competing for information, resources, and even commitment. Each coalition will also fall apart once the particular issue uniting its members is resolved. Thus, the fragmented voices of reform are put in the practical position of constantly having to reinvent the wheel.

The new social movements have had genuine success in mobilizing people and rendering public what were previously understood as private issues ranging from incest and rape to prejudice and sexual preference. Beck is completely justified in claiming that they have radically transformed everyday life for the better. It is also legitimate to claim that support for these movements and their tactics is necessary. Uncritically valorizing their tactics or turning necessity into a virtue, however, is self-defeating. It is necessary to state the obvious: precisely because existing social movements cannot contest the structural imbalances of power informing the "old" institutions, they cannot offer a "new" politics.

Institutional politics is neither rendered powerless nor "loses its function" due to the new "sub-politics." Thinking about social movements without making reference to the organizational form in which they can institutionally express their concerns is misguided. Not only powerful corporations, but every movement—even those from below—will take the organizational form of an "interest group." Each will also have a vested *material interest* in its own autonomy, which probably has less to do with the onset of a "risk society" than the self-perpetuating dynamics of bureaucracy delineated by Max Weber or the type of pluralist analysis elaborated by Robert Dahl and Charles Lindblom. But Beck deals with none of this. His primary (sub-) political concern is with furthering a "life politics" capable of liberating the repressed possibilities of the individual. Institutions collapse into everyday life, politics into culture, and bureaucratically organized "interest groups" into the movements whose concerns they institutionally express. Political parties no less that constitutional regimes are, for this reason, underestimated along with the role they play in adjudicating grievances, organizing interests, and stabilizing democracy.

The year 1989 witnessed a new nonviolent form of revolution unmistakably influenced by the 1960s. But things have changed. Power has now fallen into the hands of political parties, and in Russia and a host of other countries along its borders, forms of what might be termed "authoritarian democracy" are taking shape. Elsewhere things have changed as well. Precisely because no party can exert identity claims in the manner of times past, it would seem, emancipatory forms of political theory must begin to develop criteria and insights capable of furthering the unity of economically disadvantaged elements within each of the social movements while privileging none. Theoretically and practically, however, this presupposes a willingness to begin connecting social movements with class and interest groups with a more inclusive and invigorated organizational notion of action.[37]

A new moral sense exists. Beck is right in speaking about environmentalism in terms of something like a "red-cross consciousness." He makes mention of universals and the manner in which particularism rests upon them, but only barely. Historical reality is ignored, and political priorities are reversed. Especially when one considers the civil rights movement, feminism, or 1989, for example, the greatest successes were achieved by employing the language of equality and human "rights" rather than the rhetoric of particularism. An emancipatory encounter with those extraordinary developments in gene technology or eugenics so eloquently discussed by Beck must logically also be dealt with in terms of "rights" and the substantive equality of access to them.

Technological development may be taking on a life of its own, thereby strengthening existential fears and, especially in the face of new environmental dangers, demanding new notions of liability. The bourgeois individual—the universal subject of Kant or the citizen of Hegel—may no longer be a viable unit of analysis in a period marked by individualization of needs. But the fundamental problems of our times are not the product of some indeterminate contradiction between the political institutions inherited from an industrial order and the possibilities generated by the new risk society.[38] It also makes little sense bemoaning how commitment to the principles of constitutionalism threatens the political system with "disempowerment."

Individualism is taken for granted in America while class contradictions are not. The situation is almost the reverse in Europe. Fusing these two perspectives rather than simply emphasizing one over the other must inform new modes of theorizing. Maximizing the free choices of individuals *equitably* is the goal. *Only* with republican institutions and—yes— socialist notions of economic equality predicated on universal principles is it possible to ensure the greatest exercise of identity and difference by all individuals.

The new reflexivity and the institutional impulse to self-correction coexist, after all, with increasing functional and secondary illiteracy as well as what Theodor Adorno called the "non-conformist conformism" generated by the mass media. The new individualism stands connected with a new pseudo-individualism, and theoretical categories, which Beck does not provide, are necessary to distinguish between them. In similar fashion, perhaps, the risk society has generated new circumstances in which "either all are experts or none." But is it realistic to speak even of a "latent" democratic potential in this manner given the obviously falling "material level of culture" (Marx)? The point is to render technological subsystems accountable *through institutions*. But must this not call into question the idea that "organized irresponsibility" rules them all in the same way? Creating sustainable forms of ecologically guided economic growth is clearly *the* goal for the future. But isn't it somewhat difficult to believe, in keeping with Beck, that industry under pressure from social movements will somehow internally regulate itself and bring about a "self-abolition" of the ecological problem? Disciplinary boundaries in the sciences may be collapsing. But how then is it possible for an industry to use the critique of, say, gene technology to combat the risks of gene technology? Beck's idea of treating technology in the manner of "art for art's sake" is fascinating. But he never deals with how structural imbalances of institutional power influence the setting of priorities for scientific research or what Tom Ferguson once called the "political economy of knowledge."

The 1980s are over. President Clinton, however, did not win the election with the ecological equivalent of a "New Deal."[39] Ecology, for all the talk, was a relatively minor issue. The memorable line summing up the 1992 campaign was "It's the economy, stupid!" Growth is the problem. No one believes any longer that technology can break the business cycle, and if ecology has created a new "moral milieu," it needs regenerating in the face of economic stagnation. Beck's famous slogan "need is hierarchical, smog is democratic" has lost its punch.[40] And, come to think of it, smog was probably never so democratic anyway. Just breathe the air while taking a ride down the New Jersey Turnpike from Elizabeth, which has one of the highest cancer rates in the country, to the lovely beach towns on the southern shore of the state.

Times have changed. Perhaps it no longer makes sense to speak of a proletariat, but it certainly remains legitimate to talk about capital. Questions of class, in fact, have assumed a new relevance. Beck thinks that, mistakenly, in my opinion, social inequality might become more acute in the risk society and he claims that "material need is being circumscribed among the marginal groups (*Randgruppen*) of society."[41] But the dynamics are never explained. His position, for all the qualifications, ultimately rests on presupposing the types of sustained growth and economic affluence usually associated with traditional forms of critical theory and so much of contemporary sociological thinking.

There is a sense in which capitalism is becoming both more humane and more exploitative.[42] But suggesting that poverty is being isolated and overcome through new technological forms of productivity, or that the question of risk has supplanted conflicts over distribution, overstates the case.[43] Income differentials have exploded in the United States; one in four working Americans has become a member of the "poor." Crime, incivility, the deterioration of public spaces, the crisis of housing, the loss of privacy, and the increasing idiocy of most mass media have also produced a new brutalization of the "nonpolitical" usually associated with "civil society" and the "quality of life." Indeed, the "double theater" cannot convey the real connections between "sub-politics" and institutional politics.

Apathy is pronounced. Perhaps, to use Beck's formulation, "progress has replaced voting."[44] But the social democratic welfare state is not some doddering old fool watching new movements pick up the slack. Nor is its waning merely the product of its achievements.[45] Those were never etched in stone. The deterioration of the welfare state was the product of a concentrated *political* assault by various interests, and it had a disastrous impact on participation from below and the various attempts to liberate everyday life. Beck never really considers any of this. It would prove difficult from his standpoint. Dealing with such matters would force him to question some basic assumptions and would obviously contradict his claim that the "political" system has lost its function. It would even raise the question of whether the most radical nonviolent changes in everyday life were actually brought about less by individuals engaged in a "turning back to society" than those like Reagan and Thatcher and Kohl who were involved in the institutional conquest of the *political*.

Issues have become more complicated, interests are more difficult to discern, and the old certainties have passed into history. A willingness to admit "uncertainty" is only sensible. There is no room for dogmatism in talking about the possible role of intermediate institutions or "secondary associations" between the state and the everyday life of its subjects. There are also no longer any organizational tricks for bringing about civic responsibility. There are a thousand new problems. We must begin anew, and certainty is indeed the enemy. Informed judgment, however, is not. Kant was right when he claimed that making judgments is both an inherently uncertain enterprise and a "practical" necessity. The same is true of politics insofar as it involves specifying and then judging differences of moral and practical interest. Certainty has nothing to do with the relevance of *values* such as economic equality, political accountability, and internationalism for the development of policies. "Left" and "right" emerge from a normative engagement with these ideals.

Labor is becoming destandardized.[46] The communist and fascist movements of the past are obviously dead. But even if the burgeoning international right is merely the last expression of industrial society, contemporary economic, political, and social interests are not quite so indeterminate or prone to compromise as Beck makes it seem. Commitment to realizing the ideological, political, and economic conditions for the emancipation of individuality will create profound forms of political division. There is a material substratum, a structural imbalance of economic and political power, underpinning the division between the "secure" and the "insecure." Beck takes the symptom for the cause: the interplay between organized interests in institutional arenas still produces the most decisive "moments of decision." Struggles in the future will not simply transcend structural conflicts between the privileged and the underprivileged. New traditions will, in the same vein, not mechanically divorce themselves from those of the past. Compromise and consensus have their limits. Abstractly seeking to move "beyond" the designations of the "left" and "right" will only lead back into Hegel's night in which all cats are gray. And there we cannot remain.

4. CONCLUSION

For all of its problems, the work of Ulrich Beck retains an electric quality. Idea after idea jumps off the pages of his work. Some lack precision, others never receive justification, and still others contradict one another. Qualifications sit on top of one another; arguments disappear only to appear once again; fuzzy slogans compete with the claims of common sense. But then come the golden nuggets of dazzling insight. Beck's notion of "organized irresponsibility" and the new implications of risk for decision making can only prove seminal for any future form of emancipatory thinking. His views on the simultaneous fragmentation and globalization engendered by the "risk society" will also serve as a point of departure for any new theory of politics and social movements. His concern over the way ecology is divorced from social questions is legitimate. It is the same with his advocacy of "ecological democracy" and his belief that the degree to which technical decisions rest on nontechnical ones will become the future standard for substantive democracy.[47] The sheer number of ideas is surely what makes for the misunderstandings, the controversy, and also the allure of his work. Underpinning all this, however, is a genuine theory. Antisystematic in spirit, experimental in intention, it is guided less by logical rigor than a certain deeply anti-dogmatic form of thinking. The risk society offers a general framework to understand the trajectory of modernity without offering linkages to the constitution of particular events. It tries to deal with everyday life and perhaps it sacrifices history in the process. Nevertheless, paradoxically, its strengths are generated by its indeterminate categories and its inability to confront structural imbalances of power.

Beck's aim is, after all, less a confrontation with the present than an analysis of how the present is giving rise to a new future. He is less concerned with social scientific certainty than with making provisional claims capable of furthering debate and taking it in a new direction. For Beck, critique is the source of progress, and his concept of the "risk society" is less a fixed construct than a formulation seeking to show how other, more traditional paradigms can neither keep pace with technology nor comprehend its implications. Chernobyl and the collapse of communism are, in this vein, seen as the historical watersheds for the risk society. They have exploded the utopian ideologies inherited from industrial society along with their assumptions. Nevertheless, the thinking of Beck has little in common with the cynicism of postmodernism.

There is nothing fatalistic about his work. He is enthusiastic about the "new" and committed to a project of enlightenment capable of furthering the "reflexive" elements of modernity and squarely confronting the atavistic remnants of the past. His theory of a "half-finished" modernity is not predicated on some mechanical rejection of the past, but on a willingness to confront what old forms of bureaucratic thinking could not take into account. Beck remains concerned with the ideas of autonomy, participation, and alienation so often associated with 1968. But he refashions them for the world of 1989. Beck is unwilling to hang onto the past. There is no place for nostalgia in his thinking and even less for provincialism or the anti-Americanism so popular among certain European intellectuals. The vision of Beck is built on a belief in tolerance, multiplicity, and an "unfinished" notion of democracy.

He sees great scientific and environmental challenges before us. And, ultimately, he is right. The everyday life of the future will not look like that of the present. Confronting global issues ranging from inequality and ecological threats to sovereignty and immigration will require new international institutions, innovative policies, cosmopolitan values, and a renewal of idealism perhaps tempered by the skepticism of Beck's beloved Montaigne. Above all, however, solving the problems of the future will require imagination and intellectual bravery. Ulrich Beck possesses these qualities in abundance and if only for this reason, his thinking can play an important role in the battle for tomorrow.

PART III

In Pursuit of Progress

13

TRANSFORMING THE STATE

Reflections on the Structure
of Capitalist Democracy

I. INTRODUCTION

NORMATIVE ASSUMPTIONS about the state underpin every notion of
political practice. Any theory seeking to inform social change must,
for this reason, offer more than attempts to establish purely analytic relationships between economics and politics. Aristotle sought to show, long
before Marx, how different empirical combinations of classes tended to
produce different governmental forms. But the real task is to explain
how economic imbalances of power affect the possibilities for political
resistance within any given system and how governmental institutions
can serve diverse structural purposes. Intervention of the state into the
workings of the market is, in this regard, basic to capitalist democracy.
The degree of such intervention is radically variable, however, as are the
priorities of such action. The state has a phenomenological character,
but it simultaneously presents itself in a variety of guises capable of privileging qualitatively different interests and norms. Thus, the bureaucratic
state can no longer be seen simply as a locus of alienation, a mechanism
of legitimation, or a prop of the market. A genuinely critical theory of
the state can no longer remain content with viewing it as a monolith or
some inflexible set of institutions divorced from other elements of
society. It must instead offer a model capable of illuminating institutional possibilities for change, distinguishing between interests, and
judging alternative forms of policy.

The state offered a new form of social organization limited neither
by the geographic provincialism of the Greek city-state nor the abstract
universalism of the Roman Empire.[1] Its phenomenological essence
derives from its structural imperatives as surely as, employing the
parlance of Max Weber, its ability to monopolize the "legitimate" powers

The original version of this essay appeared in *New Political Science* (summer
1991): 17–40.

of coercion. Its diverse forms of expression were simultaneously determined by the fact that the burgeoning international capitalist system in which it developed during the sixteenth and seventeenth centuries did not spread in uniform fashion. An "uneven development" occurred instead wherein given states, alone or in combination, constantly sought to delimit the ambitions of their enemies. Only by recognizing this international context can a picture emerge of how particular governmental forms arose as the products of historical conflicts between various domestic classes and groups. States emerged in a context defined domestically by a variety of traditions, religious forms, and social structures, as well as internationally by their power in relation to other states. This complex of external and internal "mediations" ultimately establishes the uniqueness of the given state.

As a consequence, just as critical theory cannot identify the state with the indeterminate domination of instrumental rationality, it also cannot attempt to analyze a particular state's governmental form from a general view of its economic system. No necessary relation exists between the general economic organization of civil society under capitalism and the primacy of any particular governmental form. Monarchy, dictatorship, fascism, and representative democracy of various types are all possibilities for a capitalist economic system at particular times and under particular circumstances. No necessary correlation need, for this reason, exist between any particular state form and a "socialist" economy that employs the same criteria of accumulation as its adversaries within an international capitalist system of trade.

This does not deny the impact of the economic system on the workings of institutions. But the issue is not which elites are in better positions than others or what political implications, which are inherently contingent, the ascendancy of one capitalist "sector" over another may have. Here the concern is structural. It involves the relation between classes or, to put it another way, the relation between state institutions and the modern accumulation process. The more "modern" a system becomes the more it will stand defined by a system of wage labor and the instrumental rationality of the "commodity form."

Labor and capital are the two dominant classes in this system. Workers will ever more surely sell their time—or "labor power"—for a wage, while employers will buy it in order to create products salable on the market for more than the price of wages plus the cost of machinery and resources necessary to produce them. This difference constitutes the "surplus" or profit that, even as it is socially produced by workers, is appropriated by individuals or firms. Its use is, in principle, privately determined, beyond any broader social implications, according to market imperatives.

Jürgen Habermas and Claus Offe argued in the aftermath of the 1960s, when the welfare state was still relatively unchallenged, that commodification was giving way to "decommodification."[2] Capitalism would undermine its own assumptions, and, in the future, labor power would increasingly withdraw from the market. But their prophecy has been contradicted by the drastic decline of unions during the 1980s as well as the trend toward "privatization" advanced by a triumphant conservatism. The logic of the capitalist accumulation process remains what it always was. Only now it is impossible to presuppose the necessity of "welfare" any longer let alone the future elimination of labor's dependence on market uncertainties. The policies of Franklin Delano Roosevelt or Léon Blum look more radical than ever in the light of the conservative onslaught. The patronizing attitude with which so many thought of them in the 1960s, the sense that all this was "just" liberalism or social democracy, makes even less sense now than it did then. A critical theory of the state, now more than ever, must prove capable of distinguishing the interests served by given policies or what Marx called the "political economy of labor" against that of capital.

The "affluent society" of John Kenneth Galbraith is already being denied in the name of austerity programs, and nothing guarantees a consistent improvement in the condition of working people. Such a stance, implicit in most mainstream notions of reform, is as impoverished as the traditional Marxist belief in an "inevitable" collapse of the capitalist system. The condition of workers is still structurally defined by material uncertainty. Technology still simultaneously threatens jobs even as it offers the prospect of greater prosperity.[3] Investment still fuels employment though, especially with the weakening of the welfare state, the prospect of disinvestment remains even more frightening than before. Of course, in contrast to the aristocracy or other dominant classes of previous historical epochs, capitalists must reinvest at least part of their profit for research and development in order to produce more efficiently and ward off competitors. Appropriate levels of investment in the present, however, depend upon the likelihood of appropriate profits in the future. Prospects of instability or increasing state expenditures will still lead capitalists to disinvest. Thus, whatever the level of investment or disinvestment, workers still remain dependent upon the unaccountable actions of capitalists whose decisions are determined by private advantage rather than any consideration of the public good.[4]

Establishing a new relationship between liberalism and socialism is necessary for any theory seeking to contest that dependence. The private character of investment decisions is still the barrier liberalism sets to democracy. The issue for socialists and other progressives, in this vein, should revolve around the attempt to demand public accountability for such choices and mitigate the impact of economic imbalances of power on the political process. Ironically, however, seeking genuine accountability is possible only through the liberal state.

2. SOCIALISM, LIBERALISM, AND DEMOCRACY

Socialism and democracy were originally seen as intrinsically linked by the early and nonecclesiastical partisans of the working class. Both drew their inspiration from the philosophy of the revolutionary bourgeoisie while it was still an emergent class in need of specific, nonaristocratic, coalitional support. Under those historical circumstances, theory and practice complemented each other in the attempt to constrict the arbitrary exercise of power. The English, the American, and the French Revolutions ultimately fostered a worldview that declared every citizen equal—not only before the law, but also in council. Indeed, the socialist project begins with the desire to extend the most radical values of that very class which it would ultimately oppose.

Even before Marx had fully elaborated his method, or the categories for making sense of the new capitalist production process, he acknowledged the advances of the early liberal capitalist state whose principles achieved their most radical articulation in the French Revolution. Against the ancien régime with its emphasis on a "natural" hierarchic order, based on birth and sanctioned by the Church, the idea of a new secular state projected the vision of democracy along with the universal, political rights of the "citizen" under the "rule of law." Such a state would abolish slavery, base itself on secular principles of "right,"[5] and institute civil liberties and regular elections. Indeed, it would actualize "liberty, equality and fraternity" in the political realm while protecting the right to privately accumulate whatever wealth was produced in the economic realm of "civic society."

By specifying the contradictory relation between the state and civil society, Marx implicitly provided the future movements of social democracy with theoretical focus and political purpose. If liberty was to reign in the political realm, even though the principles of "laissez-faire" substantively denied the "right to work" (Louis Blanc), work was actually compulsory in civil society. If equality was promised under the "rule of law," the economic system denied any principle of distributive equity and so guaranteed socioeconomic inequality. Finally, while the state projected a concern with the "common good" and fraternity among citizens, economic life in civil society demanded that these same citizens act as "bourgeois" competitors and engage in an egoistic struggle that might be likened to Hobbes's notion of "the war of each against all." [6]

The socialist movements emerging during the first industrial revolution basically tried to resolve this set of contradictions. The failure of the 1848 revolutions along with the rise of Napoleon III in France and later Bismarck in Germany, however, soon made it clear that the bourgeoisie had surrendered its most radical democratic and political legacy of the nineteenth century. The socialist movement thus found itself shouldering a dual burden: attempting to pursue the particular economic class interests of the proletariat, it was simultaneously put in the position of seeking to fulfill the unfulfilled universalistic political promises of democracy fostered in the bourgeois revolutions.[7] Resolving the problem seemed possible only through transforming the existing antidemocratic European states whose various socialist parties were based in a rapidly expanding industrial proletariat. Indeed, the seemingly unstoppable expansion of the working class provided a materialist incentive for the commitment of all socialist parties to republicanism even as it allowed them to frame this generalizable political demand as a class issue.

Teleology was not, as so many critics would have it, bound up with totalitarian thinking.[8] Quite the contrary. The social democratic parties infused with a profound belief in Marxian "science" were, in fact, the first democratic mass parties on the continent. "Revolution" was, furthermore, never conceived in economic terms. Around the turn of the century, it was always connected with a commitment to republicanism. Its relevance was a function of the degree to which workers were permitted to organize politically in the pursuit of their class interests. The need for revolution thus stood in inverse relation to the degree of democracy offered by any given state. That is why Marx could visualize a democratic path to socialism in the United States but not in Germany: it is also one of the reasons why the socialist movement was weaker in the United States than in Germany.

Viewed as a "state within a state" by its class enemies, with a "public sphere" so remarkable that Otto Neurath could speak of a "workers' world," European social democracy paid the price for its optimism. It was not simply that the industrial proletariat ceased to grow. Class consciousness was taken for granted, and in anticipation of the later communist movement, one compromise after another was discounted as a mere "tactical" deviation. Complacent regarding its oppositional character, narrowly identifying the interests of the class with its own, socialist parties everywhere in Europe other than Italy ultimately wound up supporting their respective nation-states in the First World War. A policy of caution and timidity, which gradually ceased to emphasize the generation of what Rosa Luxemburg termed "class friction," culminated in the "great betrayal" of international socialism. Indeed, this act ultimately led the Bolsheviks and the Third International to supplant social democracy as the perceived revolutionary alternative to capitalism.

Perhaps those early socialist movements were naive in equating democracy with capitalist democracy and the industrial proletariat with the working class. Their ideology was almost crudely humanist and inspired by teleological optimism. But they still provide some laudable ideological elements for the socialist heritage. These movements, after all, genuinely believed that democracy was the prerequisite for socialism and that the realization of the one necessarily implied the realization of the other. In the modern epoch, of course, it is no longer possible to assume that capitalism will "inevitably" collapse or that the interests of the party and working people are synonymous. But classical social democracy showed how the workers could become a political force, change the face of the state, and provide its members with a dignity and sense of purpose they never had before. Then, too, whatever the legitimate criticisms of the movement, it always maintained that the "socialist" transition must stand in some plausible relation to the democratic values and concerns that a new emancipatory order would seek to institutionalize. Finally, its unambiguous commitment to socialism as an extension of democracy rather than its negation offers a transcendent perspective with which to judge not merely authoritarian forms of communist practice but the turning away from genuine reform by social democratic parties during the last decade of the twentieth century.

Marxian teleology veiled the essentially ethical and idealistic character of the socialist project.[9] And this has led to important misunderstandings. The "science" of historical materialism did not merely assume that socialism would "inevitably" emerge from capitalism, after all, but also that it would incorporate the most progressive achievements of past historical stages. Orthodox Marxism could so take its commitment to retain and radicalize liberal values for granted, in this vein, that it no longer even seemed necessary to speak the language of rights or employ its categories. But with the collapse of teleology, just as socialism becomes nothing more than a contingent possibility lacking any "scientific" guarantee, its connection with the progressive unfolding of the past can no longer be taken for granted. This is why contemporary socialists must insist upon specifying the indebtedness of their vision to the liberal ideas of the Enlightenment and the great bourgeois revolutions.

Revolution was once the ideal. The collapse of teleology, however, makes it impossible to embrace a vision in which all "reformist" tactics are subordinate to that strategic end. Revolution may still prove relevant under conditions of authoritarian rule and economic underdevelopment or under conditions in which the promulgation of reforms is impossible. But the primacy of revolution is no longer prescribed. It has become no less a tactic than reform, and the choice between them depends upon a speculative judgment based on which can best deal with a particular set of contingent circumstances.

Prior to the choice of tactics is the matter of purpose. The formal values of democracy are far easier to define than the substantive ones. In keeping with the logic of the existing accumulation process, however, they must obviously center on mitigating market discipline and liberating working people from conditions in which they are treated as a simple cost of production. The issue involves how to further substantive concerns like the fight for time or the "right" to health service without sacrificing the formal guarantees of democracy.

Democracy, in fact, is both the means and the ends of the socialist project. But this begs any number of questions. For, if the socialist project is indeed political, it must accept the need for an organization capable of developing policies enforced by the state and also offer categories of unity for its constituencies with their diverse interests. The connection between socialism and liberalism, in this way, immediately presents itself. Just as the concern with limiting the arbitrary exercise of state power drove the former, inhibiting the arbitrary use of economic power informs the latter. The great political contribution of the liberal philosophy deriving from Locke and Kant was its insight that a commitment to the universal presuppositions behind the rule of law alone guarantees the freedom of the particular. Juxtaposing the universal against the particular, or identity against difference, simply confuses matters.

The real question involves the spheres in which particular forms of agency and action are relevant. Non-class-based social movements, for example, are enormously valuable in raising particular grievances and contesting various types of formal discrimination or exclusion. But the particularist and transclass ideologies employed in fighting these battles militate against the universalism required by workers to contest the inequities of the accumulation process. As bureaucratic interest groups strive for autonomy, in this vein, the power of capital still rests on the degree of organizational and ideological disunity exhibited by working people. If this explains why reactionary cultural barriers for particular constituencies have fallen, even while a successful assault has been waged against the gains achieved by workers, it becomes necessary to consider the need for categories capable of linking the needs of social movements with those of workers. This is a complicated business. It is rendered even more difficult by the undeniable importance of these new social movements as well as the lack of either a preconstituted revolutionary "subject" or an existing political party whose interests are "objectively" commensurate with those of workers. Although the electoral strategies of European socialist parties determine whether workers will vote from a class standpoint, for example, it is contingent whether socialist parties will actually pursue such strategies.[10] It is, for these reasons, possible to unify the contradictions only speculatively or from the standpoint of a *class ideal.*

Predicated on the need to constrain the arbitrary use of economic power, and the desire to generalize interests from the standpoint of the most disadvantaged worker, the class ideal projects an ethical principle of unity.[11] It becomes the speculative point of reference with which to foster formal equality for all groups and the interests specific to the working people in each without privileging any. It thereby endorses the commitment to shouldering that dual burden inherited from the working-class movements of the last century. Even in its most advanced expressions, after all, "capitalist democracy" has not fulfilled its original democratic aspirations with respect to questions of race and gender. Hegel was, in this vein, simply mistaken in believing that the "contradictions" of one "stage" must become reconciled before the next appears on the historical scene.[12]

"Precapitalist" prejudices obviously still exist, and socialists no less than the partisans of identity politics should admit in theory what they engage in practice. They should admit their reliance on the state and the values of liberalism in their attempts to seek remedies for the injustices experienced by people of color, women, and gay people. Liberalism alone provides the avenue for using the state in order to further intraclass equality and thereby provide the foundation for any successful movement with genuinely socialist aims. The class ideal offers a new recombination of liberalism and socialism.

Objective conditions make necessary a revision of old assumptions. The resilience of capitalism, the empirical transformation of the working class, the compromises made by its political representatives, and the change in ideological climate are real. Marxian "science," in this way, calls for its own extinction. An idealist reinterpretation of socialism is demanded on materialist grounds, and, for this reason, the class ideal is—as previously suggested—an explicitly speculative proposition. Insofar as it strives to inspire practical action, however, it necessarily harbors an objective or material assumption. The class ideal privileges "class" not merely because of its intrinsic connection with the "point of production," but also because it is the most general determinant of the political possibilities of the disempowered given the constraints of the existing accumulation process.

3. CAPITALIST DEMOCRACY AND THE IMPERATIVES OF ACCUMULATION

A distinctly "capitalist democracy" has increasingly been identified with democracy as such. That is a mistake. There are severe structural imbalances of power in the current system, which militate against addressing the substantive interests of working people. But it is insufficient simply to inveigh against the "false consciousness" of the masses without analyzing how ideological support for the system is maintained. The question involves how the system reproduces itself and secures the consent of subaltern groups in the process.[13] The most obvious answer might be developed in the following way. Capitalist society is a system whose institutions are neither the tools of particular capitalists, a mere reflection of "class" interests, nor an all-embracing phenomenon incapable of reform. But, in order to specify the possibilities for reform, it is initially necessary to consider capitalist democracy as "neither just capitalism, nor just democracy, not just some combination of the two that does not change its component parts. Indeed, even to think of such separate 'parts' is to miss the vital integrity of the system."[14]

The state is neither structurally "neutral" in relation to civil society nor directly "determined" by its workings. The state has its own processes and integrity; in short, whatever the ways in which external conditions affect it, the state retains what the Austrian socialist theorist Max Adler called an "internal dynamic." This dynamic stems from the prerequisites for instituting and maintaining the given process of production and accumulation. As Jürgen Habermas has cogently argued, the state rises above the "selfish" interests of particular competitive capitalists precisely in order to realize the political hegemony of the capitalist class as a whole.[15] Or, to put it another way, the state lifts itself beyond the immediate interest of this or that particular capitalist in the short run in order to maintain the character of the existing accumulation process in the long run. If the state must represent the interests of the dominant class in relation to other classes, however, it needs a certain independent power or relative autonomy.

The ability to enforce economic compromises on particular issues is necessary in order to deflect the potential for political struggle from below. The modern state must, after all, prove capable of responding to the inherent tendency of capitalism toward overproduction. Usually, in Keynesian fashion, this has resulted in the introduction of policies intent on building the purchasing power of the populace. Such policies, however, will necessarily place costs on particular capitalists that they obviously do not wish to bear. Just how responsive the state will be cannot be determined a priori. This is always a contingent and historical matter. It is the point at which politics becomes important.

An investigation of the specific situation thus becomes necessary with respect to the international context, the institutional possibilities for expressing class interests, the character of existing parties, the particular forms of class interaction, the strength of democratic traditions, and the given ideological climate. Generally, however, state intervention has occurred most successfully under conditions in which the organizational and ideological unity of workers was strongest. Distribution of wealth is, in short, dependent not merely on productivity and economic growth but on the political power exercised by workers.

Implementing legislation regulating the market strengthens the state and, arguably, fosters bureaucratic interests with a stake in maintaining the reforms previously achieved. Especially under a republican state, however, this does not result in undermining personal freedom.[16] Economic costs become the issue. The state exists off revenues culled from a certain combination of profits and wages. If investment diminishes, which can result from an undue desire to tax profits, it will lead to a decrease in revenues. Maintaining an acceptable rate of profit for capital, which involves either shifting the burden of taxes toward wages or limiting its responsibilities, thus becomes a central concern of the state.

Where the economy is growing and social costs are relatively low, of course, spurring purchasing power and employment through government-sponsored programs will receive consideration. The problem is that such programs are most necessary in periods of economic downturn when they most directly threaten the ability of capitalists to maintain an acceptable rate of profit. It is possible to pressure the state when great masses find themselves ideologically and organizationally united. But where a welfare state already exists, and workers are unwilling to engage in disruption from below, its organizational representatives will find themselves with only two options:

they can either assume a compromise posture of "austerity," which can easily lead to the disillusionment of their mass constituency, or they can remain adamant in support of the existing welfare apparatus, which might lead sectors of the dominant class to reject the existing form of conflict resolution and perhaps even the existing democratic state structure as well.[17]

Capitalist democracy remains democratic only insofar as the state is capable of preventing economic conflicts over the distribution of public revenues from becoming political conflicts over production that would threaten the very possibility of privately appropriating the social surplus. Capitalist democracy is a system whose operational dynamic informs all of its institutions. Its state is fundamentally informed and profoundly influenced by the interests of particular capitalists and sectors of capital on particular issues. Securing the stability of the accumulation process, however, necessarily involves the state in a technocratic resolution procedure wherein interests beyond those of particular capitalists become manifest. The power of the state is subsequently irreducible to those of its actors. The need to secure consensus makes it into more than the locus of the legitimate powers of coercion and more than a simple expression of class interest.

This explains why the state in capitalist democracy has been able to provide civil liberties, organize the market to relieve competition by individual capitalists, institutionalize investment outlets, mitigate the threat of crisis by fiscal means, and forge social legislation to channel and defuse political pressure from below. These activities have solidified the system that Rudolf Hilferding originally termed "organized capitalism." Indeed, if the need for social programs identifies labor with an activist state, a significant capitalist interest in "distorting" the market with respect to defense and various other concerns is just as profound. The issue then is no longer the "watchman state." Economic policy has become a political battle over priorities in spending. The question is no longer whether "growth" and a bureaucratic "plan" for economic development are necessary, but the quality of growth, how it will be defined, and whether that plan will be democratically controlled or left in the hands of elites whose particular concerns are often uncritically identified with the "national interest."

Capitalist democracy ensures consensus by institutionalizing the contradictions between formal and substantive democracy. It creates a situation in which the control exercised by a dominant class over the existing state apparatus formally depends upon the degree of cohesion and organization of subordinate classes even if the substantive possibility of forging that unity is undermined by its incentives and structures. Or, better, the legitimation of the state depends upon its ability to maintain the disproportionate substantive power between representatives of the major classes in the production process while providing them with formal equality in the administrative adjudication of conflicts.[18]

The state engaged in serving the "national interest" of a capitalist democracy will subsequently become involved in a twofold task. It must, first of all, prevent internecine conflicts among sectors of the dominant class from developing over compromises with other classes and groups. It must, however, also secure an ideological consensus in support of the existing structural arrangement on the part of subordinate classes and groups. The contest between sectors of capital is precisely what permits the entry of other classes and groups—albeit in a subaltern manner—into the political arena and the decision-making process. Various sectors seeking to extend their control over the political process and intent on identifying their particular interests more closely with those of the"nation,"[19] in fact, will often welcome allies in the form of subaltern classes for their own legislative and reformist purposes. There is even a sense in which it is possible to claim that in the liberal state:

> The democratic process compels each social group to strike for mass support. Each group, therefore, must present its egotistic interests as universal. Politics in a democracy, the struggle for political power, thus becomes far more ideological than in any previous period in history. What was obvious for the ancients, and clear to the feudal system, becomes hidden in the democratic process. But the valuable side of this process must equally not be forgotten. The very need to appeal to social groups larger than the immediate interest group compels adjustment of various interests. Politics becomes more democratic.[20]

Capitalist democracy has clearly improved the economic conditions of working people. These gains were assuredly the products of struggle, but they were also achieved only insofar as the structural conditions for profitable investment were maintained. Internalizing the preoccupation of capitalists by all participants in the procedures of conflict resolution is a prerequisite for the consensus underpinning capitalist democracy and, perhaps, the idea of a "national interest" as well.

To claim that the state incarnates the "national" interest is tautological unless that interest becomes concrete. Indeed, this is where the collective interest of capital in the accumulation process comes into play. If investment serves as the primary condition for employment, then whatever the formally democratic elements of liberal capitalist states, and the differences between them, a structurally enforced imbalance of power between classes will exist. And if this implies that workers must temper their demands accordingly even before they reach the bargaining table, it also suggests that the satisfaction of capitalist interests regarding profitable investment will serve as the prerequisite for the satisfaction of all other interests under capitalist democracy. This structural condition, of course, also retains an ideological complement. Thus, where the collective capitalist concern will define the general or "national" interest, all other interests will necessarily appear as subordinate or "special."[21] This is precisely what progressives and socialists must work to contest.

4. AMERICAN "EXCEPTIONALISM": AN EXCURSUS

Capitalist democracy has any number of variants, and the United States is unique insofar as no viable socialist movement has ever taken root here. The explanations for America's "exceptionalism" are varied: the lack of a feudal tradition, the "open frontier," the heterogeneity of the American working class, the existence of an individualist entrepreneurial spirit, and its wealth. But where the lack of a feudal tradition and the open frontier aid in understanding the genesis of the American order, they cannot explain the institutional processes that have maintained it to the present. As far as the issue of heterogeneity is concerned, in Austria-Hungary where there was a huge labor movement no less than in Imperial Russia where a revolution took place, the working class was even less homogeneous. The original socialist rationale for having a party in the first place was to surmount the disparate interests and fragmented character of the "objective" working class and so strengthen its "subjective" power, unity, and common purpose. It also appears highly questionable whether the American entrepreneurial spirit is much stronger than that of the Japanese or the Germans. Even if Werner Sombart was right, and the ship of socialism "flounders on the reef of meat and potatoes," he clearly underestimated the way in which wealth has been distributed in the United States and the sacrifices made by generations of workers in producing it.

Perhaps the crucial source for American "exceptionalism" derives from the fact that industrialization preceded the rise of the modern state. Where the opposite occurred, as in Germany, a "strong" state arose. Following the Revolution of 1776, however, a weak state developed in the United States. A fundamental transformation of prior class relations was unnecessary in this first "anti-imperialist" revolution.[22] Even more important, however, was the political decision to secure its existence through a republic without ministerial parliamentarism and proportional representation. A single-district, "winner take all" format was instituted, which made for weak parties and strong interest groups. This structure militates against the formation of parties with distinct class orientations as well as "ideological" third parties with a realistic chance of winning elections.

Differences between parties become less important than between candidates, and ideological rigor vanishes in the attempt to fashion compromises or coalitions among interest groups whose concerns are often mutually exclusive. Capital, of course, retains differentiated interests in both parties whose structural weakness renders them unable to enforce discipline on members with respect to platform or campaign promises. Repression has also been employed to quell dissidents far more than is generally assumed.[23] All this helps translate into consistently low turnouts at the polls and the disaggregation of voters.[24] It also gives greater substantive power to smaller and better organized interests, and especially without public financing of campaigns, politicians are driven to secure the allegiance of dominant constituencies in the positions they take. Though voters will obviously make the final choice between candidates, it is a mistake simply to believe that the party system is driven by the electorate.[25] There are, structural impediments to creating a party capable of expressing the interests of workers as a class or developing a political tradition of struggle. The inability to constrain capital is a logical consequence of this situation. The United States, in fact, still lags behind countries with class-based parties on a host of social welfare issues ranging from national health insurance and vacation time to health-safety standards and input on corporate decision making.

Unions have been the only organizational vehicle for workers in America. But they were never national in character and always took the form of just another interest group. They were, for this reason, always weaker and more corrupt than their European counterparts even before the cold war and the disastrous impact of McCarthyism.[26] Well over twenty individual states still deny unions the right to organize in the United States, and an array of administrative rules furthers the fragmentation process.[27] All this has also made it more difficult for unions to deal with both the change from blue- to white- and pink-collar jobs and the devastating effects of the shift from industrial production based on steel to an information society based on computers. Instrumentalism and timidity are only strengthened by this situation, and, as a consequence, unions have increasingly lost the emotional allegiance of workers even as their membership is dwindling.

The decentralized structure of politics in the United States, interestingly enough, makes it more difficult to organize broad masses around issues of public concern than elites around issues of narrow private interest. With the lack of strong unions and a class party, moreover, workers will ever more surely find the general "cost" of gathering information on specialized issues higher than that of capitalist firms whose interests are directly affected. Organizational weakness will also increase the fear of force or reprisals in the event of radical action from below, which, in turn, only strengthens conservative and localist proclivities on the part of labor bureaucrats.

Under the circumstances, it is not at all surprising that the major inspiration for radical reform of the existing structure should originally have come through spontaneous strikes from below, mass associations like the civil rights movement, or unions outside the mainstream like the CIO and smaller political organizations like the IWW as well as the Socialist and Communist parties. Nor is it surprising that these movements should have seriously thought to contest the political system and its structural incentives for constantly choosing the "lesser of two evils." Overvaluing the possibilities for third *parties* in a system marked by "winner-take-all,"single-district elections is a mistake. But it is also a mistake to undervalue *movements* working outside the institutional arena. Their radical potential will be channeled and their successes will be "integrated" into programs like the New

Deal and the Great Society. But this only begs the question: have the changes really been integrated or has the system been changed?

With a "nonideological" party structure, weak national parties, and a fragmented union movement, working people have been fundamentally unable to understand their position in class terms. Most define themselves as "middle class," while even union members, following the dominant organizational tendency fostered by Samuel Gompers, view their concerns as those of an interest group. This ideological self-perception, strengthened by the media and the academy, further cements the structure of consent. Indeed, especially when one considers the United States, it becomes ever more apparent that Machiavelli was correct in his perception that ideology exists not for the prince but for his subjects.

5. Bureaucracy, Administrative Rationality, and Resistance

The American case is of interest because it exemplifies the manner in which economic gains by subaltern groups and classes do not mechanistically translate into political power. In fact, the lack of political power by workers creates a situation in which even the reforms that have been achieved are easier to roll back. This has become particularly apparent in the 1990s, and it suggests that the often implicit assumption of mainstream social democracy regarding the gradual and unlinear progress of reform stands in drastic need of correction.

"Compromise" is a complex phenomenon. It takes place not only in the formation of progressive proposals but also in attempts to undermine them.[28] Not every compromise is a "sellout," and not every administrative decision is made in favor of capital. But the basic reality is undeniable. Conflicts originating in a substantively biased accumulation process are adjudicated in a formally neutral fashion as a compromise between equal participants. The institutional procedure must, for this very reason, suspend consideration of structural imbalances of power in the act of reaching a decision and perhaps even of defining a problem. State institutions explicitly dismiss the structural imbalance of economic power in theory even as it becomes of obvious importance for political practice.

Ideological domination takes two forms. It emerges initially insofar as the apparatus suspends long-term and political in favor of short-term and economic concerns. It also occurs insofar as the substantive imbalance of power is veiled in the adjudication procedure. The ability to illuminate actual power relations is bound with the ability to rectify them. Disruption from below can generate new organizations or spur existing organizations into action. But still, only institutions can check the ambitions of other institutions in a sustained manner, and power is necessary to contest power. Thus, in contrast to the views of classical liberalism, "the problem of modern democracy is much less the [abolition] of political power than its rational utilization and provision for effective mass participation in its exercise."[29]

That this point is so often ignored is not due to the simple malevolence of reformers or some conspiracy on the party of the ruling class. It is rather a matter of the instrumentalist assumptions with which politicians and prevailing organizations engage the state. Ideology is not some residual product of economic activity but a lived reality and a constituent element of political practice. In this vein, what Max Weber called an "elective affinity" exists not merely or even principally between instrumental rationality and reformism,[30] but rather between instrumental rationality and the willingness to compromise existing gains. Such rationality is inherently reductive and antispeculative. It allows for predictability and calculability, and as it reduces structural and political issues to discrete and economic ones, it subordinates the concern with the mass exercise of power to issues of expertise. It also uncritically assumes the existence of those institutions and modes of thought through which reforms can be exacted. Thus, the "fit" between the bureaucratic state's attempt to eliminate the "long run" and reformist attempts to mitigate existing inequities in the "short run." The exclusive reliance on instrumental rationality inhibits the development of a coherent view of social interaction even as it threatens the free discourse on values and goals that is essential for elaborating the democratic purposes of the socialist project.

Employing bureaucratic rationality need involve neither exploitation nor oppression. Even the most emancipated society will need to structure responsibilities and routinize tasks. Coming to terms with "reification" is possible only by analyzing how specific institutions function and receive their substantive ends. Employing such a perspective, however, assumes the existence of "neutral" administrative rules and criteria. These transcend the given sociohistorical context of exploitation in which they are currently embedded. Certain administrative proposals, like public control over investment, can mitigate the structural imbalance of power in ways that others do not. Control of the state by the working class, in the same vein, speaks to reshaping those systemic processes of persuasion, political power, and accumulation from a stance committed to extending formal democracy, substantive equality, and cosmopolitanism, or the principles underpinning the class ideal.

Participation in the operations of society is always limited by time, skill, and interest. The right to participate is also not morally superior to the right of leisure. The primary concern for liberal socialists is, for this reason, the accountability of institutions even if this itself is often dependent upon the possibilities for participating in their operation. The unqualified assault on the universalistic assumptions behind the liberal rule of law loses its radical veneer once they are seen as essential to restricting the arbitrary exercise of power. Identifying the alienation of the working class, or the "people," with bureaucracy and instrumental rationality undermines the ability to forge a progressive politics: better to advocate a position that calls for an attack on the state to introduce more reforms when times are good and defend gains against possible cuts when times are less propitious.

Decentralization is no response to the existing order whether voiced by classical liberals, anarchists, or ultraleft Marxists. It is too often forgotten that the simple demand for decentralization—or "small is beautiful"—can easily produce provincialism, domination by cliques, and even the rejection of universal democratic norms. Nor can it adequately address international problems ranging from an increasingly interdependent economy to ecological concerns. Even the need to create mechanisms for the reproduction of a new order is obscured by the dogmatic insistence on decentralization. Constricting arbitrary exercises of power presupposes coordinating and supervisory institutions with the authority and capacity to impose sanctions.

Unless the ideological battle is waged for principles and goals, however, politics will become the province of technocrats. The best way of combating the technical fetish, lies in forming democratic organs from below such as workers' councils, consumer cooperatives, and the like. But if there is no longer a reason why such organs should stand in inimical opposition to parliamentary forms,[31] it is a mistake to maintain that freedom is simply identifiable with such an institutional arrangement. Workers' councils can exist under a variety of regimes, laws on the books can go unenforced, the most progressive institutional arrangements can petrify, and political traditions can wither. There are no organizational tricks to avoid bureaucratic petrification.

The question is how to maintain the democratic accountability of such mechanisms. Both the traditional anarchist and the classical liberal perspectives, Kropotkin no less than Nozick, miss the point. Such thinkers only pay fundamental attention to the quantity of centralized restrictions on the free display of individual or group energies. What really matters, however, is the quality of political institutions and bureaucratic mechanisms. In fact, just as there can be too much power inscribed in a centralized apparatus, there can also be too little. The 1980s and 1990s have shown how private associations can supplant national or international functions at the expense of the least fortunate. Thus, now more than ever, it is necessary to begin thinking about *political power* and its relevance for the furtherance of liberal and socialist goals.

14

AFFIRMATIVE ACTION
IN RADICAL PERSPECTIVE

A FFIRMATIVE ACTION has generated a bitter, protracted, and well-publicized debate. All the more remarkable then are the illusions still surrounding it. The policy still is stubbornly identified as the brainchild of left ideologues who craftily foisted it upon an innocent and unwitting nation. But the reality is very different. Affirmative action was less a product of deceit by radicals, or a programmatic push by the mass movements of the 1960s, than the design of moderate politicians and business elites. Following the logic of crisis management, seeking to maintain order and control,[1] this coalition conceived of affirmative action as an appealingly inexpensive way to both appease an increasingly militant black constituency and soothe the consciences of privileged sectors of white America.

Civil rights activists, the New Left, and progressives in the Democratic Party were actually wary of the policy. At best, they regarded affirmative action as a stunted and risky means for drawing racially excluded groups into the mainstream. Affirmative action was understood to be a pallid substitute for a far broader set of interlinked social programs predicated upon the creation of full employment. Such a program would have proved far more ambitious and inclusive than the short-lived War on Poverty whose funds for the nonelderly poor never came close to 1 percent of the federal budget.[2] Affirmative action was, from the beginning, a policy premised on "removing barriers" rather than dispensing additional aid. It was also, from the beginning, politically fraught: a public policy favoring any other than the dominant skin color inevitably invited trouble, especially for Democrats.

Republicans were well aware that affirmative action was a potentially divisive enterprise; in fact, they counted on it. Several decades later this mild measure to level the playing field of life enabled the right to capitalize

The original version of this article, written in collaboration with Alba Alexander and Kurt Jacobsen, appeared in *Critical Sociology*, no. 23 (1998): 85–102.

on a backlash of indignation stirred by hard times and by the beliefs of Americans in individualism and meritocracy.[3] It remains an open question whether the willingness to compromise on the part of the left was smart or foolish, justified or illegitimate, clear or short sighted. But the reality remains that the right would ultimately use this issue to divert attention from the dubious purposes and impact of "supply-side" policy and other conservative nostrums. Affirmative action would add grist to the neoconservative mill: American economic woes, by their account, would now be seen not as the product of greed, mismanagement, or antagonistic interests at the top, but derieved from the triple plagues of rapacious welfare mothers, wily immigrants, and the lazy able-bodied poor.

How did a relatively minor ameliorative measure become elevated to the epitome of progressive political action regarding racial injustice? The most obvious answer is the most persuasive: it came to the forefront in a nation sadly lacking remedies for its racist history and inclinations precisely because it was a rearguard action. The fizzling of the "golden age of growth" in the 1970s, the Democrats' retreat from their original commitment to the welfare state, the rise of single-issue movements, and the surreal restoration of a nineteenth-century market ideology in the guise of neoliberalism combined to produce a new historical constellation. In this new context, for want of anything better, affirmative action acquired a powerful symbolic importance as a last line of defense. Certainly, the Republican assault on affirmative action was an attempt to exploit racial prejudices and to undermine two of the Democrats' key constituencies: minorities and women. Nevertheless, the refusal of the Democratic Party to entertain a genuinely progressive tax policy left especially white skilled workers wary of new social programs and the party's willingness to lavish funds on "others."

Perhaps in order to justify their own timidity, many liberals and radicals mistakenly tended to deride or dismiss aggrieved working-class "Reagan Democrats" as victims of incorrigible racism or else of fleeting fits of false consciousness. Already at the raucous Democratic Convention of 1972 many in the mainstream seemed to concede the claim of an incipient neoconservative movement that the social aims of a rainbow of minorities were irreconcilable with the economic interests of blue-collar ethnics in thrall to corrupt city machines, conservative unions, and knee-jerk anti-communism. And so, when hard times inevitably set in, it mattered little if affirmative action programs formed a bulwark for minorities or provided them with a vital avenue of access: old alliances became extremely fragile in the new circumstances.[4]

Progressives now believe themselves caught betwixt and between, and in a way, they are. The mass media trumpet the entry of minorities and women into public life, and, partially through affirmative action, radical changes have obviously occurred. With these progressive social and cultural changes, however, economic and political regression has taken place. The decline of unions and the collapse of the New Left coincided with the transformation of the Republicans from the "pragmatic" party of Richard Nixon and Nelson Rockefeller into a saber-toothed reactionary organization in which the Christian right and what once were fringe figures like Newt Gingrich and Trent Lott could play a robust, if now slightly chastened, role. The revival tent ideology of a free marketplace also insinuated itself into receptive sections of the Democratic Party and, by the mid-1990s, Republicans were no longer simply content with a rollback but instead became intent upon demolishing the gains made by wage earners since the New Deal.

Affirmative action was the ideal rallying symbol for this campaign. Opponents pretended that its programs had not bettered the lot of many African Americans, which is manifestly false, and in the same breath argued that they are vastly more effective than they are to the point that the irrepressibly erroneous Dinesh D'Souza could call for an end to affirmative action because now "African Americans routinely receive racial preferences in universities and the work place."[5] The argument is confused, of course, but confusion of this deliberate kind is not always costly in a blinkered body politic. The illusion that affirmative action is some huge socialist scheme for equality is belied by the reality: affirmative action was never part of a scheme seeking the extension of economic security for all but rather, from the first, was intended to channel minority recruits into the university, public services, and corporate culture. It was predicated on assisting individuals rather than minority workers or employees in general. Affirmative action was the product of a hostile climate that turned "liberal" into the un-American "L word" and, regarding issues of race, led many progressives to surrender their earlier concern with substantive policies that would aid workers in favor of strategies primarily directed to the talented tenth among minorities.

Affirmative action reflected the shift from full-employment industrial policy, single-payer health care, urban reconstruction, and family support programs to what would become an increasingly symbolic politics. In practice, the policy worked to fill the ranks of the middle class with minority "representatives" by setting people against those in the economic stratum just below them. With good reason Nixon sensed in it a wonderful "way to confound the Democrats."[6] Internal bickering over a host of issues, with affirmative action in the forefront, soon enough led the right wing to get a firm grip on the Democratic Party and push through a short-sighted program that would cater to an influential portion of the middle class in terms of regressive tax cuts, public service cutbacks, and privatization.

Affirmative action fit into this shift in power and program in the following way. Insofar as its various measures never considered the question of class, and also ignored questions pertaining to the business cycle, the general policy enabled conservatives in both parties to conduct duels over the nature of "racism" on advantageously narrow ground. As economic downturns occurred, in this vein, affirmative action kindled resentment over "favoritism" among working people—a quarter of whom earn full-time wages very near the poverty line. Affirmative action, by the same token, helped produce a politics of illusion in which right-wing critics would no longer need to appear malicious or mean-spirited. Future supporters of "compassionate conservatism," themselves adept at employing a symbolic multiculturalism, would now be free to champion seemingly legitimate objections to the terrors of "reverse discrimination." Especially now, when affirmative action has supposedly served its purpose, conservatives can take the offensive: anyone who believes racist structures and attitudes persist can be condemned for living in the "haunted house of the past."[7]

By any serious empirical appraisal, however, racism is more entrenched than ever. Economic setbacks generated a backlash that began with *Bakke* in 1978 and continued through the striking down of affirmative action at the University of Texas Law School by the Court of Appeals and in California's referendum repeal of affirmative action criteria via Proposition 209 in November 1996. Indicators ranging from prison internment to infant mortality to real income evidence the impact of what can only be described as "institutional racism." Further competition between hard-pressed wage earners and oppressed groupings can be envisioned given the new downturn in the business cycle of 2001 and the continuation of a trend toward domestic downsizing and globalization of production. In these straitened circumstances the temptations of particularism and what might be termed the moral economy of the separate deal have the potential of sabotaging the unity required by any new progressive coalition.

Perhaps the greatest liability for defenders of affirmative action is its inescapable taint of special pleading. The right delightedly decries the plight of a gracious nation that is oppressively "governed by quotas" that "violate fundamental norms of justice and fair play" and then invokes prominent blacks—Clarence Thomas or Shelby Steele or Stanley Crouch—who support their cause whether out of a genuine hatred of being patronized or simple self-interest, or both. These claims, while exaggerated, do reflect a profound sentiment. Justice Thomas detests affirmative action insofar as he sees the program as based on a patronizing belief in black inferiority, and he has argued "there is a 'moral [and] constitutional equivalence' between 'laws designed to subjugate a race and those that distribute benefits on the basis of race to foster some current notion of equality.'"[8] Thomas, a fan of Ayn Rand's romantic brand of Manchester capitalism, can be seen as a predictable opponent, but his concerns are genuine and widespread. A 1995 survey in the *Washington Post* indicated that 46 percent of blacks and 75 percent of everyone polled oppose preference based on past discrimination.[9]

It remains essential to remedy increasing racial divisions and growing economic inequalities through public policies. Colin Powell, to the dismay of fellow Republicans, noted on 8 June 1996 in the *New York Times* that when half of all African American men between twenty-four and thirty-five years of age are without full-time employment, we still need affirmative action. But it would seem that more generous and universal programs are in order. Martin Luther King Jr., recast dizzyingly by conservative cosmetologists today as a "moderate," was more to the point long ago when he called for a new Bill of Rights for the Disadvantaged that would speak to the interests of the "forgotten white poor" as well as disadvantaged minorities.[10] His was a rainbow, not race-based, program. No less than Nixon, in fact, King anticipated the way in which affirmative action might disrupt the liberal coalition.[11]

In a precarious period, when even coveted middle-class occupations no longer seem so safe, a chief selling point for progressives should be that such programs as King envisioned would serve citizens of all races, colors, or creeds from languishing in the ranks of the disadvantaged. The market has no self-correcting mechanisms. Even if it has been colonized and then demonized by conservatives, in what can only be conceived as the niftiest of public relations campaigns, the only institution capable of mitigating the whip of the market and of softening the deleterious effects of the business cycle on working people is the state.[12] And there is evidence that people are becoming aware of this. Surveys indicate that two-thirds of all Americans would be willing to pay higher taxes for a universal child care system; even higher percentages would do the same for a national health system and improved education.[13] A defense of preferential hiring that is nondiscriminatory stands in accord with the commitment to democratic beliefs, and audiences in a liberal society might well prove receptive to the idea that government should live up to the nation's "basic opportunity principle" by providing adequate education, income, health care, and housing for citizens that can serve as the "background conditions" for fair competition over resources.[14]

Nonetheless it must be clear by now that until this set of policy options enters the mainstream dialogue, *any critique of affirmative action must at the same time endorse its continuation.* The right has increasingly tended to pounce on any concession by liberals in order to channel it— quite expertly—into its own agenda for shrinking the public sector, as when deinstitutionalizing the mentally ill became a pretext for emptying public wards and inflating the ranks of the homeless, or when reforming "welfare as we know it" came to mean nothing more than slashing it.[15] A different approach is needed that speaks to the interests as well as the ethics of citizens outside the investor class, in order to build a political program for alleviating the plight of the "lower 80 percent " of wage and salary earners losing ground or treading water since the late 1960s.[16]

DUBIOUS LEGACIES

Following the early successes of civil rights struggles in the South, which engendered the Civil Rights Act of 1964 and the Voting Rights Act of

1965, next on the movement's agenda was a multipronged attack on employment, housing discrimination, educational improvements, and community development. Housing was to have been the centerpiece, but ferocious resistance in northern cities, especially Chicago, demoralized a civil rights movement whose driving concern then was to develop a color-blind and inclusive political agenda reminiscent of social democracy. A narrowing of alternatives ensued from what was an already narrow range of policy choices set in the late 1940s.[17] Affirmative action, which highlighted the individual and emphasized formal discrimination, became a substitute for the original social democratic agenda.

Even the original strategy, however, had its flaws: it assumed the possibility of simply extending civil rights legislation into the social and economic sphere. No sooner were legislative edicts passed than they were gutted, retracted, or else ever more weakly enforced as in the case of the Fair Housing Act. The Kerner Commission in 1968 deplored two "increasingly separate Americas," but the 1960s ended with an increase in segregation in urban areas. Even more daunting is that in the economic boom years from 1945 up to the first oil embargo, blacks had twice the unemployment rates of whites. Assuming that a flourishing economy alone will "lift all boats" is questionable. In the absence of a flourishing economy and universal programs capable of quelling charges of race-based favoritism, however, there is clearly little political space available for targeted types of programs.

Still, "colored only" signs were taken down, and from 1960 to 1970 the proportion of African Americans in white-collar jobs rose from 11 percent to 24 percent and the ratio of black median family income to median white family income went from 55 percent to 62 percent. African American families making $25,000 or more rose from 8.7 percent of all black families in 1960 to 25 percent by 1982. About 38 percent of employed African Americans hold middle-class jobs versus only 13.5 percent in 1960.[18] In the military, Colin Powell witnessed real change as the percentage of black officers went up from 2 percent in 1970 to 12 percent by the 1990s. Progress of this sort, however, made the shortfalls even more disheartening. The result has been a crisis of rising expectations.

African Americans are 12 percent of the population yet constitute one-third of recipients of food stamps, Medicaid, and public housing. Black unemployment averages twice the rate of whites, and black family median income today is still about three-fifths of white income. Some ten million blacks live in poverty, 31 percent overall and half of all black children (Jervis Anderson, "Black and Blue," *The New Yorker*, 29 April–6 May 1996, 63). Black youth unemployment has soared to six times that of whites. One black male in three in his twenties is either in jail, on parole, or under court supervision. A survey finds that 58 percent of blacks see their social conditions as getting worse and 74 percent say they have experienced housing discrimination.

Residential segregation becomes a key culprit given the intersection between race and class. Economic progress and justice for many blacks are impeded when poverty becomes concentrated in an area because, *in the absence of integration,* it builds a set of mutually reinforcing attitudes of despair and self-generating spirals of decline.[19] Inner-city communities thus become defined by subtle networks of prejudice leading middle-class blacks to move to other segregated areas like suburbs.[20] These departures leave the inner-city ghetto worse off as well-paid blue-collar jobs vanish and the municipalities where minorities collectively have become majorities are increasingly hamstrung financially. Some critics point fingers at upwardly mobile blacks as if they were to blame for the persistence of inner-city blight, but this is to misapprehend the way in which individual choices of black working people are determined from the outside. Investment produces employment, and lack of investment produces unemployment. Government can channel investment if the political will exists to do so. Affirmative action like all policies relating to the workforce is fundamentally influenced by the choices of capital. If the market cannot do the job, then the state must enter with something more than the exploitative arrangements such as those incorporated in the cramped version of "free enterprise zones." Or, to put it another way, the less a society meets the demands of basic opportunity, the more defensible policies based on preferential hiring become. Ironically, however, it is precisely under circumstances in which such hiring is most necessary that citizens are most indisposed to help any but themselves.

There are multiple barriers to economic progress for inner-city minorities: increasing automation, the internationalization of industries, and the transition from goods to service production where automation now likewise penetrates. Chicago lost over 320,000 industrial jobs from 1967–1987, while New York lost half a million. It is possible to argue over whether class or race has primacy: the answer, however, depends upon the issue under consideration. Confronting the inequitable distribution of wealth from which blacks suffer so severely depends upon the ability to craft policies capable of facilitating a multiracial coalition building upon the general interests of working people. Precisely because Americans remain largely unsympathetic to special claims, furthering the interests of impoverished minorities requires a new general commitment to universal health care, meaningful educational reforms, and what might best be termed an encompassing program of "affirmative action based on need." It is principally through government action that minorities—and wage earners in general—have made economic and political progress. And it is a good deal likelier that Americans will favor state guarantees of equitable background conditions if they too are eligible for educational, health, and other social support benefits.

American conservatives have successfully framed the issue of affirmative action as one of defending merit and equal opportunity, thereby ignoring the exclusion of people on the basis of economic inequities. At the same time, however, conservatives have used a selectively activist state to hold down wages, cut welfare to the poor, increase after-tax profits, dividends, and upper-level incomes, weaken unions, and reduce public resistance to their ideological agenda. If cascades of money really had been showered on minorities, so they argue, then any economic stragglers have only themselves to blame. Thus, the conservative position becomes couched in respectable language; the problem, according to this inspired spin, is that "freedom of conscience, good will and persuasion [have been] replaced by regulatory and judicial coercion."[21] Citizens and voluntary organizations are exhorted to exert their initiative on the question of poverty and take steps to "eliminate the lack, not overlook it." Nevertheless, the right always seems speechless when the initiative is not forthcoming and the moment arrives for considering the costly changes needed to deal with what is materially lacking.

Their argument is pitched at the individual level and cannily held there: it is the same with affirmative action. Excesses are denounced, while structural imbalances of economic and political power disappear with a rhetorical snap of the fingers. Conservatives insist upon the need for "color-blind" hiring and cull sympathy from white ethnic groups unmindful that their own boot-strapping activities in earlier generations, for all their undeniable hard work, were historically helped along by urban patronage, war mobilizations, and federal programs. There is nothing paranoid about suggesting that the underlying objective is to pit minorities against one another and to discourage white voters from forming alliances with minorities. Republicans attack crime, quotas, and "taxes," thereby diverting focus from the role corporate and financial interests play in bringing attention to the increasingly strapped circumstances in which a majority of Americans must live. If your wages stagnate, your firm skips the country, your potential employer chooses someone else, or your taxes rise, blame affirmative action or else immigrants. This always makes a brutal sort of common sense to citizens who know no other way to frame their problems in a political climate dominated by neoliberal discourse and neoconservative diagnoses.

FLANKING ACTIONS

Affirmative action started with President Kennedy's Executive Order 10925 in March 1961 eliminating racial distinctions by government contractors. The term first occurs in the National Labor Relations Act of 1935, and it is applied to employers who had discriminated against union members and thus were ordered "to place those victims where they should have been without discrimination."[22] In 1965 Lyndon Johnson issued Executive Order 11246 in an affirmative action package establishing the

Equal Employment Opportunity Commission and the Office of Federal Contract Compliance in 1967, and called for the passage of the Fair Housing Act. All this took place at a turbulent moment with action in the streets, when the civil rights movement was at its apex, and political support from the black constituency had become necessary for Democrats given the commitment of the administration to continue the escalating Vietnam War. The ultimate failure of what would become known as a "guns and butter" strategy is not the point: the economy was booming and there seemed room for the play of conscience and for new forms of coalition building in the Democratic Party.

Important is the way in which the "Southern strategy" of Richard Nixon would, in response, drive a wedge between the white working class and the Democratic Party, and affirmative action—in the guise of "goals, not quotas"—proved to be a superb device. It let conservatives off the hook on questions about their regressive social policies. The bootstrap message was more than merely implicit: correcting historical imbalances of opportunity will alleviate the economic deprivation of African Americans and so, in the future, the need for affirmative action will wither away. In this cool technocratic spirit even liberal Democrats can argue that "a policy that isolates the requirements of relevant qualifications or equal consideration is now justified in order to create a society in which those requirements can be satisfied without wronging any (or as many) citizens."[23] Nevertheless, it is hardly hypothetical if critics ask what might happen politically should a considerable majority of the citizenry believe it is being wronged.

Implicit in affirmative action is the notion that other groups require new forms of public policy to gain access to opportunities hitherto denied them. Women were included for EEOC protection under Nixon. A combination of interest groups and government agencies emerged with a distinct interest in preserving such programs, and this interest has only grown stronger with the extension of the idea of affirmative action to other oppressed groups (Native Americans, Asians) during the simultaneous rollback of the welfare state. Many see an expanding set of cumulative claims as creating an "overload" on the system. But military expenditures, business subsidies, and tax loopholes miraculously remain largely intact and unchallenged. The debate over affirmative action and social policy begins only *after* these budgetary expenses are tactfully factored out or taken as given. Only then is it customary to decry wasteful "add-ons." Working people and disadvantaged groups, including the "working poor," thereby become called upon to battle one another: it is indeed possible to argue that from this vantage point, the urban racial struggle has been "essentially a struggle among the have-nots over access to and control of decent housing and decent neighborhoods."[24] Or, to put it another way, if the playing field is now deemed level by fiat and the labor market is tight, then any edge will matter desperately. Thus, the scramble for scarce resources among increasingly atomized constituencies.

The dilemma inherent in playing on the given terrain is cast into bold relief when one examines the wobbly assumptions behind prioritizing members of a systematically deprived group at the expense of opportunities for a worker whose parents did not experience discrimination. One official of the U.S. Department of Labor instructively and offhandedly remarked regarding the 1970s Weber case—which was defined as a clash of working-class white and working-class black in the quest for job preferences—that "If someone has to bear the sins of the fathers, surely it must be the children."[25] This is disingenuous and brimming with class disdain. Exactly whose fathers discriminated against whom else and with what accrued benefits? A punctilious ranking of relative levels of suffering is impossible, and it would only impair any nascent coalescence of groups into a movement for reform. Everyone gets buried beneath a blizzard of competing claims of more-sinned-against-than-thou. The person representing the Department of Labor was obviously oblivious to the overarching system of "divide and conquer" in the very act of perpetuating it. Contrast this smug attitude with Martin Luther King's concern to incorporate poor whites who "were the derivative victims of slavery" because its brutal legacy "corrupted their lives, frustrated their opportunities, and withered their education" and "confused so many by prejudice that they have supported their own oppressors."[26]

The degree to which such integration takes place is the degree to which constraint on the customary exercise of class power becomes possible. The foundations for reinvigorating a progressive agenda exist. Take the fact that for blacks the low-to-high income ratio of students in college changed from 7:10 in the mid-1970s to less than 4:10 by 1983. This is clearly unacceptable. But for whites the ratio of low-to-high income enrollment in the early to mid 1970s was about 6:10, which in 1983 declined to less than 5:10 (Michael McPherson and Martin Owen Shapiro, "The Student Finance System for Undergraduate Students: How Well Does It Work?" *Change* (May–June 1991): 16–22). They also slipped, if not quite so drastically. In such circumstances an exclusive emphasis on affirmative action can only pit aspiring white against aspiring minority workers in a rigged game where both are bound to lose. Little wonder that by 1980 many working-class whites who voted Republican said it was because the "Democratic Party was too concerned with blacks"—as if the latter had come a long way, or far enough—even as the Democratic Party was retreating from the more radical social programs associated with the welfare state.

Some analysts speak of a shift from a "reparations policy to a diversity policy" in the history of affirmative action whereby the "peculiarly horrid history of treatment of blacks" is seen in more relative terms as women, Native Americans, Latinos, and others climb aboard. The real problem, however, is that plenty of white men are not advantaged in any discernible way. If there is such a thing as a "standard left critique of group preferences," it would be that unless class is factored skillfully into the debate, multiracial support for programs of socioeconomic reform falls by the wayside.[27] By the same token, it is mistaken to believe that the lack of a level playing field implies that progressives must uncritically embrace affirmative action in its present form. A politically sensible approach for the left is one capable of configuring ameliorative policies such as affirmative action in such a way that they can heal divisions, promote coalition-building, and foster support for policy measures that in our deficit-obsessed discourse are treated as taboo.

BREAKING POLICY TABOOS

Progressives are currently in the untenable position of defending ameliorative programs that split their own constituencies. Portraying this fractiousness as being premised exclusively on racism is to distort the situation and ignore the wider forces at work. Solutions cannot usefully be cast as race-based versus class-based policies; and resorting to the mantra whereby race and class are mechanically linked with one another will not do either. The task is to define those conditions under which affirmative action is helpful and those problems for which policy departures are necessary.

Traditional affirmative action involves issues of access for groups rather than compensation for individuals; and it is an effective way of contesting the abuse of civil rights. It does not merely apply to blacks. Gays wishing to operate openly in the military, lesbians seeking to adopt children, ethnics wishing to study their cultures, and the disabled seeking sloping curves for their wheelchairs are also the domain for affirmative action committees. There are always targeted elements in any program and in the most universalistic of plans. These elements are what affirmative action highlights. Its function becomes critical precisely insofar as its partisans call on the current system to actualize its own ideal of fairness. Preferential hiring cannot be justified as a permanent feature, but it can be "justified by showing that the basic opportunity principle [providing adequate educational, health, and employment opportunities] is not fulfilled."[28] This requires nothing less than an integrated set of social democratic policies.

Invoking "diversity" solves nothing if each group aims to justify the resources it seeks by arguing its oppression must take precedence over that of others. Accepting the logic of affirmative action in its narrow form creates a situation in which progressives wind up apportioning austerity among the have-nots and hangers-on; each group can thereby become targeted in different ways by right-wing groups that thrive on anxieties about "quotas" and "reverse discrimination."[29] The task is to break the momentum of this pernicious particularistic logic. Progressive politics must explicitly express its normative character and yet also garner support from the bulk of the working population. With respect to affirmative action, the goal should not be discarding it but rendering it irrelevant by raising the availability of training, jobs, and housing standards. This would diminish material motives for discrimination and simultaneously pump funds and new demand into the economy, raise general wages, and begin to break down resistance to programs targeted against ghetto barriers.

Targeted programs become politically problematic when not packaged in universal programs. There is no reason why such programs should not create good jobs for ghetto men at good wages, and it is certainly arguable that the efficacy of such programs is greater than the far more "convoluted" attempts to aid black families.[30] The real problem is that such programs lack the symbolic character required by the proponents of identity politics. Proponents need to execute their own rhetorical move and raise the class interest of policies like day care, child support, job training, single-payer health care, and a federal labor market guaranteeing good jobs at good wages. The life chances of minorities have more to do with economic class position than with their day-to-day encounters with white exploitation, segregation, and discrimination. Nevertheless, the uniform reliance on class to "explain all forms and degrees of racial conflict can be as misleading as a uniform reliance on race"[31]: universal programs are inadequate without targeted and regional programs embedded within them as well.

How do "we" pay for educational upgrades, jobs and job training, student loans, urban renewal, subsidized housing, and R & D? Still too few Americans understand that in the last decade the income of the wealthiest 1 percent doubled and that virtually all income gains went to the top 20 percent.[32] Affirmative action has served important functions in the past by helping bring the excluded into the mainstream of economic life. But that mainstream is increasingly suffering drastic class and income divisions. Affirmative action, in the future, must be connected to larger spheres of the distribution of political and economic power. Raising the highest marginal tax rates from 39.6 percent to a 50 percent range can generate $20 billion to $30 billion per year. A 13 percent cut in Pentagon spending over the next seven years would provide $248 Billion and still allow a military budget three times larger than the nearest military competitors.[33] Closing loopholes for multinationals in conjunction with legislation to tax capital gains at the rate of income tax would bring in another $400 billion. The practical ideas are already out there. Edward Wolff has proposed a direct tax on wealth (exempting the first $100,000, taxing the second $100,000 at a 0.05 percent rate, and rising to 0.3 percent above $1 million) such as in Switzerland, which would raise another $40 billion. Other ideas like taxing all stock transfers—other than by pension funds—and a tax on all financial foreign exchanges, which would curb speculation, are also highly revenue-enhancing options.[34] These are our contemporary policy taboos. Soaking the poor is pragmatic everyday politics; soaking the rich—that is, getting a fair tax share from them for public purposes—is reprehensible class warfare.

It is time to revive what Martin Luther King called a "Bill of Rights for the Disadvantaged," modeled on the GI Bill, to "usher in a new era in which the full resources of the society would be used to attack the tenacious poverty which so paradoxically exists in the midst of plenty."[35] No conceivable utopia can obviate the pathological need of some injured and deprived people to fear the other, displace feelings of unworthiness, or exploit physically distinguishable and weaker people for gain.[36] However, it is possible to reduce the pool of recruits for racist movements by ensuring universal application of educational, employment, health, and community development programs. One payoff is a reduced appeal and susceptibility to right-wing nostrums by working-class whites who might then vote their pocketbooks over their cultural prejudices.

CONCLUSION

Martin Luther King saw "two concentric circles" of poverty and race within which blacks were caught, and he believed it impossible to confront racism without beginning at the wider concentric circle of poverty and picking up needed allies along the way inward. Contemporary progressives must, in this spirit, begin connecting affirmative action to the larger sphere of political power and economic distribution that, in its present forms, this policy actually obscures. When funds pour into military projects, savings and loan bail outs, and jails, these are *political* decisions. There is a right-wing campaign to kill high expectations among wage earners because a downsizing corporate world desires tractable and disposable employees. Affirmative action cannot be treated separately from the wider democratic project of controlling the economy. It also appears that programs targeted on a regional basis may be the best way to get around, while incorporating, race as a criterion. Hard-core neglected areas do require special attention to eliminate de facto redlining, steering, and other systemic discrimination.

But progressives must resist a particularistic "logic of fragmentation" that pits working-class and struggling middle-class whites against the urban working poor. Gains from affirmative action must be retained but it is important to incorporate a wider band of qualifications for enabling a new war on poverty and disadvantage. Finally, this agenda must be tied to universal health care, educational reforms, well-paid state-funded employment programs, and race-neutral policies of redistribution. The disjunction between analysis of what has been called the "culture of poverty" and of structural conditions maintaining it remains a weak point for progressive reformers. Support for affirmative action, even in its present form, is preferable to its simple abolition. The point, however, is to shift the discussion. As long as debate is constricted to dividing a shrinking pie, and not talking about how the bakery operates, racism will appeal to people grasping for easy explanations to difficult problems.

15

THE RHETORIC OF REACTION

ALBERT O. HIRSCHMAN is one of this country's most distinguished political thinkers. A member of numerous commissions and task forces, a prolific scholar known for his ongoing attempt to link theoretical concerns with policy formation, his elegant new book, *The Rhetoric of Reaction*, seemingly appears under the most favorable circumstances. The international triumph of conservatism in the 1980s legitimates an investigation into its assumptions and rhetorical modes of explanation. Professor Hirschman seeks to accomplish this task by illuminating the "imperatives of argument" employed in opposing what T. H. Marshall saw as the extension of democracy from the civil to the political and ultimately to the social spheres of existence. The ideology of reaction will thus, according to the author, justify itself in terms of either the *perversity*, the *futility*, or the *jeopardy* thesis. His approach reduces the ideology to its general lines of argument and abolishes the unique political views, the specific interests, and the distinct political style of differing reactionary theorists. Nevertheless, when dealing with each of these rhetorical modes, Professor Hirschman brings intelligence and discernment to bear.

His comments on the perversity thesis, which maintains that attempts at reform only worsen the conditions they wish to remedy, are telling. The French Revolution created a new concern with the unintended consequences of action. And numerous thinkers, beginning with Joseph DeMaistre, would afterward assert that the road to hell is paved with the terrible consequences of good intentions. They feared the worst: extending civil liberties would produce chaos; universal suffrage would usher in the rule of bureaucracy; the welfare state would aid the middle classes more than the poor and ultimately destroy traditional social structures.

The Rhetoric of Reaction: Perversity, Futility, Jeopardy was published in 1991 by Harvard University press. This review appeared in *Political Theory* 21 (February 1993): 132–135.

Hirschman nicely exposes the dogmatic quality of such arguments. But his critique of the perversity thesis essentially rests on the counter-argument that unintended consequences, like the effect on literacy of universal military service, can also prove positive in character. And that is insufficient. Obviously there are counterfactual instances for every general claim. But these alone neither subvert it nor provide an immanent critique of the given argument. A stance results from this critique of the perversity thesis in which choosing between reaction and reform actually means little more than deciding whether caution is preferable to daring.

Plus ça change . . . This cliché basically defines the futility thesis. It superficially appears more moderate than the perversity thesis. But, in fact, the futility thesis is more insulting to those seeking progressive change. After all, even if the social world is moving in the wrong direction, "hope remains that it can be steered correctly" (p. 45). If nothing really changes, however, then reformers become little more than fools. Great events, from the perspective inaugurated by Alexis de Tocqueville in *The Old Regime and the French Revolution*, become stripped of their radicalism; they surrender to the commonplace or a set of deeper laws that supposedly make society impervious to any serious transformation like Michels's "iron law of oligarchy."

The futility thesis contradicts any commonsense understanding of extraordinary events (p. 70), and it is interesting to consider how a partisan of the futility thesis might respond to the revolutions of 1989. But, still, the author is aware that claims deriving from it, especially with respect to the welfare state, are generally bereft of empirical justification and tend to ignore the ability of planners to learn or improve any given policy once it is in place. Hirschman also notes that the perversity and futility theses are basically mutually exclusive; it is, after all, somewhat difficult to claim that the unintended consequences of a reform will simultaneously prove disastrous and change nothing at all. Then, too, where the perversity thesis views the world as volatile and retains an affinity to mythic explanations, the futility thesis conceives of the world as highly structured and defers to the authority of science and laws (pp. 72–73).

Hirschman's analysis of the manner in which these theses of reaction stand in combination with one another is quite insightful. But enough reactionaries, from Gobineau over Spengler and down to the present, have tended to fuse mythical with scientific forms of explanation. Hirschman also unwittingly extends his own rationalist assumptions regarding the importance of empirical support and logical coherence to the ideologists of reaction. And that is of some importance. Reactionary thought, after all, has consistently prized intuition over reason as the criterion of truth and also staunchly opposed the Enlightenment tradition along with its political implications.

Of course, there have always been reasonable conservatives willing logically to justify their positions. The stated purpose of this book, however, is to deal with divisive ideological tendencies. There is subsequently something very strange about the refusal to confront the rhetoric of anti-Semitism, religious fundamentalism, elitism, racism, sexism, and xenophobia. They clearly exhibit an historical affinity with conservative theory and practice. Moreover, they demand neither empirical justification nor logical consistency to justify their appeal. This neglect sanitizes the object of inquiry: reactionary ideology becomes unintentionally cleansed of its most dangerous implications.

A word is still necessary, however, about the most sophisticated form of reactionary rhetoric. The jeopardy thesis, in contrast to the others, does not attack the desirability of change; it maintains instead that the costs are too high or that the reform in question will endanger progress already achieved. This thesis, which presupposes a context in which the past is honored, appeals to the plausible belief that an ancient liberty is somehow more valuable than a new one. Supporters of the jeopardy thesis will thus, for example, view the extension of democracy into economic life as a threat to individual liberty and property.

Hirschman speaks to certain material interests protected by the jeopardy thesis and offers illuminating studies of the English Reform Bills of 1832 and 1867 to substantiate his analysis. Still, he does not actually contest the reactionary position in normative or "political" terms. He instead simply claims that neither the extension of suffrage nor the welfare state has caused any noticeable harm to civil liberties (p. 105). In fact, or so he suggests, reform can provide "mutual support" for various traditions and institutions inherited from the past. There is nothing particularly remarkable about this claim. Nevertheless, it provides the first hint that the analysis of reactionary rhetoric will undergo a startling turnabout.

Hirschman's argument originally suggested that reactionary rhetoric was a response to those seeking the extension of democracy. But, soon enough, he notes that much of "progressive or liberal rhetoric can be *generated* from the various reactionary theses here spelled out by turning them around" (p. 143). The jeopardy thesis argues, for example, that social action is always disruptive; dogmatic progressives will claim, in the same vein, that reform inherently produces a type of "synergy" or "mutual support between past and present" and that it is necessary precisely to forestall the dangers of unrest. By the same token, where the futility thesis maintains that immutable laws doom all attempts to improve society, progressive thinkers like Hegel and Marx will discover laws placing history on their side. Finally, if the perversity thesis implies that the unintended consequences of action make caution necessary, its theoretical counterpart discards the very possibility of unintended consequences coming into play. Each becomes defined by the other, and, in the thinking of both, Hirschman finds a "rhetoric of intransigence." Trying to be evenhanded, however, he forgets not merely the divergent interests being served, but what he claimed in the beginning: reactionary rhetoric is driven by a reaction against the proponents of "progress."

Necessary in his view is a "mature position" capable of recognizing that both action and inaction pose risks and that the consequences of either can never be known with certainty in advance (pp. 153–154). The point is to find "feasible combinations of the old and the new ... [through] practical historical invention" (p. 127). After all is said and done, however, this really does not amount to much more than asking political people to be pragmatic and keep an open mind. In a way, of course, that is fair enough. Even without considering the sententious quality, however, it avoids some important issues.

Is it really the case that American democracy is threatened by extremist worldviews? Isn't conflict over single issues and a basic ideological bipartisanship the norm? Doesn't the "nonideological" or technical definition of problems expel real interests from the discourse and so produce a "pragmatist" dogma of its own? Is it really the case that having an overarching worldview, whether of the right or the left, necessarily closes the mind? And isn't placing reactionary and progressive rhetoric on the same plane unfair to both? Doesn't the possibility of understanding and judging their qualitatively different political and normative interests tend to vanish?

Albert Hirschman's book begs questions such as these. Perhaps that is part of its purpose. It demands tolerance from political people on both sides of the spectrum and calls on them to reflect on their assumptions. That is no small feat. It is what makes *The Rhetoric of Reaction* a work from which all of us can profit.

16

CONFRONTING NATIONALISM

NATIONALISM REMAINS the issue for our time. The allure of imperialism and concern with the national interest by the "great powers," no less than the vision of sovereignty and the right to self-determination by the colonized, has dominated the politics of modernity. By the same token, beneath the surface, an opposing vision was also taking shape. And so, even while recent events center on the role of nationalism, a new internationalism is becoming anchored in a host of transnational political institutions and the increasing economic interdependence among nations. The question is how to judge these two trends from the perspective of general strategies consonant with the expansion of global justice, republicanism, and economic equality.

Nationalism and internationalism have preoccupied socialists and progressives alike for generations. Volumes have been written on these subjects, and the controversies have been heated. Moving forward calls for a historical critique. But that initially requires surrendering the assumption that internationalism never gripped the masses and that the labor movement traditionally ignored the national question. Remaining content to cite from the sacred texts of Marxism and then look at the support socialist parties extended to their respective nation-states in World War I, of course, can lead to such conclusions. Such an approach, however, ignores how the labor movement dealt with internationalism and nationalism in practical political rather than merely ideological terms. Only by taking this hidden reality seriously is it possible to think about rectifying in the future the mistakes made in the past.

Every important representative of the three international organizations of the working class, whatever the faction, recognized the power of nationalism in practice even when opposing it in theory. Democratic socialists like Eduard Bernstein and Rudolf Hilferding, who presupposed the nation-state as *the* arena for struggle, as well as totalitarians like Stalin and Mao,

This article was originally published in *New Politics* 4, no. 1 (spring 1992): 60–65.

are obvious examples. Marx himself, while primarily committed to the international revolution, still believed that it would initially break out within national borders and publicly supported the struggles for independence in Poland and elsewhere; Otto Bauer, a leader of the Austrian movement and perhaps the most insightful socialist analyst of nationalism, sought to tame nationalism through federalism; Jean Jaurès, the most important figure of French socialism, coupled his internationalist commitments to a form of democratic Jacobinism; Lenin, while often stressing the dangers of nationalism, viewed it nonetheless as the ideological fulcrum for any practical revolutionary strategy; indeed, contrary to legend, Trotsky was not blind to nationalism and even Rosa Luxemburg—the socialist internationalist par excellence—was willing to endorse cultural claims regarding national autonomy.

Against the accepted wisdom, with respect to the political history of the labor movement, past problems concerning nationalism had less to do with ignoring it than leaving internationalism on the purely ideological level. Current interpretations arguing that nationalism is the secular religion of modernity or, conversely, that it is a merely an ideological way of obscuring economic problems don't help matters. Nor is it legitimate to claim, in some new version of the old orthodoxy, that nationalism will magically disappear with the abolition of the "commodity form." Dealing politically with nationalism in the present and understanding it historically are flip sides of the same coin. Or, to put it another way, demystifying nationalism depends upon analyzing the manner in which its supposedly progressive function has changed.

Nationalism was always linked with imperialism and militarism in the foreign policies of the great powers. When considering colonized territories, however, it became the ideology of anti-imperialist movements often inspired by vague notions of revolutionary socialism. Nationalism has, of course, also influenced movements for democracy. In fact, during the period in which the bourgeoisie was seeking coalitional support from other members of the "third estate," nationalism was combined with a decidedly radical set of progressive imperatives. Nationalism in its progressive guise married the liberal doctrine of resistance to the prevailing institutional sources of arbitrary authority, which was predicated on universalist principles of natural right, with the organizational expression for the "common good" or the "general will." Thus, the modern state became the institutional referent for a "bourgeois" nationalism intrinsically connected with an internationalist commitment to republicanism and the needs of "the people."

With the failure of the revolutions of 1848, however, even liberal nationalism lost its interconnection with republican and internationalist values, which would soon become embraced by an insurgent labor movement. The nation-state remained its primary institutional arena for political action. No international organization of the working class ever dedicated itself to more than coordination among various national parties and a generalized resistance to capitalism. Viewing the failure of the three internationals in ideological rather than institutional terms is thus a mistake. Each of these international organizations received support from a variety of national parties and groups; indeed, while internationalism was forcefully emphasized in propaganda and theory, the nation-state was *always* the referent for the activities of the various international organizations of the labor movement. Neither the First International led by Marx nor the Second International of the socialist labor movement was ever conceived to supplant the positive functions of the nation-state. Only the Comintern, which quickly subordinated any genuinely internationalist concerns to the national interests of the former Soviet Union, was ever able to enforce sanctions on its members.

As World War II ended, in any event, these old forms of organization lay in ruins, and, lacking any institutional referent, internationalism increasingly became little more than a ritualized article of faith among Western radicals. The new revolutionary nationalism of anti-imperialist movements intent upon instituting their own nation-states, by the same token, lacked any reference to the democratic and internationalist origins of the idea. That was in part because most movements of national self-determination identified themselves with Leninism, in part because the prime imperialist culprit was the West, and in part because the colonized territories mostly lacked the republican traditions and the conditions for a mass-based social democratic labor movement. Nor is it all that different for those variants of nationalism which, serving with religion as virtually the only ideological rallying points against communist authoritarianism, played such a profound role in the events of 1989 and the dissolution of the Soviet Union. Perhaps elements of the old vision remained attached to the new: internationalist values and transnational organizations were embraced by certain movements for national self-determination in Africa and Latin America, while "human rights" was of ideological importance to the uprisings in East Germany and Czechoslovakia. Nevertheless, the genuine driving force for internationalism in the second half of the twentieth century clearly came from a different quarter.

Just as the bourgeoisie was pivotal in bringing about the nation-state more than three hundred years ago, building on its failed attempt in the 1920s to institute a League of Nations, its representatives were decisive in introducing new initiatives in the aftermath of World War II. Out of the devastation, the fear of future conflict between the superpowers, the prospect of disintegrating imperial empires, the economic vagaries of reconstruction, and a host of other concerns, a new set of international and transnational institutions emerged. These included the United Nations and the European Economic Community, which would serve as examples for other institutional developments. All of them are still new and weak relative to the nation-state. Nevertheless, it would prove a dreadful mistake for socialists and progressives to turn their backs on such transnational organizations.

No "socialist" institutions currently exist for the exercise of internationalism, and waiting for the "revolution" to bring them about is not a serious option. Only by making use of existing institutions is it possible to link the theory with the practice of internationalism. Socialists worked within the nation-state, and precisely insofar as the communist experience has shown the illegitimacy of identifying internationalist aspirations with any nation-state, so must they work within the new institutions—even when not of their making. An organization like the United Nations alone can adjudicate between conflicting national claims, and legitimate concerns regarding existing imbalances of power within it will not change that. Nor will existing transnational organizations simply disappear. The United Nations is currently involved in more peacekeeping efforts than ever before, and its other activities are too numerous to mention. Increasingly staffed by a professional bureaucracy with international commitments, no less than other transnational institutions, it now has a vested interest in expanding its power and distancing itself from democratic oversight. The political question for the next century is whether progressive forces will prove capable of fighting for their interests within the new international institutions and proposing ways to ensure their democratic accountability and commitment to economic justice.

Uncritical opposition to bureaucracy, whether launched from the speculative perspective of "bioregions" or still newer forms of transnational organization is unproductive. Peacekeeping missions like those of the United Nations in areas ranging from what was once Yugoslavia to Cambodia will still need armies, disaster relief will still need experts, and it will still remain necessary to deal with the rapacity of bourgeois interests within organizations like the European Union or a burgeoning Association of Southeast Asian Nations (ASEAN). Redressing global imbalances of wealth will ultimately call for bureaucratic agencies to regulate multinationals, assist in the settlement of Third World debt, and extend the most basic achievements of the welfare state to the international arena. Policies are necessary for placing international banks under public control, refinancing and democratizing organizations like the International Monetary Fund, forging innovative policies for coming to terms with changing migration patterns, ensuring transnational standards of health and safety, and confronting the ecological degradation of the planet. New transnational organizations will need to levy taxes, curb domestic capital flight, and come to grips with "unequal development" through capital transfers.

Economic and environmental reforms of global magnitude presuppose the political power to enforce them. And that will demand powerful international parties and unions. Especially given the increasing concentration and mobility of capital, which is occurring in concert with the intensification of competition and fragmentation among workers, those are the only reasonable organizational forms for pressing the common interests of the exploited and persecuted. A role obviously exists in this regard for various international environmental agencies as well as for Amnesty International and the Red Cross. Western progressives and socialists, however, must nonetheless begin to make the most of the new possibilities for forging transnational ties among themselves and linking up with democratic forces in the economically devastated regions no less than a host of emerging transnational interest groups like the global women's movement. In keeping with the activities begun in Seattle and carried on elsewhere, the left will either reorient its strategy or face an even harder road in the future.

That is the practical challenge. But it retains an ideological dimension. Nationalism, after all, remains the dominant ideology of our time, and the more interdependent the world, the more sensitive nations might become to one another's actions, and the greater the occasion for insecurity and conflict. The nation-state will not vanish. Vested bureaucracies have an interest in its perpetuation while its traditions and customs retain a sense of immediacy impossible to deny. Thus, if the ideological conflict between nationalism and internationalism will undoubtedly continue into the next century, it is necessary to draw the consequences.

Only federalism can offer the institutional form for a genuinely democratic internationalism. Its partisans must therefore prepare themselves for ongoing conflicts involving the separation of powers between various transnational organizations and national units. And the outcome is not certain. Internationalism projects a threat as well as a promise. Attacks on "foreigners" have escalated dramatically in Europe over the last twenty years, and just as serious is the palpable growth of a climate defined by intolerance, provincialism, and what Hitler's minions called "thinking with one's blood." Adapting to the new political environment of the next millennium is, indeed, not just an economic or organizational question but an existential one as well.

Pandering to the various identity claims of entrenched interests while "free riding" on the coattails of a burgeoning internationalist bureaucracy will only strengthen the forces of reaction. A new commitment to cosmopolitanism and international organizations has become necessary. There is a pressing need for ideas about how to employ the mass media and render accountable multinational information businesses. Even more than that, however, it is necessary to begin appropriating a set of forgotten traditions and an internationalist legacy that extends from Paine and Simón Bolívar to Goethe and Rosa Luxemburg to Martin Luther King and Dag Hammarskjöld. Democracy and socialism were both movements of the lowly and the insulted. Their purpose was to ensure institutionally that the voices of the forgotten would be heard and that the arbitrary exercise of power would be constrained. No less than conflicts within a state, conflicts between nations demand institutions for redressing grievances according to principles of reciprocity and the rule of law; indeed, whatever the justifications in theory, the refusal to support empowering such institutions will subvert in practice any equal recognition of diverse national claims.

Judging conflicting claims in a principled manner between an authoritarian form of organization committed to economic reforms and a capitalist dictatorship is, of course, relatively easy. That is also the case when a democratic movement confronts an equally democratic state with demands for independence as in the case of Scotland. A purely empirical or tactical judgment comes into play when neither side offers the prospect of either political democracy or economic reform. The ethical problem really arises only when a formally democratic regime confronts an authoritarian mass movement unwilling to divulge the form of government it ultimately seeks to institute as in the case of the Palestinians. Here, too, tactical matters enter the picture along with the degree of repression employed by the state. Nevertheless, in the new context, support for national claims will ultimately rest on the degree to which the institutions and the policies of any given movement or state converge with the empowerment of international institutions committed to the constriction of arbitrary power.

Internationalism is not reducible to any set of national claims or loyalties; it is a phenomenon sui generis. It is always predicated in practice on a judgment about how the support for any national actor will affect existing possibilities for the democratic organization of working people. And, from a socialist perspective, this only makes sense. It should have become apparent by now that the teleological vision of orthodox Marxism is no longer viable and that the authoritarian voluntarism of Leninism belongs in the dustbin of history. No longer is it sufficient to suggest that economic development is the precondition for republicanism; the time has come again to suggest that republicanism is the precondition for any meaningful notion of socialism.

Internationalism can reinvigorate both. For just as socialism originally sought to better conditions and enhance solidarity among the exploited, so can a new internationalist commitment speak to what will further socialist and democratic possibilities in the poorest of nations. But that will not occur automatically. Internationalism can stagnate and even assume reactionary forms. Economic and political superpowers can dominate the United Nations; the European Community can become a "Europe of the bosses"; transnational organizations in the Third World can become the playground of the "comprador bourgeoisie." Proposals to strengthen the World Court, expand the Security Council, empower the General Assembly are steps in the right direction. But they are not enough. Success in confronting both reactionary tendencies in the planetary arena and a rising tide of nationalism will depend not merely on a tepid pragmatism but on the commitment to a new internationalist idea.

17

NEOCONSERVATISM AND THE NEW RIGHT IN THE UNITED STATES AND ABROAD

RIGHT-WING EXTREMISM happens in waves. It splashes on the front page, receives ritual condemnation from the mass media, and then recedes from view. But it never disappears entirely: its frustrations and motivations are rooted in the contradictory legacy of modernity. Coming to terms with the phenomenon is particularly difficult, however, insofar as studies usually remain provincial and limited by narrow empirical assumptions. Numerous books have charted the rise of the new right in one country or another; articles have sought to explore the economic or tactical support given by one movement to the other. Pictures of bombings in Germany, rallies in France, desecration of cemeteries in Italy, racial strife in the United States, the cult of the samurai in Japan, the Nazi flag in South Africa decorate the covers of popular magazines and play on the lingering—if misguided—fear that tomorrow will prove a repeat of yesterday. Thus, the singularity of the new movement gets lost.

No less than any other mass movement of the twentieth century, neofascism has taken an international form. Not every nation, of course, must simultaneously evidence a strong neofascist movement or a rising conservative tide. With the increasing interdependence of the economy and mass media, however, it is becoming ever more important to understand how political developments are being refracted through a global prism. The problem is that progressives and socialists seem ever more fearful of making generalizations and dealing with international trends. Inhibitions of this sort only intensify the fragmentation fostered by the very systems they seek to contest. They also undermine the ability to develop a set of principled and coherent responses. New planetary conditions are taking shape as the new century dawns and keeping pace, while making sense of the past, demands a new and more radically internationalist vision.

This essay was first published in *Neonationalismus und Neokonservatismus: Sondierungen und Analysen*, ed. Michael Kessler et al. (Stauffenberg Verlag: Tübingen, 1997), 9–21.

*   *   *

Challenging the politics of the New Right initially calls for explaining how the forces of reaction rose from the dead. After all, when World War II came to an end, the dawn of socialism seemed on the horizon. The war had discredited fascism, and with the memories of past betrayal and compromise still fresh, conservatism was on the defensive. Economically, the free market seemed an anachronism; not unlike Leon Blum in France and Franklin Delano Roosevelt in the United States during the 1930s, by the 1950s Konrad Adenauer in Germany was using the state to build purchasing power, administer reforms, direct investment, regulate competition, and reconstruct a shattered continent. Politically, labor parties were recognized as important actors everywhere on the continent, collective bargaining was universally acknowledged, and Stalin wore the mantle of a war hero in the East. Socialism, in fact, dominated the intellectual scene as conservative commitments to elitism and various forms of traditionalism fell out of fashion.

A little more than a decade before the collapse of communism, however, the situation was already quite different. The mass mobilization of the 1960s had received a certain indirect establishmentarian expression in the electoral victories of John F. Kennedy and Willy Brandt. A burgeoning "eurocommunist" tendency was introducing a more modern, democratic, and flexible style of politics, while a romantic aura still surrounded the anti-imperialist struggles of the Third World. But this began to change by the middle of the next decade. President Jimmy Carter exemplified the same trend toward technocratic progressivism as Helmut Schmidt, while the deterioration of the Soviet Union under the Brezhnev regime was becoming ever more apparent. Young people were no longer looking for inspiration to the dottering authoritarians ruling China, and fewer were enamored of the revolutionary experiment in Cuba. Soon enough, the Sandinistas in Nicaragua and the FMLN in El Salvador would also fade as symbols of hope. The bipolar world of the postwar period dominated by the United States and the Soviet Union was passing into history. Transnational organizations like the United Nations and the European Community began assuming institutional power and, in conjunction with increasing immigration, threatening national forms of identity. The longing for security and community intensified even as they were disappearing.

As capitalism changed its face toward the end of the 1970s, shifting its emphasis from industrial products like steel to informational systems and computers, progressives were caught unawares. Traditional industrial jobs started to disappear, and if a minority of skilled workers benefited, the majority of unskilled workers did not. International competition became more pronounced as new production techniques were introduced, thereby generating demands by capital for a reduction in the welfare state even as ever more workers became reliant upon it. Resentment and uncertainty grew in response to these developments. A form of right-wing politics, delegitimated since the close of World War II, surfaced once again and gripped traditional right-wing constituencies: the atavistic sectors of the economy, the provincial communities once insulated from change, religious extremists, and malcontents on the fringes. But now, without any new or consistent ideological alternative posited on the left, even segments of the working class began to express their frustration by turning to the right. An increasingly small skilled labor force thus became pitted against the remainder whose members would bear the brunt of economic dislocation.

With the more radical visions of social democrats tempered by the cold war, with traditional communism appearing increasingly sclerotic, progressives were thrown on the defensive and suffered a host of drastic political setbacks. Trade unions in the United States declined and began suffering under a score of intense institutional attacks, of which the crushing of the air controllers' strike by Ronald Reagan, whose victory in 1980 capitalized on what Carter himself termed a "malaise," was only the most memorable. Poll taxes were introduced in England. Following his party's victory in 1980, and the sobering experience of capital flight on an unprecedented scale, François Mitterrand immediately transformed his ambitious politics of socialist reform into "austerity politics." Conservatives everywhere began a counterattack on the legacy of the Popular Front and the New Deal. An attempt was made to portray all forms of progressive social policy as futile, self-defeating, and ultimately opposed to the interests of the oppressed themselves. This rhetoric of reaction was indeed strikingly successful in its impact on the masses of voters.[1]

As the costs of the welfare state rose, particularly in America and England, capital fled the cities and the infrastructure fell into disrepair. An attack on the state and its regulatory functions, in short, was already under way as the "free market" ever more surely began to define the economic discourse. Conditions were created, especially in nations where tax codes were most regressive, for a reaction against the liberal or social democratic welfare state, while competition over jobs and the deterioration of established communities produced new demands for protectionism and immigration quotas. Everywhere this new context offered opportunities for employing nationalism, racism, and an assault on progressive values and policies in the political campaigns of the last decade.

Ronald Reagan certainly made the most of them. Jokes concerning his intellect and age by more progressive opponents betray nothing more than a vulgar resentment. His eight years in office led to a transformation of the American economic landscape comparable in effect to the change brought about by Roosevelt; it has now been estimated that 1 percent of the population garnered roughly 60 percent of the wealth produced during the 1980s. There was no "trickle down," and while the gross national product grew, the real wages of average people precipitously declined.[2] National growth soared, and income disparities widened. Cutbacks in state spending helped hasten an already decaying quality of life in the cities and among minorities. Strong evidence suggests that the majority of voters were less supportive of the austerity measures advocated by Reaganism than is generally assumed.[3] This provides an initial indication less of the cabals by some conspiratorial elite than of the lived reality of ideology and its ability to override material interests.

Ronald Reagan was charismatic and a man of enormous personal appeal. But his ideological success as president derived from his ability to unite the two dominant tendencies of American conservatism—the first committed to the free market and the second to social and religious ideals associated with "family values," which had for so long opposed each other. With its classical liberal emphasis on laissez-faire, and the protection of the individual against intrusions by the state, what C. B. Macpherson initially called "possessive individualism" appealed to the interests of big business and theoreticians of capitalism like Milton Friedman, but also to political libertarians like Senator Barry Goldwater, who headed the Republican presidential ticket in 1964. Its advocates previously lacked a mass base and were branded as elitists by supporters of the second tendency within American conservatism until its antistatist philosophy was seemingly justified by events. And, in fact, this second tendency had little to offer on the programmatic level. The populist tradition of conservative thinking harked back to the "Know-Nothing" movement of the nineteenth century. Steeped in anticommunism and fears of international conspiracy,[4] perhaps best exemplified by Joseph McCarthy during the late 1940s and early 1950s,[5] the tradition was nourished on contempt for the "Eastern establishment" and "Washington" politicians and, perhaps above all, what Norman Podhoretz termed the "adversary culture" of the 1960s.

Ronald Reagan fused these two forms of conservatism into a new "neoconservatism." It is, of course, true that state spending exploded under Reagan and his idea of "supply-side" economics was discredited even by important members of his own cabinet.[6] A disciple of the master, however, became a master in turn. And so, even while abandoning supply-side economics in favor of a balanced budget, Newt Gingrich adapted Reaganism to the 1990s. The result was a "Contract with America," which not only spurred the Republican congressional landslide of 1994,[7] but gave the party the high ground on policy and ideas.

Driven by perhaps the single salient concern upon which possessive individualists and populists can fully agree, hatred of bureaucracy, a political worldview took shape. It involved: (a) giving "government" back to the people and attacking "politicians"; (b) shrinking the state while proclaiming the virtues of a new nationalism; (c) combating "special interests" and attacking the new social movements; and (d) rejecting all forms of progressive ideology in the name of traditional values like "family" and "religion."

Ideology powered the "Reagan revolution." The welfare state was castigated as an example of "big government." Deregulation was undertaken in the name of the market. Affirmative action was attacked as an insult to American individualism and a form of "reverse racism." A new militarism was justified by crude nationalism. The assault on abortion was legitimated in terms of the family and religion. Nationalism and religious fundamentalism, an often overt racism and a form of economic Darwinism, and anti-intellectualism and elitism ultimately merged in a new neoconservative worldview. This right-wing ideological trend in the West, moreover, was only strengthened by events in the East—and vice versa. The world watched with joy as an authoritarian state crumbled. But, soon enough, a sense of national emergency combined with an intense anticommunist nationalism. Capitalist "shock therapy" and the abrupt introduction of market values were initially greeted with jubilation as any alternative bearing even the faintest connection with the communist past and the "left" stood discredited in the public eye. But the euphoria dissipated quickly as standards of living plummeted and the impact of an increasingly severe *identity deficit* gripped the masses.

Unfathomable economic collapse has generated a new siege mentality in many of the former communist states. Ultranationalism, ethnic provincialism, and religion rushed to fill the void. Preoccupied with conspiracy theories and the quest for scapegoats, which build on precisely the same assumptions about "us and them" formerly employed by the arch-reactionary Carl Schmitt, the quest for scapegoats combines with a certain nostalgia for the past. Reactionary values or concerns have been fanned by the Polish church,[8] anti-Semitism has become part of the mainstream discourse in Russia, dangerous trends exist in Hungary and Romania, and what has already been called an "anti-Russian apartheid" is taking shape in Latvia, Lithuania, and Estonia. Egoism and cynicism complement paranoia and xenophobia, and, in such a climate, the more liberal public sphere generated under Mikhail Gorbachev has lost its appeal. A climate of this sort always threatens civil liberties. It justifies the impatience with genuine republican institutions like competitive parties and an independent judiciary. A trend exists toward rule by decree and the plebiscite or "referendum." It is perhaps time to recall Charles de Gaulle and consider a new category, *authoritarian democracy*, for making sense of the former Soviet Union and other states as well.

*   *   *

The New Right is a unique phenomenon. A number of factors define it. If some show continuities with the past, others differentiate the new movement from its predecessors: (1) the context in which the New Right operates, whatever its connections with the past, is not that of the 1930s; (2) the New Right is not revolutionary and it projects a new style; (3) the New Right is often religious and culturally conservative; (4) the New Right is an international phenomenon; and (5) the New Right harbors a symbiotic attachment to establishmentarian conservatism.

The 1930s still weigh like a nightmare on the living. Understandably so. The last years have not been kind. Skinheads have desecrated hundreds of synagogues in Europe, racism remains a cancer in the United States, and "ethnic cleansing" in the former Yugoslavia elicits memories of an even darker time. Pogroms have been recorded in Romania. Street gangs recall the Brown Shirts elsewhere in Eastern Europe. The sentiments of those "scholars" who deny the Holocaust ever happened receives its silent echoes among certain sectors of the populace at large.[9] *The Protocols of the Elders of Zion* sells briskly not only in the Baltic states but also in the United States both among the extremist "militias" in the western part of the country and among supporters of the Nation of Islam in the ghettos of the inner cities.[10]

The new reactionaries still castigate declining "morals." They call for the constriction of civil liberties, the abolition of trade unions, and withdrawal from the United Nations. They inveigh against immigrants, employ homophobia as a weapon, and attack the separation between church and state. Their intolerance poisons the cultural atmosphere and undermines faith in "politicians" if not yet democratic government. There is indeed something generally legitimate about the claim of a French intellectual in 1994 that "it sometimes seems as if the extreme right holds a virtual monopoly on the definition of the nation."[11]

But we should not be misled. Political institutions are not the same either in the United States or the European Community as they were in Weimar. The labor movement no longer poses the same threat it once did, communism is dead, and cultural conditions have also changed. Roaming groups of thugs obviously remain dangerous especially when, in some cities, their assaults on immigrants are given tacit and sometimes even explicit support by the police and the populace. But current estimates are that hard-line advocates of the far right explicitly indebted to the prewar movements only number a few thousand, if that, in most nations of Western Europe. They constitute a lunatic fringe, without serious institutional influence, that is condemned from all sides.

The situation is somewhat different and perhaps more dangerous with the broader and more sophisticated neofascist parties. The Lega Lombardia of Italy has significant mass support in its home province.[12] That is only slightly less the case with the far cruder Vlaams Blok of Belgium. The Norwegian Progress Party and the Danish political organization of the same name both have received about 10 percent of the electoral vote. The German Republicans received two million votes in the European parliamentary elections of 1989 and, as the last decade of the century slowly comes to a close, the National Front of France has over 100,000 members, hundreds of elected officials, and a remarkably powerful bureaucratic and cultural apparatus.[13]

These are no longer the explicitly revolutionary grassroots mass parties of the interwar period. They lack the apocalyptic and hysterically anti-modernist ideology of their predecessors. They may cynically use the rednecks and neanderthals in the streets, but they will always disavow them later. Their neofascist leaders like Jean-Marie Le Pen and Jörg Haider may hold democracy in contempt, but they are willing to call themselves "republicans" or even "liberals" and refuse to endorse dictatorship. They are racists, but shy away from rigid ideological doctrines to support their views. They hate the masses, but smile when asked about "the leader principle." They seek radical change, but are neither explicitly revolutionary nor supported by paramilitary organizations. They oppose "politics," but seek to present themselves as politicians on a par with their more established conservative colleagues. In short, for want of a better term, they wish to present themselves as the representatives of what Bertram Gross originally called "friendly fascism."

These neofascist parties, at least for now, are content to play power broker. They may have no other choice. Little suggests that the extreme right can actually seize hold of a major European government. A greater danger is its potential impact on the respectable establishment. There are ways, of course, in which even liberal institutions can employ racism with an eye toward curtailing dissent.[14] But the more pressing problem is the influence organized and well-financed right-wing movements exert on mainstream conservative parties whose more reactionary factions actually helped legitimate the activities of the far right in the first place.

Max Weber was surely correct when he noted that ideology is not like a taxicab, which the driver can simply bring to a halt at any given corner. And the taxi has picked up speed. It travels faster when economic conditions grow worse. Deregulation and the market have brutalized everyday life,[15] and even if xenophobia is not reducible to economics, the anxiety generated by the one surely influences the other. Attacks on foreigners increased tenfold between 1990 and 1991 in the former East Germany where unemployment hovered near that of the Weimar Republic during the Great Depression. The new American bigotry directed against Japanese and other Asians, often legitimated by influential business leaders and major politicians from both parties, is similarly an expression of fear of Japanese economic might. It is no different with respect to the assaults on Pakistanis in London or the ongoing violent conflicts, heightened by competition over decreasing city services, between Jews and blacks in Brooklyn.

The New Right offers a vision. Racism or anti-Semitism or an anti-foreigner attitude is only part of the worldview, which extends to gays, lesbians, the "reds," and other nonconformists. The triumph of establishmentarian conservatism has fostered a climate conducive for those who would take its cultural and religious values to the extreme. Furthermore, without a coherent ideological alternative, the attraction of such values becomes all the greater. It is thus only logical that the Christian Coalition should have won roughly 40 percent of the local races in which it participated in 1992, took control of the Republican Party machine in a number of states, and put anti-gay legislation on the ballot in more than twenty states in 1994. Its support for religious teaching in public schools and Operation Rescue, the most militant antiabortion group, and for laws restricting the civil liberties of gays in Colorado, which have recently been overturned by the Supreme Court of the United States, have received national recognition.

Religious fundamentalism is a hallmark of the New Right. It is also perhaps the dominant ideological phenomenon of the age. Disdain for "secularism," "hedonism," "decadence," civil liberties, and the demarcation between church and state is common to the movement beyond the obvious differences among Christians and Moslems, Hindus and Jews. Religious fundamentalism is always a movement of the masses. But, just like the indirect connection existing between establishmentarian conservatism and the far right, it is also indirectly tied to developments occurring within traditional religious organizations. Islamic fundamentalism has become the dominant force in the southern parts of the former Soviet Union. Its attraction was strengthened by the continuing economic underdevelopment of the region, the decay of secular authority, the success of the revolution in Iran and the struggles against secularist waged in many parts of the Arab world. An increasingly conservative Catholic Church, which often served as the cultural and political locus of anticommunist resistance, has also received new legitimation in Eastern Europe. Conservative religious trends, in short, have mirrored political ones. They too have proved international in character.

The international dimension of the right-wing drift during the last decade was obvious given the victories of Reagan and Bush in the United States, Margaret Thatcher and John Major in England, Brian Mulroney in Canada, Kohl in Germany, and Shamir in Israel, and the success of Jacques Chirac in France and Kurt Waldheim in Austria. Nor is it an accident that with those victories, everywhere the extreme right gained momentum. The symbiotic connection between moderate and extreme parties of the right is nothing new. Karl Marx already noted it in historical works like *The Eighteenth Brumaire*. It was evident in Hungary in 1919, in Mussolini's March on Rome, and in the Weimar Republic. It was manifest in Chile, where Eduardo Frei and the Conservative Party paved the way for the coup by General Pinochet, and in Peru where Alberto Fujimori suspended the constitution and opted for "plebiscitory democracy." The conservative mainstream has never had clean hands when it comes to the more extreme elements of the New Right. Bitburg increased the self-confidence of more extreme anti-Semitic groups. Likud policy justifies the dogmatism of the far right in Israel as well as the worst terrorists among the Palestinians. Waldheim certainly didn't detract from Haider. The demagoguery of national figures like Pat Buchanan and Pat Robertson has surely helped foster the ideological fantasies of groups still further on the right like the militias whose members have engaged in terroristic bombings, such as the one which shook Oklahoma City, in their war on the federal government.

Meanwhile, in France, once respectable figures like Giscard d'Estaing of the moderate Union pour la Démocratie Francaise began speaking of an Arab "invasion," while Jacques Chirac decried the "smell" stemming from an "overdose" of immigrants. Both obviously sought to cut into the strength of Le Pen.[16]

Political figures who once stood in support of strengthening the European Community now, ever more frequently, also employ organicist notions of integral nationalism and the *Volk* to denounce its supposedly imperializing ambitions. The rising conservative preoccupation in Germany with insulating the present *Volkstaat* from the Nazi past, attempts to exclude the children of Moroccan parents from French citizenship by supplanting the "law of the soil" with the "law of blood," and the racist immigration policy advocated by the English Tories are merely more sophisticated expressions of what might appear as a rising neofascist tide. This is, again, not to say that Giscard is the "twin brother" of Le Pen or Schoenhuber. Equating mainstream conservatism with a rabble-rousing right-wing extremism is a serious error.[17] Nevertheless, when dealing with either, principled opposition is not merely a moral imperative but a practical one as well.

* * *

Even though disaffection with the conservatism of the 1980s and 1990s is becoming apparent, the left is still fighting within the parameters set by the other side. The result is not merely on issues but on the principles and ethos that are the left's raison d'etre. Moderate progressives now treat issues of immigration gingerly as they rush to embrace protectionism, "welfare reform," and a host of issues important to people of color. A new cosmopolitan attitude is emphasized less by the labor movement than by representatives of multinational corporations. Indeed, the left has grown more cautious as the right has grown more bold.

Empowerment of the "other," of the immigrant, is the only way to guarantee the recognition of his or her civil rights. The left must therefore take the lead, following the Report of the European Parliament's Commitee of Inquiry into Racism and Xenophobia, in demanding that the right to vote be accorded to resident nonnationals. It must insist upon legislation making the violation of civil rights a crime—as in the United States—rather than preoccupying itself with narrowing the grounds for asylum in order to placate the elements of reaction. A regional charter for nonresidents, in the same vein, is necessary to complement the charter on social rights, and the left must bring the pressure of international organizations to bear upon those who would, through violence and hate-mongering, deny the fundamental premises of the liberal state to any given group, just as it must call upon those same institutions to direct investment to areas with high immigrant populations in order to equalize conditions of employment.

Times have changed; society has changed; the working class has changed; the new social movements are no longer quite so new. What has not changed, however, is the fact that conservative politicians have always been better than progressives at pursuing conservative aims. Confronting the extreme right today calls for contesting establishmentarian conservatism and religious dogmatism, which means breathing new life into the values associated with the great undertakings of the past; softening the whip of the market through a commitment to economic justice and the social welfare state; reaffirming the separation of church and state; rendering political *and* economic institutions democratically accountable; and tempering nationalist ambitions and provincial ideologies through a still unrealized internationalist vision.

But there is still too much timidity with respect to religious institutions. There is still too much talk about "community,"[18] and for what Richard Rorty has approvingly termed "ethno-solidarity." The ability to deal rationally with immigration and a host of other issues vanishes when leftists begin to think with what are traditionally categories of the right. Fears concerning the loss of identity and community will fester with the growing interdependence of national economies and power of transnational organizations. But progressives can no longer afford the luxury of embracing values from the right. Without a response to the current ideological malaise—emphasis on a reinvigorated public sphere, an interventionist state, and a cosmopolitan worldview for the young people of tomorrow—the future will darken and the forces of good will grow ever weaker. But, of course, none of this is certain. The future is open, and we must keep it so.

18

THE END OF HISTORY REVISITED

For Christian Fenner

"THE END OF HISTORY" itself has a history. Hegel employed the term to demarcate a unity between subject and object in which each might recognize the freedom bequeathed by the new state institutions of what might today be considered a constitutional monarchy. Marx understood the end of history—or better the end of "prehistory"—in terms of a new society in which the "invisible hand" of Adam Smith does not rule and in which meaningful decisions are not made "behind the back" of the people, but transparently by a community of individuals without reference to class interests. The most recent articulation of this idea by Francis Fukuyama, a graduate of Harvard University who worked for the State Department, caused quite a stir when it was published in the early 1990s, and my critical appraisal of it informed the last chapter of *Moments of Decision: Political History and the Crisis of Radicalism* (1992).

As far as I was concerned, with regard to my own participation in the discussion, that ended the matter. But the idea lingered. It remained the backdrop, the unspoken assumption, underpinning many important controversies including the attempt by thinkers like Ulrich Beck and Anthony Giddens to move "beyond left and right." The slick transformation of "the end of history" into the new slogan that "there is no alternative" to the forces of globalization, which was first preached by Margaret Thatcher in dismantling the English welfare state, justifies some fresh reflections on the topic.

The old ideologies had seemingly fallen by the wayside when the new version of "the end of history" first made its appearance. Fascism stood discredited, communism was tumbling, the spirit of the 1960s had waned, and only the classical liberal idea was left standing. Belief in its fusion of free markets with representative democracy, so disparaged during the 1930s, stood at its zenith. The *New York Times*, in fact, presented the cover of its

---

This text served as the basis of a talk given at the University of Leipzig on 7 June 2001.

Sunday magazine section with a picture of Fukuyama leaning on a globe: I said, at the time, that this idea was ideologically far more important than what had become an institutionalized and domesticated postmodernist assault upon universal values and "totalizing" perspectives.

Fukuyama was less interested in offering a "deconstruction" of current trends than a "grand narrative"—though one tinged with a certain post-modern pessimism—of his own. And his assertions were bold. He argued that the great battles for the future of humanity had now been decided on the basis of three propositions: (1) that the idea of freedom must now, finally, be seen as realizing itself through the planetary acceptance of liberal democratic institutions; (2) that this acceptance has resulted in a growing "common marketization" of international relations; and (3) that this common marketization is gradually eliminating the possibility of war. It is important to recall that his thesis became popular amid the triumphal cele-brations over the fall of communism by Margaret Thatcher, Ronald Reagan, and George H. W. Bush. In contrast to them and their ideologists, however, Fukuyama did not see a "thousand points of light" or a bright and open future. Instead, following Hegel and Nietzsche, he insisted that the collapse of utopian visions would result in a society increasingly defined by narrow economic calculation and self-indulgent consumerism combined with a loss of greatness and and a decline in the level of cultural produc-tion. Or, as Fukuyama put it, a "sad time" in which "daring, courage, imag-ination, and idealism" retreat in favor of the endless solving of technical problems.

Critics of this position like Samuel Huntington would argue later in *The Clash of Civilization and the Remaking of the World Order* (1994) that culture determines how and whether a country will embrace capitalism and democracy. Or putting it another way, since the chief world-wide antago-nism supposedly exists between the West and Islam, religious divisions of times past will determine future conflicts. And these will be of monumental proportions. The claims of Huntington indeed receive superficial justifica-tion from the attack on the World Trade Center and the Pentagon on September 11, 2001. These Islamic terrorists can be seen as part of a transna-tional conspiracy headed by Osama bin Laden whose ideology, in turn, reflects that of an equally transnational and militant Islamic Brotherhood with real power in any number of nations. There is some truth in asserting that the international character of the conflict ultimately proves crucial in contesting the "end of history." But it would feed into the worst ideological biases to identify the fanatics and the Wahabbi sect with a great religion and ignore the existence of democratic forces in the Middle East and the Arab World. Legitimate criticisms of the imperial policies undertaken by the United States and Israel, no less than global capitalism, can be launched from a secular and progressive stance as easily as from the standpoint of religious fundamentalism. There are tensions between those with secular and democratic yearnings as against those with fundamentalist and antidemocratic attitudes in virtually all the nations and movements of the Middle East and the Arab World. In this vein, with respect to the "end of history" and the "clash of civilizations," progressive intellectuals must draw the appropriate distinctions.

Liberty is not a western privilege and a republican state with a modern economy remains the goal of all progressive forces with any mass base. That new anti-modern concerns with ethnic and religious identity have emerged in response to the march of modernity should come as no surprise. Such criticisms do not strike at the heart of the thesis concerning "the end of history." It is a question of engaging the argument immanently. Most critics, however, are basically content to note that (1) history will continue and conflict will not disappear; (2) most states are still nondemocratic; (3) poverty is still rampant; and (4) wars remain common and "ideological wars"—inspired by national, ethnic, or religious claims—remain the most common and brutal of all. These are the criticisms of "common sense," and those forwarding them, I think, make it too easy for themselves.

History will obviously continue and conflict will, undoubtedly, not disappear. But the question concerns whether a new phase of history is looming on the horizon, a phase as different as capitalism was from feudalism, as well as the terms in which new conflicts will be framed. It is also clearly the case that most nations now attempt to legitimate their institutions and justify their policies by making reference to the language of democracy and that it has become common among political scientists to speak about a shift from the exercise of "political" to "economic" power in foreign relations. As far as war is concerned, of course, Hegel was far less sanguine than Fukuyama: he identified the "end of history" with the rise of a particular state form, constitutional monarchy, whose ability to adjudicate "ideological" and material differences might, he believed, actually produce more wars than in previous times since nation-states would become ever more obsessed with securing recognition and a sense of unique identity. If Fukuyama is clearer about the extent to which war becomes unlikely between democratic regimes, and imperialist claims along with the resort to force are increasingly subjected to criticism in the public sphere, he retains the basic point of Hegel's argument, namely, that the "end of history" is predicated on the introduction of the *idea* of a liberal capitalist state rather than its empirical realization everywhere on the planet.

Confronting the *idea* of the "end of history" immanently therefore requires a different, more speculative, approach. A number of questions deserve consideration. It is, first of all, necessary to ask whether democracy is coterminous with the liberal state: democracy is a complex phenomenon and there may be ways of deepening it and changing how it is currently understood. There is also the question of whether instrumental calculation has, in fact, proved triumphant and economics has conquered politics. Most important, however, is whether the multidimensional understanding idea of freedom—incarnated in the great mass movements of the past and most fully expressed in the tradition of philosophical idealism—has been realized in the modern liberal capitalist state and the free global market.

With respect to the first issue, in my opinion, two matters are of importance. First, while all genuinely democratic regimes provide formal rights to the disadvantaged and exploited, it is crucial to remember that some do so more and better than others. Or, to put it another way, *qualitative* rather than merely *quantitative* differences exist between democracies employing proportional representation like Sweden and others resting upon single-member districts and a "winner take all" electoral system in the United States. New forms of "authoritarian democracy" have emerged in formerly communist nations or what in Pakistan is now called "guided democracy," and constitutions and democratic trappings are regularly employed to hide profoundly undemocratic policies in nations like the Iranian "republic." Unrealized possibilities also exist for integrating more direct forms of participation, borrowed from experiences like the "soviet" or the New England town meeting, into a republican institutional structure. All these matters influence the meaning of democracy no less than the extent to which its values are propagated within civil society. Talk about "democracy" can, in short, evidence a degree of indeterminacy that makes it possible for elites to hide the ways in which they exercise their power no less than the limits on the disadvantaged in organizing themselves and articulating their interests.

Democracy is not simply a matter of civil liberties or purely formal freedoms. This was made clear in the Weimar Republic, also known as the "republic without republicans," whose democratic institutions were marked by a profoundly reactionary and anti-democratic "public sphere" and civil society no less than in the American South where, prior to the civil rights movement, the existence of civil liberties and democratic organizations on the national level had little local impact upon the life of black citizens. Civil liberties and republican institutions may be necessary for democracy, but they are not sufficient to ensure its continued existence or its everyday practice. There is nothing new about the claim that republican institutions are the precondition for any further extension of democracy into civil society: this was the view underpinning all the major thinkers of the continental labor movement from Eduard Bernstein to Rosa Luxemburg. The question is whether the republican state is understood as *both* the necessary *and* the sufficient determination of democracy.

If the answer were affirmative, then it would probably make the most sense to identify "the end of history" with the introduction of the American Constitution forged during what R. R. Palmer termed "the age of democratic revolution." Hegel would have been right, and, in the context of the United States, the same might be said for Louis Hartz. His classic work, *The Liberal Tradition in America* (1955), did not merely claim that "American exceptionalism" and the stability of its democracy derived from the lack of a feudal tradition. It also begged the Hegelian question regarding the "end of history": the fact is that no serious movement in American history—including the confederacy during the Civil War, the labor movement in the following decades, and the new social movements of the 1960s—was preoccupied with forging a "political" alternative to the institutional arrangement provided in the Constitution. It was as if the Constitution provided the undisputed political framework through which particular social demands for inclusion by the excluded and economic equality for the disadvantaged could be articulated. Nevertheless, it is also the case that the fight for political inclusion and economic equality fundamentally changed both the meaning and the exercise of democracy.

Marx had already made the point in *The Jewish Question, The Holy Family*, and other works from his early period. There he noted how the notion of democracy was truncated when left at the purely political level: liberty, equality, and fraternity incarnated in the republican state under the rule of law could still coexist with the necessity of market imperatives, inequality, and the unqualified pursuit of self-interest in the realm of civil society. The question for him was whether history had really come to an end in the constitutional state, which received its philosophical articulation in the philosophy of Hegel, or whether history—as the process identifiable with the realization of freedom—remained unfinished, and the bourgeois ideal of "political emancipation" only paved the way for a new form of "human emancipation" that would presumably result in a more radically democratic "free association of producers." The young Marx framed the issue poorly, not merely because he never articulated an institutional alternative to either the distributive mechanisms embodied in the market or the republic, but because his "radical critique of everything existing" undercut the *meaning* behind the struggles associated with political liberty and the exercise of democracy itself.

Hannah Arendt, among others, was correct in suggesting that the bureaucratic institutions associated with representative democracy distorted the democratic idea: she called for more participation and, most important, the exercise of democracy in everyday life at the local level. There is also surely a point in considering the need for integrating institutions like the town meeting or the soviet into the republican state, though the belief that "the people" will actually want to participate in endless meetings after work is, in my opinion, somewhat far-fetched. Far more important is to highlight what Arendt ignores: the way in which attempts to constrain the intervention of republican states into the economic realm have, historically, been connected with attempts to constrain the development of an organized democratic politics from below. This first became clear with respect to the policies embraced by so many conservatives and liberals opposed to the European labor movement in which, during the late nineteenth and early twentieth centuries, socialist parties sought to link the universal democratic demands associated with republicanism and the particular demands of a disenfranchised and disadvantaged proletariat. It also becomes evident in the coordinated assault upon the 1960s, which usually means *both* the new social movements intent upon expanding the boundaries of political partic- ipation *and* the radical programs generated during this time, by conserva- tives in the United States. It is obvious in the response most governments have accorded the floating demonstrations and—albeit often inchoate— demands of the "teamsters and turtles" against unfettered globalization and the market-oriented *and* antidemocratic policies of the World Trade Organization.

The critique of the market has always depended upon the *political* act of substituting ethical norms for market imperatives. In this vein, it only makes sense that those defending the market should attempt to subordi- nate "political" interests in economic justice and the public accountability of business to "economic" calculation in the name of efficiency and prof- itable investment. This idea did not arise with Fukuyama or the thinkers who would move "beyond" left and right. It is as old as liberalism itself: it is the hidden dream lurking in *The Wealth of Nations* by Adam Smith and it is articulated clearly in the Model Treaty for the Continental Congress of 1776, drafted by John Adams, which projected a world bound by commerce and devoid of traditional military and political alliances. But this general thesis ignores both the way in which economic policies have a political impact and the way in which politics itself is often necessary in order to introduce new economic priorities. Martin Luther King Jr. knew this: it was why the civil rights movement, which first sought the vote for poor blacks along with an end to social discrimination, served as the precondition for the Poor People's Movement. The political impact of economic policies is indeed greatest on the most disadvantaged: economic policies affect the time they can devote to political affairs, their ability to organize, and the confidence with which they can pursue their interests. The choice of economic policy is therefore always a political choice, or, at a minimum, it retains a political dimension.

Economic policy is not simply reducible to politics, of course, but it is a crucial determinant for the legitimacy of democratic political systems. Altering the existing economic state of affairs is again, by contrast, a polit- ical project. The inequities produced by capitalism and globalization can be contested with the most divergent means by fascists and religious funda- mentalists as well as by socialists and progressives. Few positive proposals of a cosmopolitan sort have been forthcoming from either side, however, for dealing with the economic ambitions of multinational corporations. Globalization and the general assault on the welfare state suggest that even in terms of a Hegelian "idea," in contrast to the republican state, there is no serious commitment to end economic inequality even by most contempo- rary liberals or neoliberals. When the claim concerning the "end of history" turns into the belief that "there is no alternative" to the unfettered reign of the free markets, and that political action by states or organizations is futile, political implications follow.

It makes a *qualitative* difference for the meaning of democracy whether there is free child care, a shorter workweek, and higher wages. Or, perhaps I can put the matter more bluntly: the proletariat of old might have vanished as *the* progressive force for political change, and in terms of its dominant role in the production process, but capitalism still exists and capital retains the upper hand. Employment still depends on investment, and investment still depends on the prospect of a satisfactory rate of profit. Should labor make "exorbitant" demands, capital can still either disinvest or move elsewhere. There is indeed an ideological dimension, quite traditional, in the claim that the "end of history" has arrived and that "there is no alternative": this dimension manifests itself not merely in the sense that such slogans implicitly stabilize the "free market," but—just as important—the priorities generated by the capitalist production process.

There is no reason to believe that the "booms" and "busts" of the business cycle have somehow been vanquished or that a new world depression is impossible: Simply refusing to entertain such a possibility, or hold capital publicly accountable for its investment decisions not only perpetuates the dependence of workers and the broader public on capital, but constrains the notion of autonomy, or freedom, usually associated with the idea of the "end of history." Indeed, when it comes to the welfare state, economic priorities are actually quite flexible and they are subject to political pressure. Suggesting that economics—and always economics of a particular sort—has supplanted politics essentially eradicates the sole hope of those suffering from the inequities of the existing system. Thus, when a recent cover of *The Economist* (16–22 June 2001) asked "does inequality matter?" the answer was already transparent: a new "golden age of philanthropy may be dawning" if the wealthy, who increasingly constitute "a force for the good," can "hang on to their money."

What a government excludes from taxation defines the beneficiaries of government policy as much as the choice of programs on which money is spent. While it is usually taken for granted that working people should accept cuts in wages and services for the greater good of the "economy," or in the "national interest," it is rarely suggested that capital should satisfy itself with a slightly smaller rate of profit. Furthermore, interestingly enough, the same conservatives who so devoutly condemn state intervention with respect to welfare policies are usually the same people who support state intervention when it comes to increasing the military budget, building new prisons, and strengthening the police. Their vaunted emphasis upon individual responsibility in terms of dealing with the market also turns into its opposite when it comes to abortion, drugs, suicide, and the like. The hypocrisy here is staggering: the "free market" is not "free" at all, and there are real *political* battles to be fought with normative implications over the social priorities of economic policy.

Distinctions between "left and right" come into play here as surely as they come into play when differentiating between the threes of intolerance and the forces of liberty. These distinctions highlight normative differences over questions of economic justice, the lingering conflict between "the political economy of capital" and the "political economy of labor," no less than the importance of given traditions. and the possibilities for extending democracy. Even if mainstream politicians are seeking to jettison ideological differences in their race to capture the small segment of the population known as the "center," without these categories, it becomes impossible for the public to judge policy in normative terms. The attempted abolition of "left and right" thereby feeds into the resigned belief that "there is no alternative." Thus "the end of history" along with its attendant notions turns into little more than a particularly crude elite ideology intent on securing the compliance of working people and the poor.

Confronting "the end of history" along with its political implications ultimately involves contesting the basic assumption that freedom has exhausted itself. By freedom is meant, of course, not simply personal freedom, or the freedom identified with consumer choices or personal relationships, but the notion of freedom associated with the ideals generated by the great progressive movements of the past: Jürgen Habermas once said, in this respect, that the only ideal still in need of fulfillment is democracy. As usual, though he was not directly involved in the debate over "the end of history," Habermas got to the crux of the issue. Are there any ideals other than "democracy" potentially capable of inspiring future forms of progressive political action? I believe, in contrast to Habermas, that there are.

Aside from economic equality, a goal irreducible to democracy and irrelevant to any number of genuine democrats informed by belief in laissez-faire like Milton Friedman or Friedrich von Hayek or Ludwig von Mises, there is another ideal that has been virtually forgotten by political theory: internationalism. There is something ironic about the way in which the standing of internationalism has changed. Once the special province of the labor movement of the late nineteenth and early twentieth centuries, institutionally, internationalism received its expression in three "proletarian" internationals, all of which were incapable of imposing real sanctions on the pursuit of purely national interests by their dominant participants. Today, by contrast, "bourgeois" transnational institutions have emerged with enlarged capacities for ensuring compliance on the part of member states, even while an obvious *legitimation deficit* looms on the ideological level. Internationalism was, in this same vein, previously a cherished value of every progressive. Now many on the left condemn it as "abstract" in the name of ethnic, national, and religious loyalties that previously served the right. Nevertheless this reversal of fortune offers new opportunities.

The material possibilities for pursuing a new internationalist politics are, indeed, perhaps greater than ever before. Transnational institutions are coalescing everywhere. Organizations like the United Nations, the European Community, and others are generating new and vast bureaucracies whose members will increasingly evidence transnational loyalty to their institutions. The state is no longer the only autonomous unit capable of making political decisions, which is evident not merely in the "human rights" efforts undertaken by the United Nations in so many areas of the globe, but in the growing tendency to place human rights over outmoded notions of "national self-determination." Institutionally, moreover, there has been a virtual explosion of international organizations and social movements with particular interests and concerns like "Doctors without Borders" or the meetings and activities associated with what might be termed a global women's movement. Transnationalism has also indeed, organizationally masked both the new religious terrorists and their fundamentalist mass base as surely as the secular responses to them.

Capitalism has also now for the first time become a planetary enterprise, and globalization is creating a new transnational managerial class capable of maximizing the opportunities provided by the new mobility of capital. Culture, too, is becoming a planetary commodity: movie stars, blockbuster films, popular music, and even television shows must increasingly pay their way by appealing to a world market. They are breaking down national boundaries and calling insular cultural understandings into question as surely as the new and cheaper possibilities for travel, the waves of immigration strengthened on the continent by the collapse of communism, and the new tolerance for intermarriage and what has been called "hybridity." New scientific developments in gene technology and space travel, and various other fields, are shaking the foundations of traditionalism. The assault from "the outside," so to speak, is reflected in a growing individualist response to the past—an eclectic sense of "pick and choose" among the dogmas and rites of, say, Catholicism—that would have been unimaginable in a genuinely traditional order. Traditionalism is increasingly becoming defined by modernity. Tolerance for the "other" is, by the same token, combining with a new willingness to integrate elements of differing traditions into more encompassing perspectives. What I termed in *Ideas in Action: Political Tradition in the Twentieth Century* (1999) a new "cosmopolitan sensibility" is beginning to receive greater expression in intellectual and even daily life.

All of these trends, of course, can foster confusion, unease, and, in more extreme cases, what Émile Durkheim termed "anomie." In this way, paradoxically, they can actually strengthen the retreat into established, if atavistic, forms of ethnic, national, and religious identification especially among the more economically underdeveloped segments of the society and among organizations with vested interests in perpetuating the past. The rise of religious fundamentalism precisely in a period marked by globalization with its assault on fixed and inherited forms of identity is no accident. The same can be said with respect to the rise in anti-immigrant hysteria especially given the growing inequities of wealth, the discrediting of the welfare state, and the general economic insecurity among working people produced by globalization. Even fascism, whose new forms conveniently blend a "yuppie" enthusiasm for the free market and "national pride" with aggressive assaults on immigration, has risen from the dead in Austria, France, Italy, and Switzerland.

Progressive political parties still tremble in the face of threats by capital to disinvest and respond "pragmatically" by counseling their members to accept cuts in welfare and public accountability. Trade unions have, by the same token, found it difficult to organize internationally for any number of reasons including their own refusal to employ "ideology." The inability of the new international institutions to secure an emotional loyalty on the part of citizens, counter the claim that they simply offer new layers of bureaucracy, and generate a sense of the cultural opportunities and obligations of global citizenship can be seen in a similar light. There is a lingering fear that transnational institutions can easily buttress a new world of global exploitation.

All of this having been said, however, environmental and economic and political problems are increasingly taking a planetary form. The imperatives of globalization will not vanish, and, if the left wishes to reconstitute itself both ideologically and organizationally, it must begin thinking more deeply about engaging in a planetary approach. Globalization should, in this regard, not be equated with internationalism: the latter is indeed the *alternative* to the former. Internationalism rests on political democracy and the public accountability of capital while globalization is driven by economic imperatives and informed by market imperatives. Only a *political* response can oppose the planetary ambitions of multinational corporations, some richer and more powerful than most states, whose increased mobility in the transnational arena makes it possible for them to play off increasingly immobile national labor forces in new ways. Nevertheless, the pursuit of a genuinely internationalist politics requires a fundamental change of cultural and existential perspective.

Philosophers like Martin Heidegger and Hannah Arendt, whose intellectual traditions are neither liberal nor socialist, have sought to understand the existential impact of "the world." But that is not the case with most contemporary thinkers on the left. There is still far too much romantic nostalgia for "tradition" and the wringing of hands over the dangers of modern life. This should be left to the partisans of the right. The left should embrace the new and the new can indeed be gleaned by making reference to the past. Just as the nation-state changed the existential horizons of individuals with respect to the primacy they once accorded their cities and towns so can, in similar fashion, a new planetary perspective transform the experiences of individuals shaped by provincial understandings of nation, ethnicity, and religion. Highlighting the emergence of a new cosmopolitan sensibility concerned less with the particular experience of any group than the cultural possibilities generated by new conditions of planetary life does not imply some belief that national loyalties or more local customs will simply disappear. It merely suggests the possibility that their standing can change just as the standing of painting changed with the introduction of photography and photography through the invention of film. It demands only the willingness to recognize that a new constellation of experience is looming on the horizon.

Describing and analyzing the cultural implications of this cosmopolitan sensibility should be left to other books at other times. With respect to this book at this time, however, it is sufficient to note that even cosmopolitan can easily become domesticated by globalization unless it is connected to the quest for economic equality, political democracy, and viable international institutions. There is nothing new about these goals and there is, perhaps, little drama in developing the policies and supporting the reforms requisite to furthering their realization. So long as they remain unrealized, however, it is the worst form of arrogance to speak about the "end of history" or a world "beyond" left and right in which "there is no alternative." New moments of decision still confront us, and, whatever the outrages and defeats of the present, history continues to suggest that the triumph of those who would freeze time or turn back the clock will also pass. That is why it still makes sense to say: the future is not over, indeed, it has barely begun.

APPENDIX

AN INTERVIEW
WITH STEPHEN ERIC BRONNER

Conducted by Michael J. Thompson

THE SUMMER OF 1999 saw the publication of Stephen Eric Bronner's latest book of political theory and intellectual history, *Ideas in Action: Political Tradition in the Twentieth Century*. A new edition of his *Socialism Unbound* will appear next year. Bronner has been instrumental in synthesizing democratic theory and critical theory with the theory of socialism. In so doing, he has renewed the link between theory and practice, rekindled the debate between freedom and necessity, and paved new directions for political action and commitment on the left. He is, at present, professor of political science and comparative literature at Rutgers University in New Brunswick. The following interview was conducted on the evening of 25 November 1999 at the author's home in New York City.

Q: *You say in your book that the idea of political tradition "presupposes a particular standpoint for explaining reality and the manner in which it is constituted." What gives social democracy, or liberalism in general, validity or ethical primacy over other traditions?*

A: I think there are many ways to talk about this. It is possible to construct some kind of philosophic foundation, such as an ontological foundation, or even make reference to the supposed certainty of science. But I think that the primacy of the liberal-socialist, or libertarian socialist, view is actually very simple: it stems from the primacy of its commitment to constrain the arbitrary exercise of power. This is the precondition for expanding the realm of subjective experience, and I think this was the fundamental aim of liberalism from the beginning. What is arbitrary? It can be debated meta-

This interview was published in the millennium issue of *Democratic Left* 28, no. 3 (December 1999).

physically forever. In political terms, however, most people understand the dangers of arbitrary power: this kind of power is exercised when one group of citizens receives unjust privilege or another one is picked out for punishment, exclusion, or domination by another group. What is not arbitrary? I think we can begin to answer the question by thinking about laws that treat citizens equally and render institutions accountable to their judgments. I would even claim that the extent to which arbitrary power is exercised is the extent to which terror reigns. In any event, with respect to socialists and progressives, it seems to me that the principle political aim is to make the state and other unaccountable social institutions, like capital, ever more accountable to the public.

Q: *How does that differ from the neoconservative argument?*

A: Liberalism and conservatism both start from the assumption that property is something that simply belongs to the individual and that no public accountability is necessary whereas socialists understand capital as an institution like any other, if often more powerful, and therefore just as susceptible to the demands of accountability.

Q: *If democratic theory has become "neutral" and has not given impetus to progressive movements in recent years, to what would you attribute this failure: is it inherent in the logic of democratic theory or in the manner it has been executed?*

A: There is a sense in which democratic theory was domesticated from the beginning and, if I can say this directly, it served as a kind of safe haven into which people with more radical positions could retreat and find shelter during the 1980s and 1990s. There was a time when democratic theory meant something radical—this was during the '60s and '70s when people like Philip Green and Christian Bay talked about democratic theory and attempted to connect its principal idea of participation with a burgeoning movement. With the emphasis upon discourse ethics, and the introduction of the most esoteric issues, this concern has simply fallen by the wayside. Democratic theory has come to mean everything possible to any number of different people. It poses no threat because it provides a form of artificial harmony between opposing ideas. The follower of Milton Friedman can view himself as a student of democratic theory as surely as a follower of Michael Harrington: democratic theory has become the best way to make an academic career because it seeks consensus and threatens no one. As far as I am concerned, if one wishes to speak about democracy, then it is necessary to begin with ideas concerning capitalism and class. Of course, these are notably missing from the more popular expressions of democratic theory.

Q: *How do you see the legacy of the '60s and the triumph of identity politics?*

A: Many crucial cultural gains have obviously been made since the decline of the civil rights movement and the anti-war movement. At the same time, however, the economic and political power of working people has radically declined. One of the reasons, though it is arguably less important than the ferocity with which conservatives went on the attack, is the rise of identity politics. This form of politics obscures class divisions within and between groups even as it tends to substitute symbolic for institutional power. This is a complicated question, but I will try to be clear. Different identity groups provide different possibilities of community for different individuals: the need for belonging by women, gays, and other minorities is as real as the need for white men to understand their experiences of oppression. But it is still the case that the power that capital exerts depends upon the degree of ideological and organizational disunity among workers. So, if the aim is to contest capital, it is necessary to introduce a standpoint that can identify what is common to working people within each of the new social movements, but privileges none. This, I believe, is the conceptual way to begin.

Q: *Is this your category of the "class ideal"?*

A: Yes. Its purpose is to provide some criterion for what constitutes class action. It also attempts, conceptually, to link theory with practice. The class ideal becomes translated by the work of people within the new social movements to generate common interests and a common program: nothing is more vain than simply to articulate demands in the abstract that should unify everyone. Under any circumstances, I don't think that democratic theory can provide this type of criterion for class action, at least not as it's now constituted.

Q: *You speak of the need to make the connection between democracy and socialism "explicit." What is the connection? Is it purely political, or more in the domain of political economy?*

A: Well, I think that the connection resides within the ideals embraced by socialist movements with a genuine working-class constituency: the most striking fact about the communist tradition, of course, is precisely that its revolutions were not made by a majority of the working class. As for the reason why this connection between socialism and democracy should be made explicit: ever since 1917 socialism has been tainted by what Marx might have called "equality under despotism." Its color was gray and its demand was for conformism. With respect to social democracy, especially now, the problem is less its commitment to economic reform than the abdication of that commitment. Socialists must come to terms with all this and move beyond this; that is why I titled one of my books *Socialism Unbound*. The socialist movement, when it was a workers' movement, always saw its enterprise as standing in direct connection with the political heritage of the Enlightenment. The step it made was to connect internationalism and republicanism with the commitment to economic justice.

Q: *"Genuine critique," you argue, "is the product of an ethical decision. It requires resisting a complete capitulation of what should be* to what is.*" Since the left has no monopoly on ethics, what are the ethics of socialism grounded upon that distinguishes it as a tradition?*

A: Originally the allure of Marxism rested on its ability, "objectively," to guarantee the creation of a new world. At the beginning of the twentieth century, as one prominent leader of the labor movement stated, "We can see the socialist future appearing at present." In trying to explain the popularity of the doctrine, in other words, I would suggest that workers embraced it because it seemed to be true: between 1889 and 1914, when the great socialist labor parties were on the rise, they could literally see the connection between an ideal and the way it was being realized. In Germany around 1875, there were about 30,000 organized Marxist workers and, by 1912, there were over four million. This was the case, more or less, throughout Europe: any working-class person could say, well, capitalism is indeed creating its gravediggers. What could once be understood in terms of "science," however, has become nothing more than a belief. History has lost its guarantees, and to suggest that things *might* yet work out as the great texts predicted is nothing more than an article of *faith*. Such thinking is an insult to Marx: it is better suited to a priest.

Q: *Didn't orthodox Marxists often refer to the choice between "socialism and barbarism"?*

A: Of course. But the fact of the matter was that everyone at that time believed they knew which would win out. And that was the great success of Marxism. Its teleology guaranteed commitment; people knew that down the road the creation of a just society in the future would validate their political sacrifices in the present. No one can guarantee, any longer, that the sacrifices people make in their everyday lives can ever be validated. And what that means is that you can no longer begin with the traditional assumption that you join a movement, or take a position, because you think it will be successful—especially in the short run. Instead, you join a movement, you take a position, you stake a claim, because you think it's the right thing to do.

Q: *What informs that act, to take a stance and make that claim?*

A: That is the moment of decision. From where it derives, no one can say; it retains an existential element. But it is also true that the way people are educated, the movies that they see, the books they read, the music they hear can either foster or inhibit it. I think, ultimately, a point comes when you just say to yourself: the system isn't just and something should be done to change it. Necessity is not involved here. My position doesn't offer the certitude of historical materialism. It obviously puts socialism on the defensive, and so it must since it rests on nothing more than an ultimately contingent decision. But I think that my philosophical view reflects the practical political situation in which the left finds itself. I don't think there is a single party that still works on the assumption that capitalism is going to collapse on "scientific grounds." In this vein, I believe, it also no longer really matters what progressive organization a person chooses to join: the real question is the political principles and positions he or she chooses to support within that orgainization.

Q: *You outline how the new social movements fail to live up to the progressive tradition of which socialism is a part. What, then, would a reconstituted socialist movement consist of: a vanguard political party? ethical critique? political? legal or economic reform?*

A: It makes no sense simply to castigate the new social movements: they have changed the face of everyday life and they are what we have. Most of them have progressive tendencies, obviously, some more than others. My paradigmatic movement would be the civil rights movement and the tradition of Martin Luther King. Consider where King began and where he ended—he started out concerned with civil rights, getting blacks to vote, getting them into office, attempting to change the political landscape. Next, in the face of much criticism, he linked civil rights with the antiwar movement and developed a certain vision of foreign policy that would strengthen the UN, foster a new sense of obligation to the Third World, and also bring the Vietnam War to an end. When King was killed, of course, it was in Memphis at a strike of sanitation workers and he was trying to develop the Poor People's Movement, a movement concerned with economic equality and social justice in the United States.

Transformation of the political process, the introduction of an internationalist foreign policy, and a new commitment to economic justice: these three moments, in concert with one another, offer the framework in which your new movement should operate. How will it be brought about? It would be nice to have a political party. But creating a new party is difficult given the disincentives of the existing electoral system. We might be better off envisioning what I have termed a *mass association*, something like the

Poor People's Movement, that is more centralized than a simple coalition of single interests and less centralized than a political party. It may not be able to wield political power, but it might exert political influence. In any event, clearly, the key point is to move beyond the fragmentation we are currently experiencing because I fear that, as things stand now with the left, the whole is decidedly less than the sum of its parts.

Q: *Does one dispense with the notion of crisis as the starting point for one's critique of capitalism, either economic or political crisis?*

A: Today, in my opinion, it is no longer possible to assume that the economic crisis will translate into a political crisis. The working class is more stratified, less organized, and less—well—class conscious. The issue is, in my opinion, one of making injustice visible. I really don't mean this to sound unctuous: it is very difficult to realize. But we require a new way of thinking about politics that attempts to link what needs to be done with what should be done and a sense of interest with a sense of justice.

NOTES

CHAPTER I

1. In this regard Marx specified certain transitional demands within a revolutionary context in *The Communist Manifesto*; also see his "Inaugural Address of the Working Man's International Association," both in Karl Marx and Frederick Engels, Selected Works, 3 vols. (Moscow: Progress Publishers, 1969).
2. Though the emphasis will be upon the major European currents of socialism, for some countries the term may indicate nothing more than a foreign policy alignment. In other cases, there is not even a theoretical or historical referent—for example, Islamic socialism.
3. Rudolf Bahro, *The Alternative in Eastern Europe*, trans. David Fernbach (London: New Left Books, 1978), 132.
4. Though both the social democrats and the communists provided an enormous array of clubs, functions, magazines, cultural activities, and so on, they neither linked cultural transformation to revolutionary politics nor developed a new set of social relations. The cultural tastes of the large labor parties were often conservative, as were their moral standards, and the emphasis upon productivism, efficiency, and bureaucratic hierarchy was only rarely called into question.
5. Georg Lukács, *History and Class Consciousness: Studies in Marxists Dialectics*, trans. Rodney Livingstone (Cambridge, Mass.: MIT Press, 1972), 83 ff.
6. Ernst Bloch, *Erbschaft dieser Zeit* (Frankfurt: Suhrkamp, 1973), 104–126.
7. See Karl Korsch, "Theses on Hegel and the Revolution," in *Karl Korsch's Revolutionary Theory*, ed. Douglas Kellner (Austin: University of Texas Press, 1977), 277–8; also "Marx Stellung in der europäischen Revolution von 1848," in *Politische Texte*, ed. Jurgen Seifert (Frankfurt: Europäischen Verlagsanstalt, 1974).
8. Though Marx obviously recognizes the need for a qualitative alternative to capitalism, the lack of emphasis upon the structure of industrial bureaucracy, on just how the state would "wither away," as well as on the obsolescence of the family are products of his refusal to discuss proletarian social relations of the future in a systematic manner.
9. Karl Marx, "Critique of the Gotha Programme," in Marx and Engels, *Selected Works*, vol. 3: 26.
10. Ibid., 17.
11. Bernstein's major work is *Evolutionary Socialism*, trans. Edith C. Harvey (New York: Schocken, 1961). For a biography, which shows his relation to the centers of power in the SPD and the unions, see Peter Gay, *The Dilemma of Democratic Socialism: Eduard Bernstein's Challenge to Marx* (New York: Schocken, 1962).

12. Thus, in the new foreword to his modern social democratic classic, Richard Löwenthal can write; "No doubt all our democratically organized industrial societies, from Western Europe to the U.S.A. and Japan, are still class societies. But for all that their state institutions are themselves fought over and frequently they are used to dismantle the traditional class structure" (Richard Löwenthal [Paul Sering], *Jenseits des Kapitalismus* [Berlin: Dietz, 1977], xxiii).
13. This was explicitly stated by the German social democrats in their Godesberg program of 1959.
14. On the relation between party and trade unions, following Kautsky, Lenin felt that the party must dominate the trade unions and bring in consciousness from the outside. Bebel's view was that the unions must serve as the basis for political organizing but that the party should pursue its wider goal independently. An American variant is that the union provides an entry into the political process by organizing as an interest group. For a subtle, dialectical position see Rosa Luxemburg, "Mass Strike, Party, and Trade Unions," in *Rosa Luxemburg Speaks*, ed. Mary-Alice Waters (New York: Pathfinder, 1970); also see my introduction to *The Letters of Rosa Luxemburg* (Boulder, Colo: Westview Press, 1979).
15. In the SPD's guiding document, the Erfurt Programme, written by Karl Kautsky and Eduard Bernstein in 1891, an orthodox revolutionary theory was juxtaposed with the demand for specific reforms. The two were never linked, either theoretically or in practice.
16. This argument is developed in Robert Michels, *Political Parties*, trans. Eden and Cedar Paul (New York: Collier Books, 1962).
17. The First World War marks a decisive break in the evolution of social democracy. A new generation of leaders, who rose to power through the party bureaucracies, replaced Bebel, Wilhelm Liebknecht, Victor Adler, and others. Put on the defensive by the Bolshevik victory in 1917, social democracy dispensed with revolutionary phraseology. The world was no longer to be won, but rather changed in terms of the status quo
18. Marx, "Critique of the Gotha Programme," 20.
19. Karl Marx, *Grundrisse: Foundations of the Critique of Political Economy*, trans. Martin Nicolaus (New York: Vintage, 1973), 94 ff.
20. Examples are numerous, ranging from the German USPD and SAP to the JuSos and the French CERES group in the seventies. A similar development, which is perhaps even more intense, may be observed on the more sectarian left—since the twenties—and stems from a much more obvious dogmatism.
21. "In a pluralist society based on the division of labor . . . conflicts are inevitable. . . . Each citizen must be capable of consenting to an orderly procedure of conflict settlement by compromise. He must be prepared to accept the loss of stringency and consistency that goes with that. For: no peace without compromise" (Chancellor Helmut Schmidt in *Demokratischer Sozialismus in den Achtziger Jahren*, ed. Richard Löwenthal [Frankfurt: Europäische Verlagsanstalt, 1979], 52).
22. In fact, Fritz Vilmar suggests that it no longer makes sense to speak of clear qualitative differences between parties of the left and right in the parliamentary arena of late capitalism; at best, in his view, there is only the politics of the "left—or right—middle." This view is elaborated in his *Strategien der Demokratisierung*, 2 vols. (Darmstadt: Luchterhand, 1973).
23. See V. I. Lenin, "What Is to Be Done?" and "One Step Forward, Two Steps Back," in his *Selected Works*, 3 vols. (Moscow: Progress Publishers, 1970), vol. 1; also Lukács, *History and Class Consciousness*, especially the essays "The Marxism

of Rosa Luxembourg" and "Towards a Methodology of the Problem of Organization."

24. The question is not whether but what degree of centralism and discipline is necessary, is required. Under Lenin, dissenting individuals were still allowed to voice their own opinions, though not in the manner of a faction. Of course, all this changed drastically under Stalin.

25. Still the best critique of the Russian Revolution—from a socialist stance—is Rosa Luxemburgs's posthumously published "The Russian Revolution," in Waters, *Rosa Luxemburg Speaks*. In this work, Luxemburg puts political events in the context of the tendencies extant in the domestic and international situation.

26. See "The Organizational Question of Social Democracy," in Waters, *Rosa Luxemburg Speaks*. This was one of the earliest responses to Lenin's theory of the party.

27. The differences that make for a qualitative change in the regimes of the early Bolsheviks and Stalin's apparatchiks lie in: (1) the scope and extent of the terror; (2) the continuous lying and rewriting of history; (3) the petrification of democratic centralism within the party; (4) the constraint on culture; (5) the emphasis upon nationalism; and (6) reformist policy, in conjunction with a sweeping and irrational industrialization campaign.

28. The emphasis upon the "public sphere" has become a central issue for contemporary socialist theoreticians. The modern starting point is the work by Jürgen Habermas, *Strukturwandel der Öffentlichkeit—Untersuchungen zu einer Kategorie der bürgerlichen Gesellschaft* (Darmstadt: Luchterhand, 1968). For a more radical approach, in which the "proletarian public sphere" becomes the focus, see Oskar Negt and Alexander Kluge, *Öffentlcihbeit und Erfahrung: Zur Organisationsanalyse von bürgerlicher und proletarischer Öffentlichkeit* (Frankfurt/Main: Suhrkamp, 1972).

29. "Lenin's methods lead to this: the party organization (the caucus) at first substitutes itself for the party as a whole; then the Central Committee substitutes itself for the organization; and finally a single 'dictator' substitutes himself for the Central Committee." These prophetic words were proclaimed by Trotsky long before the Russian Revolution and the rise of Stalin. Though there are many factors that make for the qualitative change from Leninism to Stalinism, a "moment" of continuity—which itself then becomes discontinuous under the pressure of external events—becomes clear in these lines. Quoted in Issac Deutscher, *The Prophet Armed* (New York: Vintage, 1965), 90.

30. In Fernando Claudin, *The Communist Movement: From Comintern to Cominform*, 2 vols. (New York: Monthly Review, 1975), the author argues that a fundamental shift in foreign policy occurred under Stalin. In contrast to Lenin, Stalin exploited divergencies between capitalistic powers without regard for contradictions existing between the bourgeoisie and the proletariat.

31. In this regard, see the current discussion on the concept that is contained in Etienne Balibar, *The Dictatorship of the Proletariat* (London: New Left Books, 1978).

CHAPTER 2

1. Enzo Traverso, *Les juifs et l'allemagne: de la "symbiose judeo-allemande" a la memoire d'auschwitz* (Paris, Decouverte, 1992), 48.

2. Stephen Eric Bronner, *A Rumor about the Jews: Reflections on Anti-Semitism and the* Protocols of the Learned Elders of Zion (New York: Palgrave, 2000).

3. Henry Pachter, *Weimar Etudes* (New York: Columbia University Press, 1982), 262.

4. Arthur Rosenberg, *Geschichte der Weimarer Republik* (Frankfurt: Europäische Verlagsanstalt, 1961), 5 ff.

5. Hannah Arendt, "Rosa Luxemburg" in *Men in Dark Times* (Middlesex: Penguin, 1973), 36 ff.; Raya Dunayevskaya, *Rosa Luxemburg: Women's Liberation and Marx's Philosophy of Revolution* (Atlantic Highlands, N.J.: Humanities Press, 1981), 79 ff.; Elzbieta Ettinger, *Rosa Luxemburg: A Life* (Boston: Beacon, 1986).

6. Rosa Luxemburg, "The National Question and Autonomy" and "Imperialism and National Oppression" in *The National Question: Selected Writings by Rosa Luxemburg*, ed. Horace B. Davis (New York: Monthly Review Press, 1976), 251 ff. and 303 ff.

7. Franz Borkenau, *World Communism* (Ann Arbor: University of Michigan Press, 1962), 148 ff.

8. Klaus Giesinger, *Eine Leiche im Landwehrkanal: Die Ermordung des Rosa L.* (Mainz: Decathon, 1993).

9. Paul Levi, *Zwischen Spartakus und Sozialdemokratie: Schriften, Autsatze, Reden und Briefe*, ed. Charlotte Beradt (Vienna: Europäische Verlagsanstalt, 1969); Charlotte Beradt, *Paul Levi: Ein demokratischer Sozialist in der Weimarer Republik* (Vienna: Europäische Verlagsanstalt, 1969).

10. Kurt Eisner, *Sozialismus als Aktion: Ausgewaehlte Aufsaetze und Reden*, ed. Freya Eisner (Frankfurt: Suhrkamp, 1979).

11. F. L. Carsten, *Revolution in Central Europe 1918–1919* (Berkeley: University of California Press, 1972), 263.

12. Marta Feuchtwanger, *Nur eine Frau* (Munich: Knaur, 1984), 133.

13. Augustin Scouhy, *Erich Mühsam: Sein Leben, Sein Werk, Sein Martyrium* (Reutlingen: Trotzdem Verlag, 1984), 10.

14. Max Nomad, *Dreamers, Dynamiters, and Demagogues: Reminiscences* (New York: Waldon, 1964), 16 ff.

15. Pachter, "Erich Mühsam; A Centenary Note" in *Weimar Etudes*, 252.

16. Erich Mühsam, *Briefe* 2 Bde. (Darmstadt: Topos, 1984) 2: 422–423.

17. Cited in Charles Bracelen Flood, *Hitler: The Path to Power* (Boston: Houghton Mifflin, 1989), 4.

18. Rosa Leviné-Meyer, *Leviné the Spartacist* (London: Gordon and Cremonesi, 1973), 6 ff.

CHAPTER 3

1. Albert Camus, "Letters to a German Friend," in *Resistance, Rebellion, and Death*, trans. Justin O'Brien (New York: Knopf, 1960), 6.

2. Ibid., 71.

3. Stephen Eric Bronner, *Moments of Decision: Political History and the Crises of Radicalism* (New York: Routledge, 1992), 57 ff.

4. "Politically, Camus' view was ridiculous. Despite his anti-fascist stand, he had not grasped the nature of the Hitler regime. Not until after the Fall of France did he realize that it was especially virulent. Moreover, he chose to ignore that France could not fight Hitler while parading her readiness to negotiate with him. While insisting that he was rejecting fatalism in the name of action, Camus was condemning himself to passivity." Patrick McCarthy, *Camus: A Critical Study of His Life and Works* (New York: Random House, 1982), 125.

5. Note the remarkable evocation of those days in Camus, "The Right Side and

the Wrong Side," in *Lyrical and Critical Essays*, ed. Philip Thody and trans. Ellen Conroy Kennedy (New York: Knopf, 1968), 5 ff.

6.   Germaine Breé, *Camus* (New York: Harcourt Brace and World, 1964), 35.
7.   Camus, "Letter to Roland Barthes on *The Plague*," in *Lyrical and Critical Essays*, 338.
8.   Camus, *The Plague*, trans. Stuart Gilbert (New York: Knopf, 1948), 150.
9.   Breé, *Camus*, 121.
10.   Camus, *The Plague*, 278.
11.   Camus, "Letter to Roland Barthes," 340.
12.   Camus, *The Plague*, 226–228.
13.   Camus, *Notebooks*, 2 vols., trans. Justin O'Brien (New York, 1991), vol. 2, 97.
14.   Ibid., vol. 2, 10.
15.   Jeanyves Guérin, *Camus: portrait de l'artiste en citoyen* (Paris: Édition François Bourin, 1993), 43 ff; Emmett Parker, *Albert Camus: The Artist in the Arena* (Madison: University of Wisconsin Press), 93 ff; McCarthy, *Camus*, 213 ff.
16.   Camus, *The Rebel*, trans. Anthony Bower (New York: Vintage, 1956), 5.
17.   Ibid., 22.
18.   Ibid., 103.
19.   Ibid., 10.
20.   Camus, *Notebooks*, vol. 2, 156.
21.   Ibid., vol. 2, 143.
22.   Ibid., vol. 1, 27.
23.   Camus, "The New Mediterranean Culture" (1937), in *Lyrical and Critical Essays*, 197.
24.   Camus, *The Rebel*, 11.
25.   Ibid., 10.
26.   Raymond Aron, *The Opium of the Intellectuals*, trans. Terence Kilmartin (New York: Doubleday, 1957), 58 ff.
27.   It is indeed unfair to ignore the differences; see Francis Jeanson, *Sartre and the Problem of Morality*, trans. Robert V. Stone (Bloomington: Indiana University Press, 1980).
28.   Jean-Paul Sartre, "Reply to Albert Camus" in *Situations*, trans. Benita Eisler (New York: George Braziller, 1965), 54 ff.
29.   Note the superb biography by Jean Lacouture, *Pierre Mendès-France*, trans. George Holoch (New York: Holmes and Meier, 1984), 211 ff.
30.   Guérin, *Camus*, 163.
31.   McCarthy, *Camus*, 276 ff.
32.   For a different perspective, Michael Walzer, "Albert Camus' Algerian War," in *The Company of Critics: Social Criticism and Political Commitment in the Twentieth Century* (New York: Basic Books, 1988), 136 ff.
33.   Guérin, *Camus*, 21.

CHAPTER 6

1.   Karl Jaspers, *The Idea of the University*, trans. H. A. T. and H. F. Vanderschmidt (London: P. Owen, 1960).
2.   Gerald Graff, *Beyond the Culture Wars: How Teaching the Conflicts Can Revitalize American Education* (New York: Norton, 1992).
3.   For an analysis of how the regulation of science and technology was linked to changes in the broader political system, see David Dickson and David Noble, "By Force of Reason: The Politics of Science and Technology Policy," in *The*

Hidden Election: Politics and Economics in the 1980 Presidential Campaign, ed. Thomas Ferguson and Joel Rogers (New York: Pantheon, 1981), 260 ff.

4. "Academics in particular, that is, intellectuals, who are professionally committed to the pursuit of truth, are not immune from aspirations for power, academic and political. . . . [Such an] intellectual deals with 'safe' issues in a 'safe' manner. On the great issues of political life, which are controversial by definition he must remain silent. He does not need to be silenced; he silences himself." Hans Morgenthau, *Truth and Power* (New York: Praeger, 1970), 24–25.

5. Julien Benda, *The Treason of the Intellectuals*, trans. Richard Aldington (New York: W. W. Norton, 1969).

6. Paul Nizan, *The Watchdogs: Philosophers and the Established Order*, trans. Paul Fittinghof (New York: Monthly Review, 1971); and Bruce Robbins, *Intellectuals: Aesthetics, Politics Academics* (Minneapolis: University of Minnesota Press, 1990), xv.

7. Karl Mannheim, *Ideology and Utopia: An Introduction to the Sociology of Knowledge*, trans. Louis Wirth and Edward Shils (New York: Harcourt, Brace and World, 1936), 15 ff.; also note the provocative piece by Martin Jay, "The Frankfurt School's Critique of Karl Mannheim and the Sociology of Knowledge," in *Permanent Exiles: Essays on the Intellectual Migration from Germany to America* (New York: Columbia University Press, 1986), 62 ff.

8. Georg Lukács, *History and Class Consciousness: Studies in Marxist Dialectics* trans. Rodney Livingstone (Cambridge, Mass.: MIT Press, 1971), 1 ff., 46 ff., and passim.

9. On the role of the committed writer, see Jean-Paul Sartre, *What Is Literature?* trans. Bernard Frechtman (New York: Harper and Row, 1965).

10. Stanley Pierson, *Marxist Intellectuals and the Working-Class Mentality in Germany 1887–1912* (Cambridge, Mass.: Harvard University Press, 1993).

11. In *The New Class: An Analysis of the Communist System* (New York: Praeger, 1957), Milovan Djilas argued that the former party of revolutionary "intellectuals" had become a ruling "class." An interesting outgrowth of this position suggested that the creation of this new class in Eastern Europe led to the abolition of the old distinction between the intellectual and the bureaucratic elite to the detriment of the former. George Konrad and Ivan Szelenyi, *The Intellectuals on the Road to Class Power*, trans. Andrew Arato and Richard E. Allen (New York: Harcourt, Brace, Jovanovich, 1979).

12. Antonio Gramsci, *Selections from the Prison Notebooks*, ed. and trans. Quinton Hoare and Geoffrey Knowles-Smith (New York: International Publishers, 1971), 3–24.

13. Alvin Gouldner, *The Future of the Intellectuals and the Rise of the New Class* (New York: Seabury, 1979).

14. Usually meant are "left" intellectuals, of course, even though they have generally been the first to criticize the division of labor and the various ideologies involved in keeping those who "do the work" in their places. Helmut Schelsky, *Die arbeit tun die anderen, Klassenkampf und Priesterherrschaft der Intellektuellen* (Opladen: Westdeutscher Verlag, 1975).

15. Richard Löwenthal, *Gesellschaftswandel und Kulturkrise* (Frankfurt: Fischer, 1979), 21.

16. Zygmunt Bauman, *Legislators and Interpreters: On Modernity, Post-modernity, and Intellectuals* (Ithaca: Cornell University Press, 1987), 21 ff., 120 ff.

17. Michel Foucault, "Intellectuals and Power" in *Language, Counter-Memory, Practice*, ed. Donald F. Bouchard (Ithaca: Cornell University Press, 1977), 205 ff. and "Truth and Power" in *The Foucault Reader*, ed. Paul Rabinow (New York: Pantheon, 1984), 68 ff.

18. Richard Sennett, *The Fall of Public Man: On the Social Psychology of Capitalism* (New York: Vintage, 1978).

19. "The term 'intellectual' appears to originate from the pen of Clemenceau in an article in *L'Aurore* of January 23, 1898, as a collective description of the most prominent Dreyfusards. The new term was promptly taken up in a pejorative sense of unscrupulousness and irresponsible disloyalty to the nation by Maurice Barres in *Scènes et doctrines du nationalisme* (Paris, 1902), 46 (where incidentally even the un-French quality of the word itself becomes part of the accusation)." J.P. Nettl, "Ideas, Intellectuals, and the Structures of Dissent" in *On Intellectuals*, ed. Philip Rieff (Garden City, N.Y.: Doubleday, 1969), 87.

20. Stephen Eric Bronner, *Ideas in Action: Political Tradition in the Twentieth Century* (Lanham, Md.: Rowman and Littlefield, 1999), 55 ff.

21. "Experience tends universally to show that the purely bureaucratic type of administrative organization—that is, the monocratic variety of bureaucracy—is, from a purely technical point of view, capable of attaining the highest degree of efficiency and is in this sense formally the most rational known means of exercising authority over human beings. It is superior to any other form in precision, in stability, in the stringency of its discipline, and in its reliability. It thus makes possible a particularly high degree of calculability of results for the heads of the organization and for those acting in relation to it. It is finally superior in intensive efficiency and in the scope of its operations, and is formally capable of application to all kinds of administrative tasks." Max Weber, *Economy and Society*, 2 vols. Ed. Günther Roth and Claus Wittich (Berkeley: University of California Press, 1978) 1:223.

22. "Nature builds no machines, no locomotives, railways, electric telegraphs, self-acting mules, etc. These are products of human industry: natural material transformed into the organs of the human will over nature, or of human participation in nature. They are *organs of the human brain,created by the human hand*: the power of knowledge objectified. The development of fixed capital indicates to what degree general social knowledge has become a *direct force of* production, and to what degree, hence, the conditions of the process of social life itself have come under the control of the general intellect and been transformed in accordance with it." Karl Marx, *Grundrisse: Introduction to the Critique of Political Economy*, trans. Martin Nicolaus (New York: Vintage, 1973), 706.

23. Yehuda Bauer, *Rethinking the Holocaust* (New Haven: Yale University Press), 33 ff.

24. Noam Chomsky, *American Power and the New Mandarins* (New York: Pantheon, 1969).

25. Edward Said, *Representations of the Intellectual* (New York: Pantheon, 1994).

26. Jean-Paul Sartre, "A Plea for Intellectuals" in *Between Existentialism and Marxism*, trans. John Matthews (London: New Left Books, 1974), 230.

27. Bauman, *Legislators and Interpreters*, 5 ff. and passim.

28. Russell Jacoby, *The Last Intellectuals: American Culture in the Age of Academe* (New York: Basic Books, 1987).

CHAPTER 9

1. Max Horkheimer, "Die Aufklärung" in *Gesammelte Werke* (Frankfurt: Fischer, 1989), 13: 571.

2. Theodor W. Adorno, *Minima Moralia: Reflections from Damaged Life*, trans. E. F. N. Jephcott (London: New Left Books, 1974), 89.

3. Helmut Dubiel, *Theory and Politics: Studies in the Development of Critical Theory* (Cambridge, Mass.: Harvard University Press, 1985), 71.
4. Max Horkheimer and Theodor W. Adorno, *Dialectic of Enlightenment*, trans. John Cumming (New York: Continuum, 1972), 9, 87.
5. Ibid., 171–172.
6. Adorno, *Minima Moralia*, 74.
7. Horkheimer and Adorno, *Dialectic of Enlightenment*, 169.
8. Nietzsche would later be termed by Horkheimer "the most radical enlightenment figure in all of philosophy." And in the general indeterminate way in which Horkheimer used the term "enlightenment" that might even be true. In terms of the values and political ideas deriving from the actual movement, however, such a claim is nonsense. Here, the unfortunate consequences of using one term in two very different ways becomes apparent. cf. Horkheimer, "Die Aufklärung," 574.
9. Adorno, *Minima Moralia*, 192.
10. Horkheimer, *Gesammelte Schriften*, 17: 873, 884.
11. Ibid., 17:687–688.

CHAPTER 12

1. "Those wishing to understand modernization as an increasingly autonomous process of creating the new must also count on modernity becoming old. The other side of this aging of industrial modernity is the establishment of a risk society. This concept defines a phase of development of modern society in which new dynamics of social, political, ecological, and individual risks are called forth and confront the institutions of control and security in industrial society" (Ulrich Beck, *Die Erfindung des Politischen* [Frankfurt: Suhrkamp, 1993], 35). Translated as *The Reinvention of the Political* (London: Polity, 1995).
2. "Modernity is, in this sense, a subpolitical 'system of revolution' without a revolutionary subject, program, or goal" (Ulrich Beck, *Politik in der Risikogesellschaft* [Frankfurt: Suhrkamp, 1991], 39). Translated as *Ecological Enlightenment* (Atlantic Highlands, N.J.: Humanities Press International, 1994).
3. Ulrich Beck, *Risikogesellschaft: Auf dem Weg in eine andere Moderne* (Frankfurt am Main: Suhrkamp, 1986), 295 ff. Translated as *Risk Society: Towards a New Modernity* (London: Sage, 1992).
4. Elisabeth Beck-Gernsheim, *Technik, Markt und Moral* (Frankfurt: Suhrkamp, 1991).
5. Ulrich Beck, *Gegengifte: Die organisierte Unverantwortlichkeit* (Frankfurt: Suhrkamp, 1988), 17, 62 ff. Translated as *Ecological Politics in the Age of Risk* (London: Polity, 1994).
6. "Reflexive modernization—simplified and in essence—means: one epoch of modernity disappears and a still nameless second comes into existence and not through political elections, seizure of power, or revolution but as the latent side effect of the normal, known, and autonomous modernization, which follows the schema and reception of western industrial society" (*Die Erfindung des Politischen*, 57 ff).
7. *Risikogesellschaft*, 40 ff.
8. "Never before was humanity forced to live under the permanent threat of self-destruction. Never before were whole oceans threatened by poisoning, entire species with overnight disappearance through negligence or wasting of the earth's surface. Never before were we threatened with a thermal overheating of the atmosphere. It is unnecessary to celebrate the past in order to see these and

other unintended consequences of modernity with eyes very, very wide open" (ibid., 35).

9. *Gegengifte*, 19 ff.
10. Ibid., 10 ff.
11. *Risikogesellschaft*, 43 ff.
12. *Politik in der Risikogesellschaft*, 16.
13. *Die Erfindung des Politischen*, 47.
14. *Gegengifte*, 115 ff.
15. Ibid., 31 ff.
16. *Politik in der Risikogesellschaft*, 28.
17. "The difference between the two phases of modern society lies subsequently here: that sometimes preindustrial traditions and other times the 'traditions' and certainties of industrial society themselves become the objects of dissolution and resolution" (*Die Erfindung des Politischen*, 71).
18. *Politik in der Risikogesellschaft*, 19.
19. *Die Erfindung des Politischen*, 39, 149 ff.
20. *Gegengifte*, op. cit, 49 ff.
21. *Politik in der Risikogesellschaft*, op. cit, 55 ff.
22. *Die Erfindung des Politischen*, 52.
23. Ibid., 162–163.
24. Ibid., 82 ff.
25. *Politik in der Risikogesellschaft*, op. cit, 23.
26. *Risikogesellschaft*, op. cit, 306 ff.
27. "Technicians must free themselves from economic domination in order to free society from alienated forms of technical domination. It may sound paradoxical: freedom of technology and social liberation from technology may coincide. Or, in other words, the radicalization of modernity—technique as l'art pour l'art—can simultaneously create the preconditions for solving the systemic problems of directing, controlling, and democratising technology" (*Die Erfindung des Politischen*, 188).
28. Ibid., 17–18.
29. "The modernization of barbarism is a not totally unimaginable variant of the future, which reflexive modernization makes possible. The entry of the *and* can lead to a renaissance of the *either/or* in numerous counter-modern forms" (ibid., 16).
30. Ibid., 249 ff.
31. Ibid., 94 ff.
32. "Imperialism thus is atavistic in character . . . It tends to disappear as a structural element because the structure that brought it to the fore goes into a decline, giving way, in the course of social development, to other structures that have no room for it and eliminate the power factors that supported it" (Joseph Schumpeter, *Imperialism and Social Classes*, trans. Heinz Norden [New York: Augustus M. Kelly Publishers, 1951], 84–85).
33. Rosa Luxemburg, *The Accumulation of Capital*, trans. Alice Schwarzchild (New York: Monthly Review Press, 1968), 366.
34. Ernst Bloch, *Erbschaft dieser Zeit* (Frankfurt: Suhrkamp, 1973), 45 ff.
35. *Die Erfindung des Politischen*, 143.
36. Beck, *Risikogesellschaft*, 319.
37. Stephan Eric Bronner, *Socialism Unbound*, 2d ed. (New York: Westview, 2000), 158–167.
38. *Politik in der Risikogesellschaft*, 62.
39. *Die Erfindung des Politischen*, 28.
40. *Politik in der Risikogesellschaft*, 63.

41. Ibid., 38.
42. Ibid., 61.
43. *Risikogesellschaft*, 25.
44. Ibid., 301.
45. Ibid., 311.
46. Ibid., 220 ff.
47. *Gegengifte*, 62.

CHAPTER 13

1. Pierre Manent, *An Intellectual History of Liberalism*, trans. Rebecca Balinski (Princeton: Princeton University Press, 1994), 3 ff.
2. Jürgen Habermas, *The Theory of Communicative Action*, 2 vols., trans. Thomas McCarthy (Boston: Beacon, 1987) 2: 374 ff. Claus Offe, *Disorganized Capitalism*, ed. John Keane (Cambridge, Mass.: MIT Press, 1985), 10–128. For a critical discussion, Adam Przeworski, *The State and the Economy under Capitalism* (London: Harwood, 1975), 73 ff.
3. Note the discussion by Henry Pachter, "The Right to Be Lazy" in *Socialism in History: Political Essays of Henry Pachter*, ed. Stephen Eric Bronner (New York: Columbia University Press, 1984), 3 ff.
4. Joshua Cohen and Joel Rogers, *On Democracy: Toward a Transformation of American Society* (New York: Penguin, 1983), 47 ff.
5. An important work for analyzing the importance of the bourgeois notion of "rights" for any form of socialist theory is Ernst Bloch, *Natural Right and Human Dignity*, trans. Dennis J. Schmidt (Cambridge, Mass.: MIT Press, 1986).
6. Karl Marx, "On the Jewish Question," in *Writings of the Young Marx on Philosophy and Society*, ed. Loyd D. Easton and Kurt H. Guddat (New York: Doubleday, 1967), 216 ff.
7. Stephen Eric Bronner, *Socialism Unbound*, 2d ed. (Boulder, Colo.: Westview, 2001); 3 ff. and passim
8. The most articulate exposition of this argument is provided by Karl Popper, *The Open Society and Its Enemies* (Princeton: Princeton University Press, 1950), 199 ff. and 3245 ff.
9. Stanley Pierson, *Marxist Intellectuals and the Working Class Mentality in Germany, 1887–1912* (Cambridge, Mass.: Harvard University Press, 1993), 258.
10. Adam Przeworski and John Sprague, *Paper Stones: A History of Electoral Socialism* (Chicago: University of Chicago Press, 1986).
11. Bronner, *Socialism Unbound*, 171 ff.
12. Note the classic discussion on "non-sychrononous contradicitons" by Ernst Bloch, *Erbschaft dieser Zeit* (Frankfurt: Surhkampf, 1973 ed.), 104 ff.
13. Adam Przeworksi, "Material Bases of Consent: Economics and Politics in a Hegemonic System," in *Political Power and Social Theory* (Greenwich, Conn.: JAI Press, 1980), ed. Maurice Zeitlin, vol. 1, 21–66; "Material Interests, Class Compromise, and the Transition to Socialism," *Politics and Society* 10, no. 1 (1980): 125–153.
14. Cohen and Rogers, *On Democracy*, 49.
15. Jürgen Habermas, *Legitimation Crisis* (Boston: Beacon, 1975), 33 ff.
16. Milton Friedman, *Capitalism and Freedom* (Chicago: University of Chicago Press, 1962).

17. David Abraham, *The Collapse of the Weimar Republic*, 2d ed. (New York: Holmes and Meier, 1986).
18. Offe, "Two Logics of Collective Action," in *Disorganized Capitalism*, 67–115.
19. It was the "parasitic" sectors of capital, cloaking their particular interests in those of the national interest, that were seen as the driving force behind imperialism in the classic account by J. A. Hobson, *Imperialism* (Ann Arbor: University of Michigan Press, 1971).
20. Franz Neumann, *The Democratic and Authoritarian State*, ed. Herbert Marcuse (New York: Free Press, 1964), 13.
21. Cohen and Rogers, *On Democracy*, 52–53.
22. Precisely because the American Revolution was not seen as a "revolution" at all, but rather a "war for independence," numerous English conservatives like Edmund Burke and Samuel Johnson supported it. For a modern analysis of this sort, see Hannah Arendt, *On Revolution* (New York: Penguin, 1963).
23. Alan Wolfe, *The Seamy Side of Democracy* (New York: John Wiley, 1978).
24. Walter Dean Burnham, *The Current Crisis in Amerian Politics* (Oxford: Oxford University Press, 1982), 121 ff.; and Martin Wattenberg, *The Decline of American Political Parties 1952–1980* (Cambridge: Cambridge University Press, 1984).
25. Thomas Ferguson and Joel Rogers, *Right Turn: The Decline of the Democrats and the Future of American Politics* (New York: Hill and Wang, 1986).
26. The labor movement bore the brunt of an intolerant assault in which "it has been estimated that of the work force of 65 million, 13 million were affected by loyalty and security programs during the McCarthy era . . . [and] over 112 thousand individuals were fired as a result of government and private loyalty programs. More than 100 people were convicted under the federal Smith Act, and 135 people were cited for contempt by the House Un-American Activities Comittee." James L. Gibson, "Political Intolerance and Political Repression during the McCarthy Red Scare," *American Political Science Review* 82, no. 2 (June 1988): 514; Robert Justin Goldstein, *Political Repression in Modern America: 1870 to the Present* (Cambridge, Mass.: Schenkman Publishing Company, 1984), 369–396.
27. Joel Rogers, *Divide and Conquer: The Legal Foundations of Post-war U.S. Labor Policy* (Ph.D. Diss., Princeton University, 1984).
28. Otto Kirchheimer, "Changes in the Structure of Political Compromise," in *Politics, Law, and Social Change: Selected Essays of Otto Kirchheimer*, ed. Frederic S. Burin and Kurt L. Shell (New York: Columbia University Press, 1969), 131 ff.
29. Neumann, *The Democratic and Authoritarian State*, 16.
30. Bronner, *Socialism Unbound*, 53 ff.
31. Joshua Cohen and Joel Rogers, *Associations and Democracy* (New York: Verso, 1995).

CHAPTER 14

1. John David Skrentny, *The Ironies of Affirmative Action: Politics, Culture and Justice in America* (Chicago: University of Chicago Press, 1996), 13.
2. Michael Sherry, *In the Shadow of War* (New Haven: Yale University Press, 1995), 261.
3. Skrentny, *The Ironies of Affirmative Action*, 5.
4. Robert Greenstein, "Universal and Targeted Approaches to Relieving Poverty:

An Alternative View" in Christopher Jencks and Paul Peterson, *The Urban Underclass* (Washington, D.C.: Brookings Institution, 1991), 437–459.

5. Dinesh D'Souza, *The End of Racism* (New York: Free Press, 1995), 489.
6. Skrentny, *The Ironies of Affirmative Action*, 14.
7. D'Souza, *The End of Racism*, 487.
8. Jeffrey Rosen, "Annals of Law," *The New Yorker*, 29 April–6 May 1996, 66; Glenn C. Loury, "Performing without a Net," in *The Affirmative Action Debate* ed. George E. Curry (Reading, Mass.: Addison-Wesley, 1996), 49–64.
9. Michael Tomasky, "Reaffirming Our Actions," *The Nation*, 13 May 1996, 21–24.
10. Martin Luther King Jr. *Why We Can't Wait* (New York: Signet, 1964), 137–138.
11. Skretny, *The Ironies of Affirmative Action*, 232.
12. Stephen Eric Bronner, *Socialism Unbound* (2d ed., Boulder, Colo.: Westview, 2001), 169 and passim.
13. William Julius Wilson, *When Work Disappears: The World of the New Urban Poor* (New York: Knopf, 1996), 205.
14. Amy Gutmann and Dennis Thompson, *Democracy and Disagreement* (Cambridge, Mass.: Harvard University Press, 1996), 308.
15. Note the interesting discussion by Jason DeParle, "The Ellwoods: Mugged by Reality," *New York Times Magazine*, 8 December 1996, 64–67, 99–100.
16. On the "delinking of wages from economic growth" see David Dyssegard Kallick, "The Budget Crisis: Politics not Economics" in *Social Policy* (winter 1995): 3. and David Gordon, "Underpaid Workers Bloated Corporations" in *Dissent* (spring 1996): 24. "Among working couples, if the lesser paid spouse were laid off, half the couples in the top fourth of earners would fall into the middle half.... Fully one-third of earners would slip into the bottom quarter." *New York Times*, 18 May 1997.
17. See chap. 3 in Alba Alexander, *Playing Fair: U.S. Tax Reform and Social Citizenship* (Ph.D. Diss., University of Chicago, 1994).
18. Robert Blauner, *Black Lives, White Lives* (Berkeley: University of California Press, 1989), 137, 165, 166.
19. Douglas Massey and Nancy Denton, *American Apartheid: Segregation and the Making of an Underclass* (Cambridge, Mass.: Harvard University Press, 1993), 2.
20. Ibid., 8.
21. Paul Craig Roberts and Lawrence M. Stanton Jr., "Color Code," in *National Review*, 20 March 1995, 36–48, 50–51, 80. Note also, by the same authors, *The New Color Line* (New York: Regnery, 1996).
22. Skrentny, *The Ironies of Affirmative Action*, 111.
23. Gutmann and Thompson, *Democracy and Disagreement*, 340.
24. William Julius Wilson, "Public Policy Research and the Truly Disadvantaged," in *The Urban Underclass*, eds. Christopher Jencks and Paul Peterson (Washington, D.C.: Brookings Institution, 1991), 477.
25. Pinkney, *The Myth of Black Progress*, 165.
26. King, *Why We Can't Wait*, 139.
27. David Hollinger, "Group Preferences, Cultural Diversity and Social Democracy: Notes toward a Theory of Affirmative Action," *Representations* 55 (summer 1996): 31–40.
28. Gutmann and Thompson, *Democracy and Disagreement*, 320.
29. Paul Berman, "Redefining Fairness," *New York Times Book Review*, 14 April 1996, 16–17.
30. William Julius Wilson, *The Declining Significance of Race* (Chicago: University of Chicago Press, 1980), 160.
31. Wilson, *When Work Disappears*, xviii.

32. Leon Friedman, "A Snare the Wealth Tax," *The Nation*, 6 January 1997, 23–24.
33. Robert Borosage, "The Politics of Austerity," *The Nation*, 27 May 1996, 22–24.
34. William Greider, "Global Warning: Curbing the Free Trade Freefall," *The Nation*, 13–20 January 1997, 11–17.
35. King, *Why We Can't Wait*, 139.
36. Bruno Bettleheim and Morris Janowitz, *Social Change and Prejudice* (New York: Free Press, 1964).

CHAPTER 17

1. Albert O. Hirschman, *The Rhetoric of Reaction: Perversity, Futility, Jeopardy* (Cambridge, Mass.: Harvard University Press, 1991).
2. Kevin Phillips, *The Politics of Rich and Poor: Wealth and the American Electorate in the Reagan Aftermath* (New York: Random House, 1990).
3. Thomas Ferguson and Joel Rogers, *Right Turn: The Decline of the Democrats and the Future of American Politics* (New York: Hill and Wang, 1986), 11 ff. and passim.
4. Richard Hofstadter, *The Paranoid Strain in American Politics and Other Essays* (New York: Alfred Knopf, 1966).
5. Michael Paul Rogin, *The Intellectuals and McCarthy: The Radical Specter* (Chicago: University of Chicago Press, 1967).
6. David A. Stockman, *The Triumph of Politics: How the Reagan Revolution Failed* (New York: Harper and Row, 1986).
7. Ed Gillespie and Bob Schellhas, eds. *The Contract with America: The Bold Plan by Rep. Newt Gingrich, Rep. Dick Armey and the House Republicans to Change the Nation* (New York: Times Books, 1994).
8. Paul Hockenos, *Free to Hate: The Rise of the Right in Post-Communist Eastern Europe* (New York: Routledge, 1993), 237 ff.
9. Roger Eatwell, "The Holocaust Denial: A Study in Propaganda Technique," in *Neo-Fascism in Europe* ed. Luciano Cheles, Ronnie Ferguson, and Michalina Vaughan (London: Longman, 1991), 120 ff.
10. Stephen Eric Bronner, *A Rumor about the Jews: Reflections on Anti-Semitism and The Protocols of the Learned Elders of Zion* (New York: St. Martin's Press, 2000).
11. Michel Wieviorka, "French Intellectuals: End of an Era ?" *Dissent* (spring 1994): 251.
12. Note the discussion in Armin Pfahl-Traughber, *Volkes Stimme ?: Rechts-populismus in Europe* (Bonn: Dietz Verlag, 1994), 83 ff and 153 ff.
13. Glyn Ford, *Fascist Europe: The Rise of Racism and Xenophobia* (London: Pluto Press, 1992), 9 ff. and passim.
14. Michael Novick, *White Lies, White Power: The Fight against White Supremacy and Reactionary Violence* (New York: Common Courage Press, 1995).
15. Francis Fox Piven, *The New Class War: Reagan's Attack on the Welfare State and Its Consequences* (New York: Pantheon Books, 1982).
16. Michalina Vaughan, "The Extreme Right in France: 'LePenism' or the Politics of Fear" and Douglas Johnson, "The New Right in France," in *Neo-Fascism in Europe*, 211 ff., 234 ff.
17. For a somewhat different view, Sara Diamond, *Roads to Dominion: Rightwing Movements and Political Power in the United States* (New York: Guilford Press, 1995).
18. For what remains the most trenchant critique of communitarian thinking, note the 1924 essay by Helmuth Plessner, "Die Grenzen der Gemeinschaft" in *Gesammelte Schriften*, Bd. V (Frankfurt: Suhrkamp Verlag, 1981), 7 ff.

INDEX